The Concept of Tolerance in Judaism, Christianity and Islam

Key Concepts in
Interreligious Discourses

Edited by
Georges Tamer

Volume 7

The Concept of Tolerance in Judaism, Christianity and Islam

Edited by
Catharina Rachik and Georges Tamer

DE GRUYTER

KCID Editorial Advisory Board:
Prof. Dr. Asma Afsaruddin; Prof. Dr. Patrice Brodeur; Prof. Dr. Nader El-Bizri;
Prof. Dr. Elisabeth Gräb-Schmidt; Dr. Naghmeh Jahan; Prof. Dr. Assaad Elias Kattan;
Prof. Dr. Christian Lange; Prof. Dr. Manfred Pirner; Prof. Dr. Nathanael Riemer;
Prof. Dr. Kenneth Seeskin

ISBN 978-3-11-077288-3
e-ISBN (PDF) 978-3-11-077298-2
e-ISBN (EPUB) 978-3-11-077312-5
ISSN 2513-1117

Library of Congress Control Number: 2025940346

Bibliographic information published by the Deutsche Nationalbibliothek
The Deutsche Nationalbibliothek lists this publication in the Deutsche Nationalbibliografie;
detailed bibliographic data are available on the internet at http://dnb.dnb.de.

© 2025 Walter de Gruyter GmbH, Berlin/Boston, Genthiner Straße 13, 10785 Berlin

www.degruyterbrill.com
Questions about General Product Safety Regulation:
productsafety@degruyterbrill.com

Preface

This volume in the series Key Concepts in Interreligious Discourses (KCID) is based on a conference on the concept of tolerance in Judaism, Christianity, and Islam, which took place on December 13–14, 2017. This was followed by a conference on the concept of peace in the three religions, the proceedings of which have been published.[1] Due to the COVID-19 pandemics, the untimely and unexpected death of Professor Dr. Christian Polke (1980–2023), whose contribution had to be completed posthumously, and some other complications, the publication of this volume has been greatly delayed.[2]

The conference and the book series Key Concepts in Interreligious Discourses (KCID) are central projects of the Bavarian Research Center for Interreligious Discourses (BaFID). The main goal of the Center is to study the fundamental ideas and central concepts of Judaism, Christianity, and Islam with the aim of uncovering their interconnectedness and highlighting the similarities as well as the differences between these three religions. By sharing the results of our research, BaFID seeks to promote peaceful relations among religious communities and to foster mutual understanding and social cohesion in pluralistic societies. In addition to the published volumes, selected highlights from each volume are made available online on the BaFID website.

BaFID aims not only to engage a small group of academic specialists in reflection on central religious ideas, but also to disseminate these ideas in a way that is accessible and engaging to the wider public. Academic research in the service of society is essential to counteract the current trend of radicalism and segregation rooted in ignorance, and to strengthen mutual respect and acceptance among different religions. This aspiration is fulfilled through the discursive exploration of concepts, as exemplified in this volume on the complex concept of predestination.

BaFID could not fulfill its mission without the generous support of the Bavarian State Ministry of the Interior, for Sport and Integration. Their support has been instrumental in advancing our research and outreach efforts, and I extend

---

[1] Georges Tamer (Ed.), *The Concept of Peace in Judaism, Christianity and Islam*, Volume 8 of the book series *Key Concepts in Interreligious Discourses*, ed. by Georges Tamer, Berlin/Boston: Walter de Gruyter, 2020.
[2] I would like to thank Dr. Friedhelm Meier (University of Tübingen) for his professional help in completing Polke's text.

my deepest gratitude to Minister of State Joachim Herrmann and his team for their unwavering commitment to promoting interreligious understanding and social integration.

I would like to express my gratitude to Walter de Gruyter Publishers for their expert management of this volume and the entire book series.

Georges Tamer
Erlangen, May 2025

Contents

Preface —— V

Menachem Kellner
The Concept of Tolerance in Judaism —— 1

Christian Polke (1980–2023)
The Concept of Tolerance in Christianity —— 43

Anna Ayşe Akasoy
The Concept of Tolerance in Islam —— 83

Catharina Rachik and Georges Tamer
Epilogue —— 149

List of Contributors —— 171

Index of Persons —— 173

Index of Subjects —— 177

Menachem Kellner
The Concept of Tolerance in Judaism

1 Introduction — The Problem

I have been invited by the editors of this volume to contribute an essay on the idea of tolerance from a Jewish perspective. This essay is being published in the volume dedicated to the notion of tolerance as part of the book series "Key Concepts in Interreligious Discourses".[1] The various books in this series are each dedicated to a key concept in Judaism, Christianity and Islam. My essay will therefore attempt to develop *a* concept of religious tolerance out of the sources of Judaism — I do not intend to present *the* Jewish concept of tolerance (as if there could be such a thing). I also make no pretensions of approaching the topic from an objective, outside perspective. This essay is a work of constructive Jewish theology. It is also a polemic, arguing for a place for tolerance that rejects both the "Scylla of relativism and the Charybdis of absolutism."[2]

My intention here is to develop a strong version of religious tolerance, without shading over into some form of pluralism and without sacrificing the idea that truth and falsity are important distinctions. My version of tolerance will not involve pity or condescension towards those who do not share my religious positions and must involve more than simply "putting up with" religions other than my own. I will explain these terms through the course of what I write here.[3] I also seek an approach to religious tolerance that could be adopted by traditionalist followers of other religions, should they choose so.

Rather than defining what I mean by a strong version of tolerance, let me cite an example of it, from what struck me originally as a surprising source: the (Orthodox) Rabbinical Council of America (RCA) issued a policy statement on inter-religious dialogue (1964).[4] After affirming, "Each religious community is endowed

---

[1] This article is based on an already published chapter in my book *We Are Not Alone: A Maimonidean Theology of the Other*, 105–36, Boston: Academic Studies Press, 2021.
[2] Kimelman, Reuven, "Judaism and Pluralism," *Modern Judaism* 7, no. 2 (1987), 131–50, 137.
[3] On these various approaches, cf. Brill, Alan, *Judaism and Other Religions. Models of Understanding*, New York: Palgrave Macmillan, 2010, 9; 16–17; Gellman, Jerome (Yehudah), *God's Kindness Has Overwhelmed Us. A Contemporary Doctrine of the Jews as the Chosen People*, Boston: Academic Studies Press, 2013, 31–42.
[4] An organization that, I suspect, would be less happy today with the statement than it was in 1964. For background to this statement, cf. Heilman, Samuel C., *Sliding to the Right. The Contest for the Future of American Jewish Orthodoxy*, Berkeley: University of California Press, 2006.

with intrinsic dignity and metaphysical worth" the RCA statement went on to maintain: "Only full appreciation on the part of all of the singular role, inherent worth and basic prerogatives of each religious community will help promote the spirit of cooperation among faiths."[5] Given the way in which it was promulgated — published as an appendix to a programmatic article on the subject of inter-religious dialogue by the leading rabbinic figure in the RCA's world (Rabbi Joseph B. Soloveitchik[6]) — this statement carried great weight.

---

5 Appended to: Soloveitchik, Joseph B., "Confrontation," *Tradition* 6, no. 2 (1964), 5–29. Cf. further: Kimelman, Reuven, "Rabbis Joseph B. Soloveitchik and Abraham Joshua Heschel on Jewish-Christian Relations," *Edah Journal* 4, no. 2 (2004), 1–21; Korn, Eugene, "The Man of Faith and Religious Dialogue: Revisiting 'Confrontation'," *Modern Judaism* 25, no. 3 (2005), 290–315. Here is the text of the full statement:

STATEMENT ADOPTED BY THE RABBINICAL COUNCIL OF AMERICA AT THE MID-WINTER CONFERENCE, FEBRUARY 3–5, 1964

We are pleased to note that in recent years there has evolved in our country as well as throughout the world a desire to seek better understanding and a mutual respect among the world's major faiths. The current threat of secularism and materialism and the modern atheistic negation of religion and religious values makes even more imperative a harmonious relationship among the faiths. This relationship, however, can only be of value if it will not be in conflict with the uniqueness of each religious community, since each religious community is an individual entity which cannot be merged or equated with a community which is committed to a different faith. Each religious community is endowed with intrinsic dignity and metaphysical worth. Its historical experience, its present dynamics, its hopes and aspirations for the future can only be interpreted in terms of full spiritual independence of and freedom from any relatedness to another faith community. Any suggestion that the historical and meta-historical worth of a faith community be viewed against the backdrop of another faith, and the mere hint that a revision of basic historic attitudes is anticipated, are incongruous with the fundamentals of religious liberty and freedom of conscience and can only breed discord and suspicion. Such an approach is unacceptable to any self-respecting faith community that is proud of its past, vibrant and active in the present and determined to live on in the future and to continue serving God in its own individual *way*. Only full appreciation on the part of all of the singular role, inherent worth and basic prerogatives of each religious community will help promote the spirit of cooperation among faiths.

It is the prayerful hope of the Rabbinical Council of America that all inter-religious discussion and activity will be confined to these dimensions and will be guided by the prophet, (Mic 4:5) *Let all the people walk, each one in the name of his god, and we shall walk in the name of our Lord, our God, forever and ever.*

This statement was made in the context of Vatican II and the many Jewish discussions of how to respond to that initiative. Rabbi Soloveitck's article laid down the parameters of permissible dialogue with (primarily in his case) the Catholic Church.

6 Much has been written by and about Rabbi Soloveitchik (1903–1993), the undisputed leader of what was once called Modern Orthodoxy. Cf. Turkel, Eli, "Partial Bibliography of works by and about Rabbi Joseph B. Soloveitchik Zt"l," published online: Eli Turkel, http://www.cs.tau.ac.il/~turkel/ (accessed on 5.08.2019). Two valuable studies: Rynhold, Daniel/Harris, Michael J., *Niet-*

I personally found this a surprising statement. It speaks of religious *communities* and religious *faiths*; it thus ignores the ethnic component of Judaism (on which, more below) and adopts the view of Judaism as a religion, like Protestantism and Catholicism (in 1964 very few American Jews had ever seen let alone met a Muslim).[7] More importantly, it also acknowledges that Christianity has a singular role[8] and inherent worth, not to mention being "endowed with intrinsic dignity and metaphysical worth."[9]

This is the strong form of tolerance that I seek: acknowledging that other religions (not just Christianity and Islam) have a singular role in their respective cultures and *inherent religious* worth.[10] Once I acknowledge that with respect to other faiths, I am on strong grounds to insist that followers of other religions acknowledge the singular role and inherent worth of Judaism.

But having said that, I am faced with a serious problem. Is it possible to arrive at the strong form of tolerance without adopting a pluralist stance towards truth? Jews, Christians, and Muslims have traditionally seen the teachings of their respective religions to be exclusively true. Indeed, this is a consequence of their monotheism. The issue of religious tolerance arises urgently in the context of western monotheisms.

Much of the essay will involve the elucidation of ideas drawn from the writings of the greatest Jewish legist and thinker, Moses Maimonides (1138–1204).[11] It

---

zsche, Soloveitchik, and Contemporary Jewish Philosophy, Cambridge: Cambridge University Press, 2018; Schwartz, Dov, *Religion or Halakha. The Philosophy of Rabbi Joseph B. Soloveitchik*, Leiden: Brill, 2007.

7 For a prominent expression of this perspective, cf. Herberg, Will, *Protestant – Catholic – Jew. An Essay in Religious Sociology*, Chicago: University of Chicago Press, 1955.

8 Of course, this could be taken as a form of *praeparatio evangelica*, which, as we will see below, is precisely Maimonides' move.

9 One could water down the admission that Christianity has inherent worth by adopting Alan Brill's locution concerning certain patronizing medieval Jewish attempts to make space for what we might call tolerance of Christianity. Brill points out that certain medieval authorities maintained that Christianity is "monotheistic enough for Gentiles." Cf. Brill, *Judaism and Other Religions*, 179. This can hardly be said of Islam as Maimonides sees it. For Maimonides Islam is every bit as monotheist as Judaism. For two of many studies, cf. Lasker, Daniel J., "Tradition and Innovation in Maimonides' Attitude toward Other Religions," in: Jay Harris (ed.), *Maimonides After 800 Years. Essays on Maimonides and His Influence*, 167–82, Cambridge: Harvard University Press, 2007; Schlossberg, Eliezer, "Maimonides' Attitude Towards Islam," *Pe'amim* 42 (1990), 38–60 (Hebrew).

10 I realize that in putting the matter this way, I am denying the claim of these other religions to universal (exclusive) validity. Judaism never made that claim about itself.

11 An excellent and relatively brief introduction to the life and thought of Maimonides may be found in Halbertal, Moshe, *Maimonides*, Princeton: Princeton University Press, 2014. Longer

is important to emphasize at the outset that I seek to build on Maimonidean ideas to arrive at a form of theological tolerance. I do not claim for one moment that Maimonides himself would be happy with what I have done with and to his writings. He was a twelfth-century figure whose life had been turned upside down more than once by Muslim persecution. Like many medieval universalists, he would probably be baffled by our interest in developing a doctrine of theological tolerance. For Maimonides, Judaism (at least as he presented it) is true; Christianity and Islam are at best pale imitations.[12]

Why write about tolerance at all? I have a problem: I would like my views to be tolerated, even respected. Does consistency demand that I tolerate and even respect views with which I strongly disagree? How should I behave if those views with which I strongly disagree result in actions which I abhor?[13] This is one way of putting what has been called the "paradox of toleration."[14] I have a second, related problem: I would like to think that truth matters[15] and that the distinction between truth and falsity remains valid, despite the attacks of contemporary postmodernism. But, if truth really matters, how can I tolerate falsity? I have a third problem: should I tolerate the intolerant?

For reasons that will become clear below, issues such as these have been less of a problem for Judaism than they have been for classical Christianity and Islam.

---

studies include Davidson, Herbert A., *Moses Maimonides. The Man and His Works*, Oxford: Oxford University Press, 2005; Kraemer, Joel, *Maimonides. The Life and World of One of Civilization's Greatest Minds*, New York: Doubleday, 2008.

12 On Christianity and Islam as imitations of Judaism, cf. Maimonides, "The Epistle to Yemen," trans. A. S. Halkin, in: A. S. Halkin/David Hartman (eds.), *Crisis and Leadership. Epistles of Maimonides*, 93–131, Philadelphia: Jewish Publication Society, 1985. Despite this view, Maimonides envisioned a role for Christianity and Islam in the messianic process. Cf. Maimonides, *Mishneh Torah*, Yohai Makbili (ed.), Haifa, 2008 (Hebrew), "Laws of Kings and their Wars," xi. 4 (uncensored version). For details, cf. Kellner, Menachem/Gillis, David, *Maimonides the Universalist. The Ethical Horizons of Mishneh Torah*, London: The Littman Library of Jewish Civilization, 2020, chap. 14.

13 Putting the matter this way frees me from the obligation of considering whether tolerance is a virtue, and, if so, deciding if it is intimately bound up with liberalism. On this question, cf. Mendus, Susan, *Toleration and the Limits of Liberalism*, Atlantic Highlands, NJ: Humanities Press International, 1989; Kymlicka, Will, "Two Models of Pluralism and Tolerance," in: David Heyd (ed.), *Toleration. An Elusive Virtue*, 81–105, Princeton: Princeton University Press, 1996.

14 On the paradox of toleration, cf. Williams, Bernard, "Toleration. An Impossible Virtue?," in: David Heyd (ed.), *Toleration. An Elusive Virtue*, 18–27, Princeton: Princeton University Press, 1996.

15 Cf. Benson, Ophelia/Stangroom, Jeremy, *Why Truth Matters*, London: Continuum, 2006. Since truth matters, normative theological pluralism is no option, based as it is on the idea that there can be many competing "truths." I will take this up below and in my conclusion.

However, I am not only a Jew, but I am also (perhaps primarily[16]) a citizen in a democratic polity. As such, the "paradox of toleration" obtains in matters not directly connected to Jewish views of other religions. Let us take examples torn from today's headlines in the West:
- I strongly support the rights of women to control their own bodies, including the right to have an abortion (at least up to the point of fetal viability). Many of those who oppose abortion maintain that there is a conflict of rights in this case: the right of the mother to her own body vs. the right of the fetus to live. Since I do not believe that zygotes and fetuses have rights, ought I tolerate such "pro-life" forces?
- I support the rights of homosexuals to live their lives unmolested and with all the rights of heterosexuals, including marriage. But, like Islam and apparently classical Christianity, my religious tradition treats male homosexuality as an abomination, worthy of capital punishment. How ought I to behave?
- To my mind, individuals who seek to impose boycotts, divestment, and sanctions (BDS) on the State of Israel in general and upon Israeli academe in particular are either culpably misinformed or simply evil.[17] A few years ago, I was confronted by a problem in this regard. Sitting on an academic committee approving grants made by the State of Israel I was confronted by an application from an Israeli academic prominent in the boycott Israeli academia campaign. Should one boycott the boycotters?

Must I tolerate those who oppose abortion and those who seek to deny equal civil rights to homosexuals and those who support "conversion therapy"? Must I tolerate (and fund!) individuals who seek to undermine the very academic world in which they (and I) function?

The three examples cited here raise the "paradox of toleration" very clearly. I may have clear opinions on how to respond to the paradox in these cases, but my opinion on these matters is of no relevance to the issue before us, namely, how tolerant can a traditionally oriented Jew be of Christians and Muslims (or, for that matter, of believers in non-monotheistic faiths)? To rephrase: what can I say to a Jew who accepts the idea that the Torah is in some real sense the record of God's revelation? How can I urge that person to acknowledge the inherent

---

16 This is why my views will be of no interest to Jewish particularists, of whom there are (too) many, and on whom, more below.
17 This, of course, is hardly the place to go into the issue. For details, cf. Nelson, Cary, *Israel Denial. Anti-Zionism, Anti-Semitism, & the Faculty Campaign Against the Jewish State*, Bloomington: Indiana University Press, 2019.

worth and metaphysical dignity of religions that deny the truth of the Torah, either because it has been superseded, or because it is a counterfeit?

It is obvious that this last question has not really confronted Jews — at the very least — since the destruction of the second temple in Jerusalem in year 70 CE. To be troubled by the question of tolerance, one must be able to tolerate. A weak and persecuted community does not have to worry about tolerating others; it is too busy, as it were, trying to be tolerated by those others. Now that the State of Israel exists, the question of theological tolerance of other religions by Jews has become a live and pressing matter.

The issue in Israel is often phrased in terms of idolatry ('*avodah zarah* "alien or foreign worship"), one of the three "cardinal sins" in Judaism.[18] The general question, what constitutes idolatry, is of great contemporary relevance in Israel: growing ties with Hindu India raise questions about the relevance of classic views of idolatry; the constantly growing contributions of evangelical Christian organizations to Israeli Jewish institutions raise questions about whether or not Christianity should be treated as idolatry.[19] In the article just cited, I had occasion to address the question of whether Christianity (in all or some of its many, many forms) is to be considered idolatry. It should be emphasized that this is not a light matter in Jewish eyes: '*avodah zarah*, as noted, is one of the three so-called "cardinal sins" of Judaism: it is settled law that one must submit to martyrdom rather than engage in '*avodah zarah*, murder, or commit certain forms of sexual immorality. Whether or not Christianity is considered '*avodah zarah* is also not a light matter considering the vast numbers of Jews who over the generations chose martyrdom over forced conversion to Christianity. Are we to say that

---

[18] The other two are murder and sexual immorality. On the three 'cardinal sins' cf. Maimonides, *Mishneh Torah*, "Laws of the Foundations of the Torah", v.2.

[19] The question of whether Christianity is '*avodah zarah* usually arises in the following contexts: May one enter a church? For one detailed discussion, cf., Kellner, Menachem, "Thinking Idolatry with/against Maimonides: The Case of Christianity," in: Alon Goshen-Gottstein (ed.), *Idolatry: A Contemporary Jewish Conversation*, 290–311. Boston, USA: Academic Studies Press, 2023. No one reading this essay will suspect that I personally consider Christianity to be '*avodah zarah*. It ought to be noted that a minority of Orthodox rabbis (some of them quite prominent) argue that Christianity is not '*avodah zarah*. Cf., for example, Chief Rabbi Herzog, Isaac, "Zekhuyot Miutim le-fi ha-Halakhah," *Tehumin* 2 (1981), 169–99; and Shapiro, Marc, "Is It Permissible to Enter a Church? First Publication of a Responsum by Ha-Ga'on R. Eliezer Berkovitz on the Matter," *Milin Havivin* 4 (2011), 43–50. Note further the views of Rabinovitch, Nachum, *Melumadei Milḥamah*, Ma'aleh Adumim: Ma'aliyot, 1992, 145; Shapiro, David, *Studies in Jewish Thought*, vol. 2, New York: Yeshiva University Press, 1981, 272–75. It may not be a coincidence that all four of these figures reached rabbinic maturity outside of Israel. Cf. further the "Orthodox Rabbinic Statement on Christianity," published online: CJCUC, https://web.archive.org/web/20221128052125/http://www.cjcuc.org/2015/12/03/orthodox-rabbinic-statement-on-christianity/ (accessed on 16.01.2025).

their sacrifice was mistaken, in vain, since God would not have been disappointed, as it were, had they submitted to baptism since Christianity is not 'avodah zarah?[20]

It is of, course, not only in the State of Israel that the issue arises. Jewish communities around the world must ask themselves how best to cooperate with non-Jews in a world in which all religion seems to be constantly under siege by the forces of secularism.

The issue of theological tolerance arises most emphatically in the context of the three Western monotheisms under study in the present volume. All three traditions present themselves as based upon divinely revealed texts. Each of these texts, especially as received by their respective traditions, claims to teach truth in some important and significant manner. While there are many areas of agreement among these texts, there are even greater areas in which they do not agree. Not all three can be equally true. Jews, Christians, and Muslims have historically claimed that their respective traditions are true and that the other two are partially or even wholly false. The issue of tolerance arises in this context.

2 Tolerance among Jews and towards Other Faiths

Most contemporary discussions of tolerance in Jewish contexts relate to intra-Jewish tolerance: can one group of Jews accept other groups as in some sense Jewishly legitimate?[21] As the old saw has it, "two Jews, three views" — there has never

---

[20] Maimonides maintained that one must die rather than submit to forced conversion to Christianity. He maintained as a religious decisor of the first rank that one ought not die rather than submit to forced conversion to Islam. Christianity in his eyes is 'avodah zarah, Islam is not. Cf. above, note 8, on Christianity and Islam. On submitting to forced conversion to Islam, cf. Maimonides, "Epistle on Martyrdom," in: S. Halkin/David Hartman (eds.), *Crisis and Leadership. Epistles of Maimonides*, 15–33, 30, Philadelphia: Jewish Publication Society, 1985.
[21] There is plenty of respectful tolerance *within* the halakhic community. The challenge, of course, is to find ways of promoting tolerance towards Jews whose Judaism is significantly different that one's own. For studies, cf. Ravitzky, Aviezer, "The Question of Tolerance in the Jewish Religious Tradition," in: Yaakov Elman/Jeffrey S. Gurock (eds.), *Hazon Nahum. Studies in Jewish Law, Thought, and History Presented to Dr. Norman Lamm on the Occasion of His Seventieth Birthday*, 359–91, New York: Michael Sharf Publication Trust of the Yeshiva University Press, 1997; Ravitsky, Aviezer, "The Question of Tolerance. Between Pluralism and Paternalism", in: *Ḥarut Al ha-Luḥot*, 114–38, Tel Aviv: Am Oved, 1999, (Hebrew). Further valuable statements and studies include Altmann, Alexander, *Tolerance and the Jewish Tradition*, The Robert Waley Cohen Memorial Lecture, 1–18, London: The Council of Christians and Jews, 1957; Kimelman, "Judaism

been a lack of debates among Jews over what Judaism is, or even whether it might be.[22] As is often the case with intra-group polemics, it may be hard for outsiders even to see the differences between the groups. Ask a contemporary Reform Jew, for example, to explain the difference between "modern Orthodoxy" and "open Orthodoxy" and you are likely to meet with total lack of comprehension.[23] Similarly, if you ask a contemporary American Orthodox Jew to explain why there are so many political parties in Israel, each of them claiming to represent "true Jewish Orthodoxy" you will probably find the same lack of comprehension. Freud's "narcissism of small differences" indeed! Luckily for us, however, these questions may be set aside, since our challenge is to mount an argument in favor of tolerance on the part of Jews vis-à-vis other religions and not towards each other.

We thus seek a Jewishly serious basis for a position of tolerance towards non-Jewish religions. Is that possible? Before turning to that question, a brief historical digression is in order. The first stirrings of an attempt to ground a Jewish vision of tolerance may be found in the writings of Moses Mendelssohn (1729–1786), strongly influenced as he was by the European Enlightenment. In his book, *Jerusalem* (1783), Mendelssohn presents a defense of religious tolerance and pluralism. His views are ably summarized by Raphael Jospe:

---

and Pluralism"; Stone, Suzanne, "Tolerance Versus Pluralism in Judaism," *Journal of Human Rights* 2, no. 1 (2003), 105–17. I present an argument in support of intra-Jewish tolerance in Kellner, Menachem, *Must a Jew Believe Anything?*, Oxford: Littman Library of Jewish Civilization, 2006².

22 Historically, Jews have not understood themselves as a religion, similar in structure to Christianity and Islam. Leora Batnitzky maintains that arguing over the issue is a mark of Jewish modernity. Cf. Batnitzky, Leora, *How Judaism Became a Religion. An Introduction to Modern Jewish Thought*, Princeton: Princeton University Press, 2011. Abraham Melamed has shown that *dat* ("religion") is a term applied by Jews to what came to be called "Judaism" from at least the fifteenth century. Cf. Melamed, Abraham, *Dat. Me-Ḥoḳ le-Emuna. Ḳorotav Shel Minu'aḥ Mekhonen*, Tel Aviv: Ha-Kibbutz Ha-Me'uhad, 2014. I have argued that Maimonides may have been the first Jew to use the term *dat* in a way like the way in which we use the term "religion" and that he certainly had a notion of what we today would call "Judaism" even if it never occurred to him to use the term. Cf. Kellner, Menachem, "The Convert as the Most Jewish of Jews? On the Centrality of Belief (the Opposite of Heresy) in Maimonidean Judaism," *Jewish Thought* 1 (2019), 33–52 and my other studies cited therein.

23 For an entry into the lively discussion around "open Orthodoxy" cf. Farber, Zev, "Torah Min ha-Shamayim. A Guide to the Four Questions," published online: *The Torah*, https://www.thetorah.com/article/torah-from-heaven-a-guide-to-the-four-questions (accessed on 16.01.2025). Two recent books by Jerome Yehudah Gellman are exemplary of the new openness: Gellman, *God's Kindness Has Overwhelmed Us*, Gellman, Jerome (Yehudah), *This Was from God. A Contemporary Theology of Torah and History*, Boston: Academic Studies Press, 2016.

[...] Mendelssohn argues that Judaism adds no dogmas, no eternal truths necessary for salvation, to the basic rational truths of natural religion, namely the existence of God, providential reward and punishment, and the immortality of the human soul, on the grounds that these truths must be rationally accessible to all humans in all times and all places, and cannot be revealed. [...] Mendelssohn's theory establishes the basis for two modern corollaries that are basic pillars of the Enlightenment ideology of religious toleration. First, since all positive religions, with their diverse theoretical doctrines and ritual practices, share a common, universal rational basis and morality, the state can and must tolerate diversity and be neutral in religious areas. Second, since the truths essential for human happiness are rationally accessible to all, there is no basis for claiming exclusivity of salvation. A different and more positive relationship among religions is therefore not only practically possible, in terms of political toleration, but also theoretically desirable, in terms of pluralism.[24]

Without specific reference to Mendelssohn, Eugene Korn cites Jacob Katz to the effect that it was the budding Christian tolerance during this period that significantly influenced the development of a positive *halakhic* (Jewish legal) attitude toward Christians held by traditionalist Orthodox rabbis who came after Mendelssohn.[25]

With the rise of reform movements in nineteenth-century European Judaism, the reaction of that stream which came to be called "orthodox" was harsh and uncompromising. Originally viewed as a form of apostasy,[26] as "demonic deviance,"

---

24 Jospe, Raphael, "Moses Mendelssohn: A Medieval Modernist," in: Andrea Schatz/Irene Zwiep/Resianne Fontaine (eds.), *Sepharad in Ashkenaz: Medieval Knowledge and Eighteenth-Century Enlightened Jewish Discourse*, 107–40, esp. 123–24, Amsterdam: Royal Netherlands Academy of Arts and Sciences, 2007.
25 Korn, Eugene, "The People Israel, Christianity, and the Covenantal Responsibility to History," in: Robert W. Jensen/Eugene Korn (eds.), *Covenant and Hope*, 145–72, Grand Rapids, MI: Eerdmans, 2012. Korn cites Katz, Jacob, *Exclusivism and Tolerance*, New York: Schocken, 1962. Further on Mendelssohn cf. Altmann, Alexander, *Moses Mendelssohn: A Biographical Study*, Oxford; Portland, Oregon: Liverpool University Press, 1973. On our issue directly, cf. Schwarzschild, Steven, "Do Noachites Have to Believe in Revelation? (a Passage in Dispute between Maimonides, Spinoza, Mendelssohn, and Herman Cohen) a Contribution to a Jewish View of Natural Law," in: Menachem Kellner (ed.), *The Pursuit of the Ideal: Jewish Writings of Steven Schwarzschild*, 29–59, Albany: SUNY Press, 1990.
26 David Ellenson, himself long-time head of the main Reform seminary, Hebrew Union College, has examined the issue objectively and in detail. Cf., for example, Ellenson, David, "Traditional Reactions to Modern Jewish Reform: The Paradigm of German Orthodoxy," in: Daniel Frank/Oliver Leaman (eds.), *History of Jewish Philosophy*, London, 1997; Ellenson, David, "The Orthodox Rabbinate and Apostasy in Nineteenth-Century Germany and Hungary," in David Ellenson (ed.), *Tradition in Transition*, Lanham: University Press of America, 1989. On the use of these motifs in contemporary Israeli orthodoxy, cf. Ferziger, Adam, "The Role of Reform in Israeli Orthodoxy," in:

over the last two centuries the attitudes of almost all exponents of Jewish orthodoxy outside of Israel have moderated dramatically.[27] There are, of course, many reasons for this change of attitude, but it certainly has taken place.[28] Thus, there is growing intra-Jewish tolerance on the part of many Orthodox figures, but, it must be admitted, not the strong tolerance of respect which I seek to ground this essay.

3 Possible Solutions for Living Together Beyond Tolerance

Tolerance is only one way of looking for ways to live with other faiths in mutual respect. I want to examine and reject several other options.

3.1 Pluralism

We can solve our problem by affirming theological pluralism, the assertion that other religions are no less true than one's own. If one can assume that other religions are also true, there is no need for tolerance towards those other religions.[29]

Michael Meyer/David Myers (eds.), *Between Jewish Tradition and Modernity*, 51–66, Detroit: Wayne State University Press, 2014.

27 Ferziger, Adam, "From Demonic Deviant to Drowning Brother: Reform Judaism in the Eyes of American Orthodoxy," *Jewish Social Studies: History, Culture, Society* 15, no. 3 (2009), 56–88. Ferziger is the author of several studies on this phenomenon. Cf., among others, Ferziger, Adam, "Religion for the Secular: The New Israeli Rabbinate," *Journal of Modern Jewish Studies* 7, no. 1 (2008), 67–90 and *Beyond Sectarianism: The Realignment of American Orthodox Judaism*, Detroit: Wayne State University Press, 2015.

28 Among the reasons advanced for this change: Orthodox triumphalism ("the Jewish future is ours, we there can and ought to be magnanimous"), the rise of world-wide antisemitism, financial need, but most of all a growing sense of Orthodox responsibility for the Jewish people. This latter was spear-headed by the Habad movement, but now finds spirited acceptance in Orthodox outreach (*kiruv*) institutions. For details, cf. Ferziger, "From Demonic Deviant to Drowning Brother,".

29 For important contemporary expositions of pluralist views, cf. Korn, Eugene, "One God, Many Faiths: A Jewish Theology of Covenantal Pluralism," in: Eugene Korn/John T. Pawlikowsky (eds.), *Two Faiths, One Covenant?*, 147–54, Lanham, MD: Rowman and Littlefield, 2005; Korn, Eugene, "Extra Synagogam Sallus Est? Judaism and the Religious Other," in: Robert McKim (ed.), *Religious Perspectives on Religious Diversity*, 37–62, Leiden: Brill, 2016; Kimelman, Reuven, "Irving Greenberg, For the Sake of Heaven and Earth. The New Encounter Between Judaism and Christianity," *Modern Judaism* 27 (2007), 103–25. On Greenberg's version of pluralism, cf. also Korn, Eugene, "Idolatry and the Covenantal Pluralism of Irving Greenberg," in: Shmuly Yanklowitz (ed.),

There are several problems with this approach (aside from the fact that it makes writing this essay otiose). Most importantly, theological pluralism is based upon a notion of epistemological relativism — truth is relative, and, hence, truth does not *really* matter.[30] As stated above, in this essay I want to avoid the challenge put so well by Reuven Kimelman of adopting neither the "Scylla of relativism [nor] the Charybdis of absolutism." I want to arrive at a position of tolerance without being forced to abandon the claim that truth matters (on which more below).

I define epistemological relativism as the claim that truth is not one, absolute, and knowable, but variable, depending upon historical circumstance, point of view, etc.: "true for you, but not for me." An epistemological relativist should have no problem agreeing with the philosopher Judah Halevi (1075–1141), who deduced from the conflicting truth claims of Judaism, Christianity, and Islam that they are all equally false.[31]

3.2 Noahides

One-way Jews have sought to avoid intolerance is by granting (some) non-Jews the status of Noahides. Jewish tradition teaches that the "sons of Noah" (i.e., all human beings after the flood and before Sinai) were given seven divine commandments.[32] Of these seven, six involve forbidden behaviors (worshiping idols, murder, sexual immorality, theft, blaspheming God, eating flesh torn from a living

---

A Torah Giant. The Intellectual Legacy of Rabbi Dr. Irving (Yitz) Greenberg, 59–70, Jerusalem: Urim Publications, 2018.

30 Raphael Jospe does not agree with this assertion. For his important (if ultimately unsuccessful) attempt to ground theological pluralism without being forced into epistemological relativism, cf. his "Affirming Chosenness and Pluralism. Ritual Exclusivity Vs. Spiritual Inclusivity".
31 Halevi, Judah, *Accepting and Excepting: Pluralism and Chosenness Out of the Sources of Judaism* (Boston: Academic Studies Press, 2025). *Kuzari*, trans. Michael Schwarz, Be'er Sheva: Ben Gurion University Press, 2017, part 1, section 1 (end) (Hebrew).
32 A vast amount has been written on the Noahide commandments. David Novak is the author of a comprehensive study of the subject: Novak, David, *The Image of the Non-Jew in Judaism. An Historical and Constructive Study of the Noahide Laws*, New York: E. Mellen Press, 1983. Cf. also Novak, David, "Maimonides and Aquinas on Natural Law," in: *Talking with Christians. Musings of a Jewish Theologian*, 67–88, Grand Rapids, MI: Eerdmans, 2005. Further on Maimonides and Noahism, cf. Schwarzschild, Steven, "Do Noachites Have to Believe in Revelation?" (above, note 25); Kreisel, Howard, "Maimonides on Divine Religion," in: Jay Harris (ed.), *Maimonides After 800 Years. Essays on Maimonides and His Influence*, 151–66, Cambridge: Harvard University Press, 2007; Frimer, Dov, "Israel, the Noahide Laws and Maimonides. Jewish-Gentile Legal Relations in Maimonidean Thought," in: Yamin Levy/Shalom Carmy (eds.), *The Legacy of Maimonides. Religion, Reason, and Community*, 96–110, New York: Yashar Books, 2006.

animal) and one positive commandment: to establish courts of law. These seven commandments are often construed as a kind of universal morality, making demands of Jews and non-Jews alike. Non-Jews who satisfy these seven are considered righteous.

I sense a heavy dose of condescending paternalism in this approach.[33] In the words of Alan Brill, Christianity (which I cite here as a possible contemporary example of Noahism) is "monotheistic enough for Gentiles," but not, of course, truly and fully monotheistic. (I hasten to emphasize that this patronizing position is not Brill's own!) Indeed, Maimonides, the greatest Jewish legal and philosophical authority of the last millennium (at least), insisted that to count as a Noahide one must explicitly accept and obey the Noahide commandments, not because they are reasonable, but because they are taught in the Torah of Moses.[34] On this view, to be a Noahide is to be a self-consciously watered down Jew. On this view also, most of the humanity who have never heard of Torah would be left out in the cold.

Further, as Eugene Korn has shown, the vast majority of medieval and early modern decisors in Christian Europe found a middle path, originally charted by the Talmudic commentators known as Tosafists, between pluralism and viewing Christianity as rank idolatry: Christianity is forbidden idolatry ('*avodah zarah*) when practiced by Jews, but not when practiced by Gentiles.[35] As noted, on this approach, "Christianity is monotheistic enough for Gentiles," but certainly not for Jews! Tolerant, perhaps, but hardly respectful.

---

[33] Elijah Benamozegh (1822–1900) would have rejected this assessment. Cf. Benamozegh, Elijah, *Israel and Humanity*, trans. Maxwell Luria, Mahwah, NJ: Paulist Press, 1995. Cf. also Luria on Benamozegh: Luria, Maxwell, "Rabbi Eliyahu Benamozegh. Israel and Humanity," published online: Institute for Jewish Ideas and Ideals (ed.), https://www.jewishideas.org/article/rabbi-eliyahu-benamozegh-israel-and-humanity (accessed on 17.01.2025).

[34] Maimonides, *Mishneh Torah*, "Laws of Kings and their Wars," viii. 11. Maimonides is often misconstrued as maintaining there that only such Noahide non-Jews have a share in the world to come. Cf. Kellner, Menachem, *Maimonides' Confrontation with Mysticism*, Oxford: Littman Library of Jewish Civilization, 241–49, 2006.

[35] Korn, Eugene, "Rethinking Christianity. Rabbinic Positions and Possibilities," in: Alon Goshen-Gottstein/Eugene Korn (eds.), *Jewish Theology and World Religions*, 189–215, esp. 196–97, Littman Library of Jewish Civilization, Liverpool: Liverpool University Press, 2012.

3.3 (Messianic) Universalism

Another way of avoiding intolerance is by adopting some form of messianic universalism.[36] A common way of presenting this view is to say that, in effect, Christianity is correct: when the messiah (actually) comes, Judaism will cease to be an ethnically based religion, but the universal religion of all humankind. Christianity's basic mistake was in thinking that the messiah has already come.[37]

This universalism is one way of construing the position of Maimonides. He included the following passage in his major exposition of messianism:[38]

> Even of Jesus of Nazareth, who imagined that he was the Messiah, and was put to death by the court, Daniel had prophesied, as it is written, *And the children of the violent among thy people shall lift themselves up to establish the vision; but they shall stumble* [Dan 11: 14]. For has there ever been a greater stumbling-block than this? All the prophets affirmed that the messiah would redeem Israel, save them, gather their dispersed, and strengthen [observance of] the commandments. But he [Jesus] caused Israel to be destroyed by the sword, their remnant to be dispersed and humiliated. He was instrumental in changing the Torah and causing the world to err and serve another beside God. But it is beyond the human mind to fathom the designs of the Creator; for our ways are not His ways, neither are our thoughts His thoughts. All these matters relating to Jesus of Nazareth, and the Ishmaelite [Mohammed]

---

36 Much, but not all the writing on Judaic universalism is apologetic in tone. In a wholly non-apologetic plane, for the Bible cf., Levenson, Jon D., "The Universal Horizon of Biblical Particularism," in: Mark G. Brett (ed.), *Ethnicity and the Bible*, 143–69, Leiden: Brill, 1996; Kaminsky, Joel S., *Yet I Loved Jacob. Reclaiming the Biblical Concept of Election*, Nashville: Abingdon, 2007. For rabbinic Judaism, cf. Blidstein, Gerald, "A Note on Rabbinic Missionizing," *Journal of Theological Studies* 47, no. 2 (1996), 528–31. Menachem (Marc) Hirshman has isolated a strain of universalism in rabbinic thought. Cf. his "Rabbinic Universalism in the Second and Third Centuries," *Harvard Theological Review* 93 (2000), 101–15. In this article, Hirshman summarizes the main points in his *Torah Lekhol Ba'ei Olam. Zerem Universali be-Sifrut ha-Tana'im ve-Yaḥaso le-Ḥokhmat ha-'Amim*, Tel Aviv: Ha-Kibbutz ha-Meuhad, 1999. Hirshman continues his examination of this strain of rabbinic thought in his "Election and Rejection in the Midrash," *Jewish Studies Quarterly* 16 (2009), 71–82. For Maimonides' views, cf. Kellner, *Maimonides' Confrontation with Mysticism*; Kellner, Menachem, *Science in the Bet Midrash. Studies in Maimonides*, Brighton, MA: Academic Studies Press, 2009, chapters 16–20. For Maimonides' geonic background, cf. Sklare, David, "Are the Gentiles Obligated to Observe the Torah? The Discussion Concerning the Universality of the Torah in the East in the Tenth and Eleventh Centuries," in: Jay Harris (ed.), *Be'erot Yitzhak. Studies in Memory of Isadore Twersky*, 311–46, Cambridge: Harvard University Press, 2005, (and the other studies cited there).
37 I ignore other mistakes of Christianity, such as original sin and the divine nature of the messiah, among others.
38 Maimonides, *Mishneh Torah*, "Laws of Kings and their Wars", xi.4. For detailed commentary on the texts cited in this section, cf. Kellner/Gillis, *Maimonides the Universalist* (above, note 12), chap. 14.

> who came after him, only serve to clear the way for King messiah, to prepare [*letaken*] the whole world to worship God with one accord, as it is written, *For then will I turn to the peoples a pure language, that they all call upon the name of the Lord to serve Him with one consent* [Zeph 3:9]. How so? The messianic hope, the Torah, and the commandments have become familiar topics—topics of conversation [among the inhabitants] of the far isles and many people, uncircumcised of heart and flesh. They are discussing these matters and the commandments of the Torah. Some say, 'Those commandments were true, but have lost their validity and are no longer binding'; others declare that they had an esoteric meaning and were not to be taken literally; that the messiah has already come and revealed their occult significance. But when the true King messiah will appear and succeed, be exalted and lifted up, they will forthwith recant and realize that they have inherited nothing but lies from their fathers, that their prophets and forebears led them astray.

Maimonides affirms that Christianity and Islam have crucial roles in the messianic advent. Since the task of the Messiah is "to prepare the *whole* world to worship God with *one accord*," and since, as Maimonides often stresses, no miracles are to be involved, for the Messiah to come the world must be monotheized, as it were. That is the role assigned by God to Christianity and to Islam.[39]

Having dismissed Christianity and Islam, Maimonides turns in the final, climactic chapter of the *Mishneh Torah* to the main contours of the messianic era. In the first paragraph of the last chapter of the *Mishneh Torah* ("Laws Concerning Kings and Their Wars", 12:1), Maimonides writes:

> Let it not enter your mind that in the days of the messiah any aspect of the regular order of nature will be abolished or some innovation will be introduced into the world of nature; rather, the world follows its accustomed course. The verse in Isaiah [11: 6], *the wolf shall dwell with the lamb, the leopard lie down with the kid* is an allegory and metaphor. Its meaning is that Israel will dwell in security with [those who were] the wicked nations of the earth, which are allegorically represented as wolves and leopards, as it says [Jer. 5: 6]: *the wolf of the desert ravages them. A leopard lies in wait by their towns.* Those nations will all adopt the true religion [*dat ha'emet*]. [In consequence,] they will neither rob not destroy; rather, they will eat permitted foods in peace and quiet as Israelites, as it says, *the lion, like the ox, shall eat straw.*[40] All similar things written about the messiah are allegories, and in the days of the

---

[39] It is of interest to note how the verse from Zephaniah contrasts with the story of the Tower of Babel, anticipating a time when peace reigns because all people speak one language (presumably Hebrew, not Esperanto). It should also be noted that this passage was censored from premodern editions of the *Mishneh Torah*. By whom? That is hard to say. Cf. Kellner, Menachem, "*Farteitcht un Farbessert* (On 'Correcting' Maimonides)," *Me'orot* [=*Edah Journal*] 6, no. 2 (2007), 2–13.

[40] Note that according to this proof-text, the lion and the ox eat the *same* food. For an alternative reading of this paragraph, according to which messianic Gentiles fulfill the seven Noachide commandments but remain Gentiles, cf. Chaim Rappoport's critique of Kellner in *Me'orot* 7.1 (next note).

messianic king everyone will understand which matters were allegories, and also the meaning hinted at by them.

What does the expression *dat ha'emet* mean in this context? In a number of places, I have argued that Maimonides means that in the messianic era (or, more accurately, by the time it reaches fruition since it is, after all, a process and not an event) all human beings will worship God from a position of absolute spiritual equality.[41] Whether that means that all non-Jews will convert formally to Judaism,[42] that they will be absorbed into Israel in some other fashion, or that the distinction will become in some way significantly less important than it is now, is open to question. What is clear is that the relevant distinctions between Jew and non-Jew will disappear by the time that the messianic process has reached completion. In making this claim, I stand opposed to those who interpret Maimonides in a more particularist fashion, according to which even at the end of days for Maimonides the Jews will remain God's chosen people, especially beloved, and distinct from the mass of humanity. I also stand opposed to those who might want to read Maimonides in a pluralist fashion, as if he holds that in the messianic era many different paths will lead equally to God. Rather, I read him as a messianic universalist.[43]

---

[41] Cf. Kellner, Menachem, "Maimonides' *True Religion* – for Jews, or All Humanity?", *Me'orot* [=*Edah Journal*] 7.1 (2008), 1–24; and Kellner/Gillis, *Maimonides the Universalist*, chap. 14.

[42] As I argue in *Maimonides on Judaism and the Jewish People*, Albany: SUNY Press, 1991, 39–58, Maimonides was not alone in this view. Cf. the surprising number of Kabbalists who also looked forward to a redemption characterized by wholesale conversion to Judaism cited by Reuven Kimelman in his study of *Lekha Dodi*: Kimelman, Reuven, "*Lekha Dodi" ve-Ḳabalat Shabat. Ha-Mashma'ut ha-Mistit*. Jerusalem: Magnes, 2003, chap. 4. Maimonides' son Abraham likely understood his father in much the way as we present him here: "And the meaning of 'a kingdom of priests' [Ex 19:6] is that the priest of a congregation is its leader, for he is its most honored member and serves as its model, inasmuch as the members of the congregation will walk in his footsteps and through him will find the straight path. Thus, God said, 'You, by observing My commandments, will become the leaders of the world. Your relationship to them [the nations of the world] will be like the relationship of the priest to his congregation. All the world will follow in your wake, they will imitate your actions, and walk in your path.' This is the understanding that I received as the explanation of this verse from my father and master, of blessed memory." Abraham ben Maimonides, *Commentary on Genesis and Exodus*, ed. S. D. Sasoon/E. Weisenberg, London, 1958, 303 (Arabic original) and 302 (Hebrew translation); note that this book is available for download on https://hebrewbooks.org/ (accessed on 03.04.2025).

[43] This essay is not about Maimonides (although some readers may be forgiven for thinking that it is), so I will not go into the question of whether Maimonides' messianism was Abrahamic or Mosaic. For discussion, cf. Kellner/Gillis, *Maimonides the Universalist*, chap. 15.

Maimonides makes our point in the resounding last paragraph of the *Mishneh Torah*:

> The Sages and Prophets did not long for the days of the messiah that they might exercise dominion over the world, or rule over the nations, or be exalted by the peoples, and not in order to eat and drink and rejoice, but so that they be free to devote themselves to the Torah and *its wisdom*, with no one to oppress or disturb them, and thus be worthy of life in the world to come, as we explained in 'Laws of Repentance' (ix.2). Then there will be neither famine nor war, neither jealousy nor strife. Good things will be abundant, and delicacies as common as dust. The one preoccupation of the whole world will be only to know [*lada'at*] the Lord. Hence [they][44] will be very wise, knowing [*yod'im*] things now unknown and will apprehend knowledge [*da'at*] of their Creator to the utmost capacity of the human mind, as it is written: *For the land shall be full (ki malah ha'arets) of the knowledge [de'ah] of the Lord, as the waters cover the sea* [Isa. 11: 9].

The peak of messianism for Maimonides is to bring all human beings to the point where they abandon idolatry (and all that idolatry stands for, namely, brutality and stupidity) and embrace monotheism. Remember, the Messiah will "prepare the whole world to worship God with one accord, as it is written, *For then will I turn to the peoples a pure language, that they all call upon the name of the Lord to serve Him with one consent* [Zeph 3:9]". This will come about without miraculous intervention.[45] If the Messiah is meant to "to prepare the whole world to worship God with one accord," then the world must be made ready to accept belief in one God to make the messiah's mission possible. Converting the entire world from paganism to refined monotheism in one fell swoop would be a miracle of gargantuan proportions. Such a change can only come about miraculously since, as Maimonides teaches in the *Guide* (iii.32, p. 526), "a sudden transition from one opposite to another is impossible. And therefore man, according to his nature, is not capable of abandoning suddenly all to which he was accustomed." Thus, for Judaic messianism to reach fruition, the world needs Christianity and Islam to pave the way for the messiah's advent. Maimonides is perhaps the

---

[44] Presumably the inhabitants "of the whole world," the *ba'ei olam* who, Maimonides says, can achieve the highest possible level of sanctity even in this dispensation (Maimonides, *Mishneh Torah*, "Laws of the Sabbatical Year," xiii. 13; and Kellner/Gillis, *Maimonides the Universalist*, chap. 7). On the textual issues here cf. Schwarzfuchs, Simon-Raymond, "Les Lois Royales De Maimonide", *Revue des etudes juives* 111 (1951–52), 63–86. On 81–2 Schwarzfuchs shows that many printed editions and manuscripts add the word "Israel" here.

[45] The claim that the messianic advent comes about without interruptions in the order of nature is, as it were, a *leitmotif* of Maimonides' discussions of messianism. Here, too, cf. Kellner/Gillis, *Maimonides the Universalist*, chap. 14.

most universalist of pre-modern Jewish thinkers, but, as a messianic exclusivist, he had no room for non-Jewish religions in his messianic world.[46]

We have surveyed pluralism, Noahism, and messianic universalism. None of them provides a basis for the strong sort of tolerance that I seek.

4 Particularism

Of course, historically, the most prevalent option has been to reject tolerance altogether and affirm some sort of Judaic particularism. Particularism comes in many varieties and flavors. We can hardly survey them all here.[47] Perhaps a useful way of entering our subject is by very briefly examining the history of two words, *ger* (stranger, alien, sojourner) and *re'a* (fellow, often translated neighbor).

The Bible teaches, *Love the ger, because you were gerim* [pl. of *ger*] *in the Land of Egypt* (Dt 10:19). That seems clear enough: the Israelites in Egypt were strangers, aliens, sojourners there. Thus, Jews of all people, should be sensitive to the needs of strangers, etc., in their midst. However, the rabbinic tradition is overwhelmingly consistent in reading this verse as if it refers to the *ger tsedek*, or proselyte, one who converted to Judaism and is thus a Jew, not a stranger, alien, or sojourner.[48]

---

46 Messianic particularists, of course, such as the Ḥabad movement, have even less room for non-Jewish religions in their messianic world. Non-Jews there will be, but they will be Noahides, subservient to the Jews. For a typical statement of Ḥabad attitudes on non-Jews in the messianic era, cf. *Sha'arei Geulah*, New York: Kehat, 1992, 188–205; Dahan, Alon, *Go'el Aharon. Mishnato ha-Meshihit shel Rabbi Menachem Mendel Schneerson*, Tel Aviv, 2004, 535–77. Not only Ḥabad affirms messianic particularism. Daniel J. Lasker is the author of an important and widely cited study showing that according to Judah Halevi, in the messianic era all humanity will accept Judaism, but the "new Jews" will constitute a separate community. Cf. Lasker, Daniel J., "Proselyte Judaism, Christianity, and Islam in the Thought of Judah Halevi," *Jewish Quarterly Review* 81 (1990), 75–91.
47 For studies of Judaic particularism, cf. Balk, Hanan, "The Soul of a Jew and the Soul of a Non-Jew. An Inconvenient Truth and the Search for an Alternative," *Hakirah. The Flatbush Journal of Jewish Law and Thought* 16 (2013), 47–76; Gellman, Jerome, "Jewish Mysticism and Morality. Kabbalah and its Ontological Dualities," *Archiv fuer Religionsgeschichte* 9 (2008), 23–35; Lachter, Hartley, "Israel as a Holy People in Medieval Kabbalah," in: Alan Mittleman (ed.), *Holiness in Jewish Thought*, Oxford: Oxford University Press, 2018; Wolfson, Elliot, *Venturing Beyond. Law and Morality in Kabbalistic Mysticism*, 137–59, Oxford: Oxford University Press, 2006. These studies all deal with Judaic particularism in kabbalistic contexts. For philosophic contexts, cf. Kasher, Hannah, *'Elyon Al Kol Ha-Goyyim. Tsiyyunei Derekh Ba-Philosophia Ha-Yehudit Be-Sugiyat Ha-'Am Ha-Nivḥar*, Tel Aviv: Idra, 2018; Kellner, Menachem, "On Universalism and Particularism in Judaism," *Da'at* 36 (1996), v–xv.
48 Deut 19:10 teaches that one is obligated to love the *ger*, since we were *gerim* in the land of Egypt. Ex 22:20 teaches that one may not defraud the *ger*. In both instances, references to these

The proselyte is, of course, the locus of many discussions of Judaic tolerance, pluralism, universalism, etc.[49] That, however, is irrelevant for our purposes here since proselytes are Jews; they may be the objects of special love, but as Jews, do not have to be the objects of theological tolerance.

It is worthwhile to digress for a moment to emphasize this point. In a famous halakhic responsum to a proselyte, one Obadiah, Maimonides writes, in response to a question about a proselyte reciting prayer text that relate to descent from the patriarchs:

> You shall certainly say the blessing, "Who has chosen us," "Who has given us," "Who have taken us for Your own," and "Who has separated us," for the Creator, may He be extolled, has indeed chosen you and separated you from the nations and given you the Torah. For the Torah has been given to us and to the proselytes, as it is said, *One ordinance shall be both for you of the congregation, and also for the stranger that sojourns with you, an ordinance forever in your generations; as you are, so shall the stranger be before the Lord* (Num. 15:15). Know that our fathers, when they came out of Egypt, were mostly idolaters;[50] they had mingled with the pagans in Egypt and imitated their way of life, until the Holy One, may He be blessed, sent Moses our teacher, the master of all prophets, who separated us from the nations and brought us under the wings of the Divine Presence, us and all proselytes, and gave to all of us one Law.

Maimonides brings this section of his response to Obadiah to a dramatic close with the following resounding statement:

> Do not consider your origin as inferior. While our descent is from Abraham, Isaac, and Jacob, your descent is from Him through whose word the world was created. As is said by Isaiah: *One shall say, I am the Lord's, and another shall call himself by the name of Jacob* (Is 44:5).

---

verses in rabbinic literature assume that *ger* in these contexts mean proselyte. Cf, for example the Talmud (bB. Mets. 59b), following the Mishnah (mB. Mets. iv. 10), and, for example out of several in midrashic literature, *Midrash Tehilim* (*Shoḥar Tov*) 146. Maimonides summarizes this tradition in his *Book of Commandments*, trans. Charles B. Chavel, London: Soncino, 1967, positive commandment 207 and negative commandments 252 and 253. Cf. also *Mishneh Torah*, "Laws Concerning Character Traits," vi. 3.

49 For an entry into the discussion, cf. Kellner, *Maimonides on Judaism*, chap. 6. An extremely important study on Maimonides on proselytes is Diamond, James, *Converts, Heretics, and Lepers. Maimonides and the Outsider*, Notre Dame: University of Notre Dame Press, 2007, ch 1. Cf. now also Kellner, "The Convert as the Most Jewish of Jews?".

50 Maimonides repeats this claim in several places. Cf. explicitly in Maimonides, *Mishneh Torah*, "Laws Concerning Idolatry," chap. 1 and Maimonides, *Guide of the Perplexed*, trans. Shlomo Pines, Chicago: University of Chicago Press, 1963, iii.32. In this he stands opposed to Judah Halevi (*Kuzari*, I. 97) who maintained that only 3000 out of 600,000 Israelites worshiped the golden calf.

Proselytes are Jews, period. In Maimonidean eyes, the best of Jews, since their Judaism is the result of conviction and choice, not simply birth.

Returning to our discussion, just as Jewish tradition narrows the focus of love of the *ger* from love of the stranger, sojourner, etc., to love of the proselyte, so does the tradition narrow the focus of the famous verse *Love thy neighbor (re'a) as thyself* (Lev 19:18). Who is the neighbor whom one must love? It is not, it turns out, the person living next door, whatever their religion or ethnicity. At the very least, it is the fellow Jew, and in some even more particularist readings, only Jews who keep all the commandments.[51]

Presenting these two terms in this fashion reflects a prejudice of mine: that the Jewish tradition, from the Bible onward, is fundamentally universalist, becoming ever more particularist as Jewish history became ever more difficult.[52] Over the generations, it became more and more difficult to see the non-Jew as a fellow creature made equally in the image of God. Thus, we find a kind of ethnic particularism developing and growing especially from the Middle Ages onward.[53] Going into this matter would take us far afield, since our interest is in finding a Jewishly serious form of theological tolerance. Explaining why that is hard to find in Jewish sources is hardly what we are about here.

---

51 Simon, Ernst, "The Neighbor (Re'a) Whom We Shall Love," in: Marvin Fox (ed.), *Modern Jewish Ethics. Theory and Practice*, Columbus: Ohio State University Press, 1975, 29–56. For a prominent rabbinic figure who includes non-Jews in the obligation of love, Cf. Ellenson, David, "Rabbi Hayim David Halevi on Christians and Christianity: An Analysis of Selected Legal Writings of an Israeli Authority," in: Franklin Harkin (ed.), *Transforming Relations: Essays on Jews and Christians... In Honor of Michael A. Signer*, 340–61, Notre Dame: Notre Dame, 2010. Rabbi Hayyim David Halevi (1924–1998) was Chief Rabbi of Tel Aviv. Ellenson cites his Aseh Lekha Rav)Tel Aviv, 1989) vol. 9, 64–5.

52 By "universalist" here I mean the view that all human beings are fully created in the image of God and all are objects of God's concern. It will be objected that my prejudice ignores the biblical doctrine of election — a popular accusation among individuals seeking to contrast Judaic narrowness with, say, Christian universalism. For accurate accounts of what biblical election entails, cf. the writings of Levenson and Kaminsky, cited above in footnote 36. For important support of my "prejudice" cf. Roth, Leon, "Moralization and Demoralization in Jewish Ethics," in: *Is There a Jewish Philosophy?*, 128–43, London: Littman Library of Jewish Civilization, 1999.

53 Ethnic particularism, often expressed in terms of ontological superiority, became dominant in the Jewish Middle Ages, but it was hardly the only view. For a detailed analysis of Maimonides' rejection of this view, and his affirmation that all human beings are indeed created in the image of God, cf. Kellner, Menachem, *Gam Hem Ḳeruyim Adam. Ha-Nokhri be-'Eynei ha-Rambam*, Ramat-Gan: Bar-Ilan University Press, 2016. In English, one may consult Kellner, Menachem, "We Are Not Alone," in: Michael J. Harris/Daniel Rynhold/Tamra Wright (eds.), *Radical Responsibility. Celebrating the Thought of Chief Rabbi Lord Jonathan Sacks*, 139–54, Jerusalem: Maggid Books, 2012. Reprinted in: Hava Tirosh-Samuelson/Aaron Hughes (eds.), *Menachem Kellner. Jewish Universalism*, 107–18, Library of Contemporary Jewish Philosophers 12, Leiden: Brill, 2015.

5 Judaic Religious Tolerance — Finally

Tolerance comes in many flavors. There is a weak version, typical of Judaism over the generations, of not being interested in other religions, so long as the Jews were left alone. This is the view expressed by the rabbi in the Broadway musical, "Fiddler on the Roof":

> the rabbi's son asks if there is "a proper blessing for the czar." The rabbi responds, "A blessing for the czar?" He ponders awhile, then pronounces: "Of course: May God bless and keep the czar — far away from us. Amen."

This is meant to be amusing, but it expresses an important point. All the rabbi wanted from the Czar was to be left alone. If the Czar was not persecuting the Jews, what the Czar did was the Czar's business. Let God bless the Czar and keep him (as in the priestly blessing, *May the Lord bless you and keep you* [Nu 6: 23]), and let the Czar leave the rabbi and his flock to their own devices. The rabbi has no interest in the Czar, certainly not in his theology, and has no objection to God showering blessings upon the Czar.

Why has the rabbi no such interest? The reason behind this lack of interest is simple to state, but rarely understood by non-Jews, and has recently become the focus of debate within Judaism on the part of scholars, some of whom have barely hidden political agendas.[54] What is that reason? Judaism, unlike Christianity and Islam, makes no pretensions of being a universal religion; indeed, it is hard to see it as "only" a religion in the sense that Christianity and Islam are religions (however one defines the term). Judaism is the religion *of* the Jewish people,[55] or the religion *that constitutes* the Jewish people.[56] Jews, defined as members of the Jewish people, have held many religious views (on which, more below) and generally have been uninterested in the religious views of other peoples. Jewish history and texts do not call for crusades and jihad against unbelievers.[57]

---

54 Cf. Sand, Shlomo, *The Invention of the Jewish People*, London: Verso, 2008.
55 Solomon Schechter (1847–1915) is often quoted as having stated, "Judaism is the religion of the Jewish people."
56 Sa'adia Gaon (882–942) stated, "Our people is only a people by virtue of its Torahs [i.e., written and oral]." Cf. Sa'adia Gaon, *Book of Belief and Opinions*, trans. Samuel Rosenblatt, New Haven: Yale University Press, 1948, iii. 7.
57 Altmann, *Tolerance and the Jewish Tradition*, put it well on page 6: Judaism "It may be said, in general, is intolerant of Israelites falling away from the God of the Fathers and of the Covenant. It shows no trace of intolerance of heathens following their customs and traditions. Ruth the Moabite is welcomed as a proselyte, but Orpah, her sister-in-law is not reproved because of her return to her native paganism. David and Solomon extended their kingdoms far beyond the

So far, the weak version of tolerance meaning lack of interest. Another version of weak tolerance can be "putting up with" or pitying.[58] This is hardly the sort of tolerance we are looking for here. I do not want non-Jews to put up with me, condescend towards me or, worse, pity me. I shall thus not seek a version of tolerance towards non-Jews that involves my "putting up" with them, condescending towards them or pitying them.

Before moving on, allow me to present one personal story illustrating the tolerance of pity. Many years ago, before making *aliyah* (moving) to Israel, my family and I were close to two other religious families in the community in which we then lived: the family of the local Orthodox rabbi, and a family of Evangelical Christians, with whom we shared many social and cultural attitudes. All three families once got together for a bar-b-cue in the rabbi's back yard. Mary, the teen-age daughter of our Evangelical friends was playing with the rabbi's son, then a toddler. Suddenly Mary burst into bitter tears. When asked why, she explained: "Ploni [the rabbi's son] is such a wonderful, sweet little boy, and is still destined to burn in hell!" Well-meaning, I suppose, but certainly condescending and pitying.

There is a second reason for the rabbi's lack of what we might call theological interest in the thinking and doing of non-Jews: Judaism, whatever it is, makes no claims of exclusivism. Jewish texts and teachers have never called upon all non-Jews to become Jewish to be "saved" (whatever that might be[59]). It has long been settled Jewish doctrine that outside of the synagogue there *can* be salvation.[60]

Israelite borders, but they did not impose their religion on the subjugated peoples." On page 7, Altmann also notes that Jonah did not demand that the inhabitants of Ninveh worship the God of Israel, let alone become Jews.

58 Abraham Joshua Heschel calls for reverence of the other, not tolerance in the sense of condescension or pity. See Heschel, Abraham Joshua, "No Religion is an Island," *Union Seminary Quarterly Review* 21, no. 2 (1966), 117–34, esp. 123.

59 Jewish texts express the idea captured by the word "salvation" by talking of having a share in the world to come. Aside from an endless stream of jokes, the Jewish tradition has never arrived at a clear understanding of what that means. Minimally, it is expected that in some fashion or other the righteous will be rewarded after death and the wicked punished. For an introduction to the discussion, cf. Schwarzschild, Steven, "On Jewish Eschatology," in: Menachem Kellner (ed.), *The Pursuit of the Idea. Jewish Writings of Steven Schwarzschild*, 209–28, Albany: SUNY Press, 1990.

60 If there is anything in Jewish theology which may be considered settled doctrine it is that righteous non-Jews (ḥasidei umot ha-'olam) enjoy a share in the world to come. For studies, cf. Korn, Eugene, "Gentiles, the World to Come, and Judaism. The Odyssey of a Rabbinic Text," *Modern Judaism* 14 (1994), 265–87; Korn, "Extra Synagogam Sallus Est?" (note 29 above); Kasher, Hannah, "Three Punishments Which are One, According to Maimonides," *Sidra* 14 (1988), 39–58;

As noted already at the beginning of this essay, I seek a strong version of tolerance, one grounded in Jewish texts and teachings, and one that a person committed to the truth of Torah could accept. Having said that, I am faced with a serious problem. Is it possible to arrive at the strong form of tolerance without adopting a pluralist stance towards truth? Jews, Christians, and Muslims have traditionally seen the teachings of their respective religions to be exclusively true. Indeed, this is a consequence of their monotheism. The issue of religious tolerance arises urgently in the context of western monotheisms.

6 Monotheism and Intolerance

On the one hand, one might expect that belief in one God who created all human beings in the divine image should lead to a universalist ethic, according to which all human beings are equal in the eyes of God and equally beloved by God. A well-known Mishnaic text (M. Sanhedrin iv.5), one that was the basis for a Qur'ānic verse (5:32),[61] makes the point emphatically and explicitly:

> How were the witnesses inspired with awe? Witnesses in capital charges were brought in and intimidated [thus]: perhaps what you say is based only on conjecture, or hearsay, or is evidence from the mouth of another witness, or even from the mouth of a trustworthy person: perhaps you are unaware that ultimately, we shall scrutinize your evidence by cross-examination and inquiry? Know then that capital cases are not like monetary cases. In civil suits, one can make monetary restitution and thereby effect his atonement; but in capital cases he is held responsible for his blood and the blood of his [potential] descendants until the end of time, for thus we find in the case of Cain, who killed his brother, that it is written: *the bloods of thy brother cry unto me:* not the blood of thy brother, but the bloods of thy brother, is said — i.e., his blood and the blood of his [potential] descendants. Alternatively, *the bloods of thy brother,* teaches that his blood was splashed over trees and stones.

Katz, Jacob, "The Vicissitudes of Three Apologetic Statements," *Zion* 23–24 (1958–59), 174–93 (Hebrew); Lubitch, Ronen, "The Righteous among the Nations of the Earth in the Thought of R. Hayyim David Halevi. Kabbalah and Natural Justice in the Question of the Attitude Towards Gentiles," in: Zvi Zohar/Avi Sagi (eds.), *Yahadut Shel Ḥayyim. 'Iyyunim be-Yetsirato ha-Hagutit-Hilkhatit Shel ha-Rav Ḥayyim David Halevi*, 215–34, Jerusalem: Keter, 2007 (Hebrew). Nehorai, Michael Zvi, "'Righteous Gentiles Have a Share in the World to Come'," *Tarbiz* 61 (1992), 465–87 (Hebrew); Nehorai, Michael Zvi, "A Portion in the World to Come for the Righteous/Sages of the Nations," *Da'at* 50–2 (2003), 97–105 (Hebrew).
61 Cf. Kellner, Menachem, "A New and Unanticipated Textual Witness to the Reading, 'All Who Kills a Single Person – it is as if He Destroyed an Entire World'," *Tarbiz* 57 (2007), 565–66 (Hebrew).

- For this reason was man created alone, to teach you that whosoever destroys a single soul, Scripture imputes [guilt] to him as though he had destroyed a complete world; and whosoever preserves a single soul, Scripture ascribes [merit] to him as though he had preserved a complete world.
- Furthermore, [he was created alone] for the sake of peace among men, that one might not say to his fellow, "My father was greater than yours."
- And that the sectarians might not say: "There are many ruling powers in heaven."
- Again, to proclaim the greatness of the Holy One, blessed be He: for if a man strikes many coins from one mold, they all resemble one another, but the Supreme King of Kings, The Holy One, blessed be He, fashioned every man in the stamp of the first man, and yet not one of them resembles his fellow.

Therefore, every single person is obliged to say: the world was created for my sake.

This text would seem to teach the following lessons (among others):
- each person is a world unto himself or herself and should, therefore, be treated as such
- every human being is, in terms of his or her humanity, equal to all other human beings — none is more noble than the other, more precious than the other, more worthy than the other
- unlike coins, each person is unique (and can never be replicated or replaced — the loss of any single human being is thus tragic)
- if each person is obliged to say that the world was created for his or her sake, then, in the words of Immanuel Kant, humans must be treated as ends also, and never as means only — after all, if I am the object of creation, so is every other human being.[62]

It would seem also to follow from the above that each person is in some sense responsible for the whole world — each human should be a guarantor for all the others.[63]

However, being the God of the western monotheist religions must be a frustrating experience. Many western monotheists have managed to avoid the universalist consequences of the notion that all human beings are created in the divine image, by arguing that if there is only one God, then there can be only one 'approved' way of approaching that God, and all other approaches are illegitimate.

---

[62] To my mind, Nazism is the clearest antithesis to this approach: stripping human beings of their identity, tattooing numbers on their arms (numbers are simply place-holders — there is nothing unique about them), killing them outright, or working them to death, all these are expressions of the idea that these people are means only, and not ends at all.

[63] The Talmud gives expression to this idea (with respect to Jews, at least): "All Israelites are guarantors/responsible for each other" (bShev 39a). (Note that in context, the assumption being discussed is whether the whole world is responsible for violations of the Torah.)

Further, if one's share in the world to come depends upon one's (correct) relationship to that one God, then theological mistakes can be eternally deadly.[64] In other words, if that one God vouchsafed to humanity a message expressing crucially important truths, competing messages are not only mistaken, but also culpably false.

Seeking to make certain that God is totally frustrated, the Jewish tradition preserves another version of our Mishnaic text. In almost all versions of the Mishnah published since the invention of printing, we find the following instead of the text cited above: "For this reason was man created alone, to teach you that whosoever destroys a single *Jewish* soul, Scripture imputes [guilt] to him as though he had destroyed a complete world; and whosoever preserves a single *Jewish* soul, Scripture ascribes [merit] to him as though he had preserved a complete world." It is easy to prove that the text cited above, and not the particularized contemporary version, was the original version in the Mishnah.[65] As with the terms *ger* and *re'a* (sojourner, neighbor), here, too, a universalist text has been stripped of its original meaning and made to serve a particularist agenda. God can only try…

Monotheism is thus part of our problem (and, one hopes, part of the solution). But so is the truth.

7 Truth

Maimonides is well known for having insisted, "accept the truth whatever its source."[66] Hidden behind this injunction is the view that truth is one, objective, unchanging, and largely knowable. This is hardly a surprising claim to find in the writings of a medieval monotheist, but it must be admitted that it has a hard edge. On the one hand, this statement leads to universalism: all human beings who acknowledge the truth are "in the club" as it were. Nevertheless, allied with this universalism, we find a sharp elitism:[67] those who fail to acknowledge

---

64 Historically this has been more of a problem for pre-modern Christianity and many versions of contemporary Islam. However, if historically, Christianity and Islam have had more opportunities than Judaism to put religious particularism into actual practice, this may have been only because Jews have not had the opportunity to do so, as Judah Halevi *seems* to admit to the King of the Khazars. Cf. Halevi, *Kuzari* i. 114–15.

65 Urbach, Ephraim E., "'Whoever Saves One Soul … [mSan 4:5].' The History of a Recension," in: *Me-Olamam Shel Ḥakhamim. Ḳovets Meḥḳarim*, 561–77, Jerusalem: Magnes, 1988 (Hebrew).

66 Maimonides, "Introduction to His Commentary on the Tractate Avot," trans. Raymond Weiss/Charles Butterworth, *Ethical Writings of Maimonides*, New York: Dover, 1983, 60.

67 On Maimonidean elitism, cf. Kellner, *Maimonides' Confrontation with Mysticism*, esp. 16 and index under "elitism"; Brague, Remi, "Athens, Jerusalem, Mecca. Leo Strauss's 'Muslim' Under-

the truth are at best mistaken and probably evil.[68] To the extent that acknowledging truth is the key to God's favor, failure to arrive at the truth is a serious matter indeed.

Can someone who accepts that her or his religion is true in some serious sense truly tolerate someone who rejects or even questions that truth? The simplest solution to this problem is to abandon the Maimonidean understanding of truth as one, objective, unchanging, and knowable. This is the epistemological relativism of various postmodernists.[69] I have yet to find a version of postmodernism which is not self-refuting, but that is not the tack to be taken here.[70] Once I am willing to accept the relative nature of truth, the need to justify tolerance disappears and this essay can end at this point. Religious pluralism, as a normative stance, simply obviates the need for tolerance.

So, why not give up on the notion of objective truth and become religious pluralists? Aside from the fact that truth *does* matter (without agreeing on some standards of truth and falsity, I do not see how any real communication can take place), for Jews the issue take on special urgency. I once heard the philosopher and theologian Emil Fackenheim (1916–2003) make the chilling point that people were killed by the Nazis because at least one of their grandparents was Jewish; had that grandparent converted to Christianity, they would have been spared. To remain Jewish, Fackenheim challenged his listeners, was to make a choice fraught with moral implications and, possibly life or death for one's descendants.

Remaining theologically Jewish without affirming at least some element of important truth in Judaism is thus actually immoral, or, at the very least, irresponsible. Allow me to elaborate. I grew up in a bubble but did not realize it. I grew up in an environment where when the older generation talked about anti-Semitism, I thought they were crazy. So, from 1946 when I was born, to 2000, when the second

---

standing of Greek Philosophy", *Poetics Today* 19, no. 2 (1998), 235–59; Freudenthal, Gad, "The Biological Foundations of Intellectual Elitism. Maimonides Vs. Al-Farabi," *Maimonidean Studies* 5 (2008), 293–324; Rynhold, Daniel/Harris, Michael J., *Nietzsche Soloveitchik, and Contemporary Jewish Philosophy*, 268–77, Cambridge: Cambridge University Press, 2018.

68 Rabbi Elhanan Wasserman, martyred by the Nazis in 1941, was a strict anti-modernist (and anti-Zionist). He held that God's existence and providence were so evident that only a hedonist, seduced by the pleasures of this world, could possibly be an atheist. Cf. the chapter on Wasserman in Diamond, James/Kellner, Menachem, *Reinventing Maimonides in Contemporary Jewish Thought*, 107–48, London: Littman Library of Jewish Civilization, 2019.

69 For as good a defense of this impossible approach as can be found, cf. Feldmann-Kaye, Miriam, *Jewish Theology for a Postmodern Age*, London: Littman Library of Jewish Civilization, 2019.

70 For a brief but telling exposition of this position, with citations of relevant studies, cf. Gellman, *God's Kindness Has Overwhelmed Us*, 33.

Intifada broke out, I can only recall two small events in my entire life which might have been caused by anti-Semitism. Until I moved to Israel, no one ever tried to harm me because I was Jewish. Now, people throw rocks, rockets and bullets at me because I am a Jew. The rise of anti-Semitism in this millennium shook my entire being. I thought that the Holocaust had made it impossible to be an anti-Semite, but I was wrong. (I am not one of those people who thinks that every criticism of Israel is anti-Semitic, but I think a lot of it is). In a world in which not only the unwashed masses, but also the perfumed elites shamelessly repeat anti-Semitic tropes only two generations after the Holocaust, remaining a Jew is a *choice* fraught with moral implications.

What can I do? I want to claim that Judaism (whatever that might be) is true (whatever that might mean) but do not want to claim that other religions are false.

8 Proposed Solution

I would like to propose a way out of our impasse. I will phrase it in terms of Jewish texts and teaching, but it could be adopted by followers of other religious traditions as well. Put simply, to say that Torah teaches truth is not to say that Jews understand that truth fully. One might even want to follow thinkers like Tamar Ross and Jerome Gellman (both influenced by Rabbi Kook) who maintain that our approximation of Torah truth grows ever greater and deeper, not the further we get from Sinai, but the closer we get to the messianic era.[71] But one need not go that far to find traditional Jewish warrant for the assertion that our understanding of Torah is far from deep and full.

8.1 Moses, Maimonides and Human Limitations

Examining the figure of Moses will elucidate the point. Maimonides was the first authoritative Jewish teacher to affirm that Judaism had dogmas in the strict sense of the term (doctrines taught by the Torah, correct acceptance of which was both a necessary and sufficient condition for being part of the Jewish collective and for achieving a share in the world to come).[72] Judaism, he taught, consists of thirteen core beliefs. Of them,

---

[71] For Ross, cf. Ross, Tamar, *Expanding the Palace of Tora. Orthodoxy and Feminism*, Walthan, MA: Brandeis University Press, 2004; for Gellman, cf. the works cited above in note 3.
[72] Cf. Kellner, Menachem, *Dogma in Medieval Jewish Thought*, Oxford: Oxford University Press, 1986, chap. 1.

> The seventh foundation is the prophecy of Moses, our Teacher; to wit, it should be known that: Moses was the father of all the prophets – of those who came before him and of those who came after him; all were beneath him in rank and that he was the chosen of God from among the entire species of humanity and that he comprehended more of God, may He be exalted, than any man who existed or will exist, ever comprehended or will comprehend, and that he, peace upon him, reached a state of exaltedness beyond humanity and became included in the level of angels. There remained no veil which he did not pierce, no material hindrance burdened him, and no defect, whether small or great, mingled with him. The imaginative and sensible faculties in his perception were stripped from him, his desiderative faculty was still and he remained pure intellect only. For this reason, they remarked of him that he discoursed with God without the intermediary of an angel [...].[73]

Despite the facts that Moses was the greatest of all prophets who ever lived or ever will live,[74] that he comprehended more of God than any other human who ever lived or will live, that he became, in effect, an angel, and there "remained no veil which he did not pierce," so much so that God spoke to him, as it were, face to face (Nu 12: 8), despite all that, there was much about God that Moses did not comprehend.[75]

This we learn from Maimonides' statement in *Guide of the Perplexed* i. 54 that despite all his greatness, Moses remained a human being, and as such was limited in what he could know of God:

> Moses our Teacher, the master of those who know, made two behests, both answered: first, that God acquaint him with His true Reality, and second (although he asked this first) to make Himself known through His attributes. God answered by promising Moses knowledge of all His attributes, revealing that His attributes are His acts, and teaching him that one cannot know Him as He really is but awakened him to an intellectual plane from which he could reach the summit of human awareness. What Moses knew then has been grasped by no one else before or since.[76]

Moses made two requests of God in Exodus 33: to know God's ways, and to behold God's presence. Maimonides interprets this latter request as a desire to know

---

[73] I cite the translation of David Blumenthal as found in Kellner, *Must a Jew Believe Anything?* (above, note 21), 168–69.
[74] Including even the Messiah; cf. Maimonides, *Mishneh Torah*, "Laws of Repentance," ix. 2.
[75] For surveys of the places in his writings where Maimonides deals with the exalted nature of Moses and his prophecy, cf. Ivry, Alfred, "The Image of Moses in Maimonides' Thought," in: Aviezer Ravitzky (ed.), *Rambam. Shamranut, Meḵoriut, Mahapkhanut*, 481–99, Jerusalem: Merkaz Zalman Shazar, 2008; Kasher, Hannah, "Maimonides' Interpretation of the Story of the Divine Revelation in the Cleft of the Rock," *Da'at* 35 (1995), 29–66.
[76] I cite the translation of Lenn Evan Goodman and Phillip Lieberman. In the translation of Shlomo Pines (Chicago, 1963), 123.

God's true reality, i.e., to know God as God truly is. God's ways, Maimonides teaches here, are what we would call the laws of nature, God's acts. However, to know God as God truly cannot be achieved by any human being, even one as supreme as Moses.

If divine truth in and of itself was hidden from Moses, how much more so it is it hidden from us![77] Ought we not extend that modesty to our claims to understand the truths taught by Torah?

God's ultimate unknowability is one of the fundamental teachings of Maimonides' entire philosophy. It also underlies his widely cited assertion that the Torah speaks in human language.[78] Why must the Torah speak in human language as opposed to expressing the truths of God in, as it were, God's language?[79] The Torah is addressed to human beings, not to angels,[80] and human beings are, by their very creaturely nature, incapable of actually knowing God as God is. This should certainly undermine any claims to theological certainty.

This point is importantly buttressed, as Eugene Korn pointed out to me, by a variety of Talmudic and later texts, which fault Abraham for having misunderstood God's command concerning the sacrifice of Isaac. Abraham was not meant to sacrifice Isaac, but to offer a sacrifice to God *with* Isaac. Given the central importance that later Jewish texts attached to the ʿaḳedah, the binding of Isaac, and its place in the liturgy, this is a striking claim, but it is found in a number of sour-

---

[77] Kellner, Menachem, "Maimonides on the Science of the *Mishneh Torah*. Provisional or Permanent," *AJS Review* 18 (1993), 169–94. Cf. Ibid., 170 and 192 on the incompatibility of astronomy and metaphysics (which explains why we, and even Moses, can never achieve full knowledge of God) and 176 ff on the fallibility of the Rabbinic sages. If the authors of Mishnah and Talmud could make mistakes on theological issues, how much more can we. Further on this latter point, cf. Kellner, Menachem, *Maimonides on the "Decline of the Generations" and the Nature of Rabbinic Authority*, Albany: SUNY Press, 1996.

[78] Maimonides took the rabbinic statement that the Torah speaks in human language to mean that much of the Torah ought to be understood metaphorically. For entry into the discussion, cf. Funkenstein, Amos, "'Scripture Speaks the Language of Man'. The Uses and Abuses of the Medieval Principle of Accommodation," *Philosophes Medievaux* 26 (1986), 92–101; Goldin, Joshua L., "On the Limits of Non-Literal Interpretation of Scripture from an Orthodox Perspective," *Torah u-Madda Journal* 10 (2001), 37–59; Klein-Braslavy, Sara, "The Philosophical Exegesis," in: Magne Saebo (ed.), *Hebrew Bible / Old Testament. The History of its Interpretation*, 302–20, Goettingen: Vandenhoeck and Ruprecht, 2000.

[79] Mystics, of course, are not restrained in this matter to the same degree as philosophers, who, by and large, aim for an understanding of God, as opposed to an experience of God.

[80] bBer. 25b and parallels; cf. Hayes, Christine, "The Torah was not Given to Ministering Angels. Rabbinic Aspirationalism," in: Charlotte Fonrobert et al. (eds.), *Talmudic Transgressions. Engaging the Work of Daniel Boyarin*, Supplements to the Journal for the Study of Judaism 181, 123–60, Leiden: Brill, 2017.

ces (known to Maimonides).[81] If Abraham could misinterpret God's message, and if Moses was unable to plumb the depths of knowledge of God, how much more should we adopt a stance of epistemological modesty when it comes to affirming the truths of Torah.[82]

There is another lesson we should learn from Moses. Not only did he "reach the summit of human awareness," but he was also the most modest of all human beings (Nu 12:3). The Mishnaic tractate Avot teaches (iv. 4) that one must be excessively humble. In his extensive commentary on this text Maimonides cites Moses as the exemplar of human humility.[83] Why was Moses so humble? Knowing better than any other human being how little he knew of God; Moses was more aware than most of his human frailty. If Moses, the greatest of all human beings, was excessively modest, so should not we be?[84]

8.2 Maimonidean Mistakes

We have now shown that according to Maimonides[85], Moses' theological apprehensions were limited by his humanity. We can also show that there is hardly a Jew alive today who thinks Maimonides himself did not err on crucial theological issues. In *Mishneh Torah*, "Laws Concerning Repentance," iii. 6, Maimonides writes that "The following have no portion in the world to come, but are cut off and perish, and for their great wickedness and sinfulness are condemned forever and ever." In paragraph 7 he specifies one of the groups of people there mentioned:

---

[81] Korn notes: "This is the interpretation offered *in b. Ta'anit* 4a; *Genesis Rabbah* 55:5 and 56:8; *Pesikta Zutra* 44." Korn also points to Rashi on Gen 22:2, and R. Abraham Isaac Kook (*Letters* II: 379) — neither of whom were known to Maimonides — about the first there is no proof, but around the second, there obviously can be no question.

[82] Cf. Korn, Eugene, "Religious Violence, Sacred Texts and Theological Values," in: Robert W. Jensen/Eugene Korn (eds), *Plowshares into Swords? Reflections on Religion and Violence*, Jerusalem: Center for Jewish Christian Understanding and Cooperation, 2014.

[83] It is of great interest, but not actually relevant to our point, that in his commentary on this text Maimonides cites a Sufi story about humility. Cf. Davidson, *Moses Maimonides*, 94, note 104. Cf. also, Weiss, Raymond L., *Maimonides' Ethics. The Encounter of Philosophic and Religious Morality*, Chicago: University of Chicago Press, 1991, 40.

[84] As Daniel J. Lasker pointed out to me, a Christian might say: Jews did not fully understand God's revelations despite all the obvious hints to their real meaning, namely Christianity. I imagine that very few Christians would want to say that Moses himself did not fully understand God's revelation.

[85] As noted above, Maimonides was an extreme intellectual elitist.

> Five classes are termed sectarians [*minim*]: he who says that there is no God and that the world has no ruler; he who says that there is a ruling power but that it is vested in two or more persons; he who says that there is one Ruler, but that He has a body and has form; he who denies that He alone is the First Cause and Rock of the universe; likewise he who renders worship to anyone beside Him, to serve as a mediator between the human being and the Lord of the universe. Whoever belongs to any of these five classes is termed a sectarian.[86]

On this text, Maimonides' acerbic critic, R. Abraham ben David (Rabad, 1125–1198), writes:

> Why has he called such a person [he who says that there is one Ruler, but that He has a body and has form] a sectarian? There are many people greater than, and superior to him, who adhere to such a belief on the basis of what they have seen in verses of Scripture, and even more in the words of the aggadot [Talmudic stories] which corrupt right opinion about religious matters.[87]

I do not believe that Rabad was affirming the corporeality of God (after all, those who do believe in divine corporeality are misled by Torah verses and aggadot "which corrupt right opinion about religious matters"); rather he was affirming that one is allowed to be mistaken about that issue. But for Maimonides God's corporeality is an issue about which no one is permitted to remain mistaken, not even "little children, women, and the dull and deficient" (*Guide* i. 35, Pines, p. 81).[88] The important point for our purposes here is that Rabad recognizes that Maimonides does not allow for inadvertence (*shegagah*) with respect to theological matters. A sincere mistake about God is still a mistake and constitutes her-

---

[86] I cite the translation of Moses Hyamson (Jerusalem, 1962), p. 84b. Hannah Kasher subjects the terms in this paragraph to detailed analysis in 'Al ha-Minim, ha-Kofrim, ve-ha-Epiḳorsim be-Mishnat ha-Rambam, Tel Aviv: Ha-Kibbutz ha-Meuhad, 2011. Zev Harvey points out that our paragraph parallels the first five of Maimonides' Thirteen Principles. Cf. Harvey, Zev, "The Question of God's Incorporeality in Maimonides, Rabad, Crescas, and Spinoza," in: S. Rosenberg et al. (eds.), *Minḥah Le-Sarah*, 63–78, Jerusalem: Magnes, 1994.
[87] I cite the text as translated by Isadore Twersky. Cf. Twersky, Isadore, *Rabad of Posquieres. A Twelfth-Century Talmudist*, Philadelphia: Jewish Publication Society, 1980, 282. A more moderate version of Rabad's gloss has been preserved. Cf. Kellner, *Dogma in Medieval Jewish Thought*, 89.
[88] Let it be noted that Maimonides, unlike almost all other medieval figures (Jewish, Christian, or Muslim), held women to be fully human, fully created in the image of God. Cf. Kellner, Menachem, "Misogyny. Gersonides vs. Maimonides," in: Kellner, *Torah in the Observatory. Gersonides, Maimonides, Song of Songs*, 283–304, Boston: Academic Studies Press, 2010. For whatever it might be worth, Maimonides' misogyny is halakhic, not philosophical. Hannah Kasher has recently addressed this issue: Kasher, Hannah, "Maimonides on the Intellects of Women and Gentiles," in: Charles Manekin/Daniel Davies (eds.), *Interpreting Maimonides*, 46–64, Cambridge: Cambridge University Press, 2018.

esy. It follows that worship of a god about which one is objectively mistaken is 'avodah zarah.[89]

I do not believe that any contemporary Jew agrees with Maimonides over Rabad. Few would be willing to *say* that Maimonides was simply wrong on the fact of God's absolute incorporeality – rather they act on that view. Proof of my claim here is that David Berger is clearly correct: on strict Maimonidean terms, contemporary Ḥabad Hasidism is heretical, and, when pressed, many would be willing to admit that this is correct.[90] Do any other contemporary rabbinic figures in Orthodoxy follow up on that admission and impose upon followers of Ḥabad the considerable restrictions that Maimonides and others would have us impose upon heretics? Hardly. Lip service is paid to Maimonides' strict criteria of theological orthodoxy, but it is only lip service.[91]

It would be easy to show (and in fact, I have shown[92]) that very few contemporary Orthodox Jews pass Maimonides' own tests for theological orthodoxy. Maimonides erred on important matters, and so can we.

9 Pluralism, Again

Why can't I simply say that Judaism is true for Jews, Christianity is true for Christians, and Islam is true for Muslims? This ignores the ethnic component of Judaism. Judaism is not only a religion, since it is also an ethnicity, whereas Christianity and Islam are indeed "only" religions. The ethnic component of Judaism is a central part of its religious self-understanding. Jews are both members of a religion and members of a nation. To put the matter simply, Judaism teaches not only that the Torah is God's revelation, but that also that the Jews are God's cho-

---

[89] In his statement at the end of this thirteen principles Maimonides defines his principles as dogmas in the strict sense of the term: beliefs taught by the highest religious authority (in this case, the Torah itself), acceptance of which is both a necessary and sufficient condition for both being part of the community of Israel and for achieving a share in the world to come. Rabad, clearly saw (and rejected) the implication that there is no possibility of *shegagah*, inadvertence, playing an exculpatory role here.

[90] Cf. Berger, David, *The Rebbe, the Messiah, and the Scandal of Orthodox Indifference*, London: Littman Library of Jewish Civilization, 2001; Berger, David, "Must a Jew Believe Anything? By Menachem Kellner," *Tradition* 33 (1999), 81–89, and my response in Kellner, *Must a Jew Believe Anything?* (2nd edition), 127–48.

[91] On this lip service, cf. Kellner, *Dogma in Medieval Jewish Thought*, 207–17.

[92] Kellner, "The Convert as the Most Jewish of Jews?" (above, note 22).

sen people. The question of what that latter claim means is no less debated than the meaning of the former, but neither claim is denied by professing Jews.[93]

No less importantly, to say that Judaism is true for Jews, Christianity is true for Christians, and Islam is true for Muslims makes a mockery of the sort of truth we have been seeking here and simply sneaks religious pluralism in through the back door.

Further, I know that I am Jewish only thanks to accidents of birth and upbringing. Several years ago, I read a book by Jonathan Haidt (*The Righteous Mind: Why Good People are Divided by Politics and Religion*) which resonated with me deeply. Haidt shows that our deepest convictions are rarely (if ever) the result of rational argument. Rationality, he maintains, is primarily used to justify our antecedently held positions, positions that are the result of many factors, rational argument often the least of them. Haidt helped me to understand why it is that people whom I respect (and often love) hold views that to me are clearly and evidently wrong. In their eyes, my views are equally wrong (about which, "of course," *they* are wrong). My Judaism may only be an accident of birth and upbringing, and has not remained static over the years, but I have never been tempted to give it up.

Despite knowing all this, I cannot free myself from the strong feeling that Christianity and Islam make demands upon my credulity that Judaism does not. I rarely rely upon Judah Halevi in my Jewish thinking, but here I do: The Khazar king rejects Islam on the grounds that he has no way of judging if the language of the Qur'ān is as miraculous as the Muslim spokesperson insists (to which I add that so much of the Qur'ān is clearly drawn from earlier Jewish sources). He rejects Christianity on the grounds of its blatant irrationality. Both the King and I, not having been brought up on these beliefs, have no reason to accept them.[94]

---

[93] This is not the place to go into the matter, but to say that Jews have understood the notion of the chosen people in wildly different ways is an understatement. For an entry into the discussion, cf. Kellner, *Maimonides' Confrontation with Mysticism*, chap. 7. Since the "chosen people doctrine" is often used by anti-Semites, allow me to point out that many nations have made the same claim about themselves. Cf. Smith, Anthony D., *Chosen Peoples*, Oxford: Oxford University Press, 2003; cf. also the interesting reflections of Paul Mendes-Flohr in Mendes-Flohr, Paul, "Israel. In Pursuit of Normalcy – Zionism's Ambivalence towards Israel's Election," in: William R. Hutchison/Hartmut Lehman (eds.), *Many Are Chosen. Divine Election and Western Nationalism*, 201–24, Minneapolis: Fortress Press, 1994. Mendes-Flohr points out the recent invention of the term "chosen people" and its reliance on Christian self-understanding.

[94] For two of many relevant studies by Daniel J. Lasker, cf. Lasker, Daniel J., "Popular Polemics and Philosophical Truth in the Medieval Jewish Critique of Christianity," *Journal of Jewish Thought and Philosophy* 8 (1999), 243–59 and Lasker, Daniel J., *Jewish Philosophical Polemics Against Christianity in the Middle Ages*, Oxford: Littman Library of Jewish Civilization, 2007².

10 Pluralism, Yet Again

I would like to take one final stab at pluralism since, by personal predilection, it is the position with which I am most comfortable. My late mentor and friend, Steven S. Schwarzschild (1924–1989), used to assert (with tongue only partially in cheek) that many people whom he admired (such as Immanuel Kant and the later Sartre) were Jewish Non-Jews.[95] Playing on Isaac Deutscher's discussion of Non Jewish Jews (such as Spinoza and Freud)[96] Schwarzschild maintained that ethnicity, religious identification and practice (or lack thereof) aside, some non-Jewish philosophers were, in effect, philosophically Jewish. By this, he meant that they preached and practiced a form of ethical monotheism.[97]

Let us seek to recast Schwarzschild's point in terms drawn from Maimonides. As noted above, Maimonides innovated the claim that to be counted as a member of the Jewish community and in order to earn a share in the world to come, one had to accept thirteen fundamental teachings. I have argued that to be consistent, Maimonides would have to admit that only the first five of his thirteen principles are actually necessary for full membership in the Jewish community.[98] These five are: God' existence, unity, incorporeality, transcendence,[99] and that God alone may be worshiped. A Jew can say, building on and out of Maimonides, that an immoral person (Martin Heidegger comes to mind) cannot really be a philosopher. Thus, to be a Maimonidean non-Jewish Jew is, once again, to be an ethical monotheist. But, if this is enough, why be Jewish? Why not be, in effect, a Noahide, a watered-down Jew?

I fear that I am stuck without pluralism, messianic or otherwise, and will have to make do with tolerance.

---

95 Kellner, Menachem, "Steven Schwarzschild, Moses Maimonides, and 'Jewish Non-Jews'," in: Görge K. Hasselhoff/Otfried Fraisse (eds.), *Moses Maimonides (1138–1204). His Religious, Scientific, and Philosophical Wirkungsgeschichte_in Different Cultural Contexts*, 587–606, Würzburg: Ergon, 2004.
96 Cf. Deutscher, Isaac, *The Non-Jewish Jew and Other Essays*, Oxford: Oxford University Press, 1968.
97 Schwarzschild was originally an ordained Reform rabbi, but of a very traditionalist bent — as evidenced by his ultimate membership in the (Conservative) Rabbinical Assembly, and his close relations with two major Orthodox rabbinic figures, rabbis Joseph Soloveitchik and Issac Hutner (for details, cf. my introduction to Schwarzschild's *The Pursuit of the Ideal*, Albany: SUNY Press, 1990, 1–14). I do not think that his basic criterion of who a non-Jewish Jew is (emphasis on ethics and philosophical monotheism) is a function of his Reform background.
98 Kellner, *Maimonides' Confrontation with Mysticism*, 233–38.
99 More literally, "ontic precedence." Is that clearer?

11 Final Thoughts

A respected friend who read this essay for me said that it appears that I am trying to square the circle. That may be a polite way of saying that I am trying to eat my cake and have it, too. Other friends have pointed out that in my day-to-day life I behave like a theological pluralist: trying to live while letting others live (up to a point, of course: I strongly believe that brutality and intolerance must be resisted). I want therefore to restate what I am trying to accomplish in this essay.

As I said above, if I want to be tolerated as a Jew by individuals many of whose beliefs contrast sharply with core beliefs of historical Judaism, then how can I not tolerate them? Why do I want to both tolerate and be tolerated (in the strong sense of the term used in this essay)? Above, I defined the strong sense of tolerance as acknowledging that other religions (not just Christianity and Islam) have a singular role in their respective cultures and *inherent religious worth*. Were I willing to withdraw behind the walls of a cultural ghetto, imposed by others or self-imposed, it would then be enough for me to leave others alone in the hope and expectation that they would leave me alone. Were that the case, there would be no problem. But –and I am sure that this is the case with the other contributors to this volume- that is not enough. Historically, it was all that could be hoped for.[100] We, however, are challenged to do more.

I want to affirm the truth of Torah, but not be so sure of myself that I can condemn every other view (within and without Judaism) as false. Why affirm the truth of Torah? I recently came across an interesting sentence in Gibbon's *Decline and Fall:* "The various modes of worship, which prevailed in the Roman world, were all considered by the people, as equally true; by the philosopher, as equally false; and by the magistrate, as equally useful."[101] If that is all we sought, this could be a very short book: each of us could undertake to "put up with" the others and be done with it. We seek more.

Thankfully, I will, of course, find truly tolerant (i.e., respectful) partners among many Christians and Muslims. However, they will not be any more representative of their communities than I am of mine. I have had this experience of-

---

100 Paul Mendes-Flohr quoted Franz Rosenzweig to the effect that "The Christian ignored the Jew in order to be able to tolerate him, and the Jew ignored the Christian in order to allow himself to be tolerated." Cf. Mendes-Flohr, Paul. "Jewish Philosophy: An Obituary," ed. Oxford Centre for Hebrew and Jewish Studies. Yarnton Manor, Yarnton, Oxford, 1999, 20, note 24, published online: https://www.ochjs.ac.uk/wp-content/uploads/2011/09/4th-Frank-Green-Lecture-Jewish-Philosophy-An-Obituary.pdf (accessed on 18.08.2019).
101 Gibbon, Edward, *The History of the Decline and Fall of the Roman Empire* (abridged edition), London: Penguin Books, 2000, 35.

ten: engaging in trialogues (Jews, Christians, and Muslims), I find much in common with my fellow participants (despite all the differences between us). We all admit, ruefully, that when we return to our synagogue, church, or mosque it will be hard to find many of our fellow worshipers interested in sharing our respectful openness towards the religious other.

For religious tolerance to be serious, each side must not be expected to relinquish the truth claims of their respective religions. To do so would be to give up devotion to the God of Abraham, Isaac, and Jacob and replace that with intellectual acquiescence to the existence of the God of the philosophers. Instead of speaking to God, we would speak about God. Instead of being believers, we would become metaphysicians. Instead of believing *in* God, we would believe *that* God exists. Judaism, Christianity, Islam would cease to be sources of knowledge and become only cultural artifacts.[102]

The solution offered here (epistemological modesty about religious beliefs) may satisfy few (it will not satisfy many of the people with whom I pray to God, not about God, in my synagogue), but it allows me (and people like me) to relate to our religions seriously while being truly respectful of others, within Judaism, and without.

I occasionally quote Oliver Cromwell. He (allegedly) exhorted his troops: "Put your trust in God but keep your powder dry." To me, that sounds like an excellent characterization of Judaism in general and of religious Zionism in particular (*ein somkhin al ha-nes* — trust not in miracles). I shall close here with another Cromwell quote, addressed to all those so confident of their faith that they are dismissive of other faiths (or other understandings of their own faiths): "I beseech you, in the bowels of Christ, think it possible you may be mistaken."[103]

Bibliography

Abraham ben Maimonides, *Commentary on Genesis and Exodus*, ed. S.D. Sassoon/E. Weisenberg, London, 1958.
Altmann, Alexander, *Moses Mendelssohn: A Biographical Study*, AL: Liverpool University Press, 1973.

---

[102] This paragraph owes much to Altmann, Alexander, "The God of Religion, the God of Metaphysics, and Wittgenstein's 'Language Games'," *Zeitschrift für Religions- und Geistesgeschichte* 39, no. 4 (1987), 289–306. Buber's distinction between belief in and belief that is developed in Kellner, *Must a Jew Believe Anything?*, chap. 1.
[103] For both Cromwell quotes: https://en.wikiquote.org/wiki/Oliver_Cromwell (accessed on 18.08.2019). I would like to thank James Diamond, Yehudah Gellman, Raphael Jospe, Eugene Korn, Daniel Lasker, Avrom Montag, and Kenneth Seeskin for their generous assistance.

Altmann, Alexander, *Tolerance and the Jewish Tradition*, The Robert Waley Cohen Memorial Lecture, London: The Council of Christians and Jews, 1957.

Altmann, Alexander, "The God of Religion, the God of Metaphysics, and Wittgenstein's 'Language Games'," *Zeitschrift für Religions- und Geistesgeschichte* 39, no. 4 (1987), 289–306.

Balk, Hanan, "The Soul of a Jew and the Soul of a Non-Jew. An Inconvenient Truth and the Search for an Alternative," *Hakirah. The Flatbush Journal of Jewish Law and Thought* 16 (2013), 47–76.

Batnitzky, Leora, *How Judaism Became a Religion. An Introduction to Modern Jewish Thought*, Princeton: Princeton University Press, 2011.

Benamozegh, Elijah, *Israel and Humanity*, trans. Maxwell Luria, Mahwah, NJ: Paulist Press, 1995.

Benson, Ophelia/Stangroom, Jeremy, *Why Truth Matters*, London: Continuum, 2006.

Berger, David, "Must a Jew Believe Anything? By Menachem Kellner," *Tradition* 33 (1999), 81–89.

Berger, David, *The Rebbe, the Messiah, and the Scandal of Orthodox Indifference*, London: Littman Library of Jewish Civilization, 2001.

Blidstein, Gerald, "A Note on Rabbinic Missionizing," *Journal of Theological Studies* 47, no. 2 (1996), 528–31.

Boyarin, Daniel, *Judaism. The Genealogy of a Modern Notion*, New Brunswick, NJ: Rutgers University Press, 2018.

Brague, Remi, "Athens, Jerusalem, Mecca. Leo Strauss's 'Muslim' Understanding of Greek Philosophy," *Poetics Today* 19, no. 2 (1998), 235–59.

Brill, Alan, *Judaism and Other Religions. Models of Understanding*, New York: Palgrave Macmillan, 2010.

CJCUC, "Orthodox Rabbinic Statement on Christianity," published online: https://web.archive.org/web/20221128052125/http://www.cjcuc.org/2015/12/03/orthodox-rabbinic-statement-on-christianity/ (accessed on 03.04.2025).

Davidson, Herbert A., *Moses Maimonides. The Man and His Works*, Oxford: Oxford University Press, 2005.

Dahan, Alon, *Go'el Aharon. Mishnato ha-Meshiḥit shel Rabbi Menachem Mendel Schneerson*, Tel Aviv, 2014.

Deutscher, Isaac, *The Non-Jewish Jew and Other Essays*, Oxford: Oxford University Press, 1968.

Diamond, James, *Converts, Heretics, and Lepers. Maimonides and the Outsider*, Notre Dame: University of Notre Dame Press, 2007.

Diamond, James/Kellner, Menachem, *Reinventing Maimonides in Contemporary Jewish Thought*, London: Littman Library of Jewish Civilization, 2019.

Ellenson, David, "Rabbi Hayim David Halevi on Christians and Christianity: An Analysis of Selected Legal Writings of an Israeli Authority," in: Franklin Harkin (ed.), *Transforming Relations: Essays on Jews and Christians... In Honor of Michael A. Signer*, 340–61, Notre Dame: Notre Dame, 2010.

Ellenson, David, "The Orthodox Rabbinate and Apostasy in Nineteenth-Century Germany and Hungary," in: David Ellenson (ed.), *Tradition in Transition. Orthodoxy, Halakhah, and the Boundaries of Modern Jewish Identity*, Lanham, Md.: University Press of America, 1989.

Ellenson, David, "Traditional Reactions to Modern Jewish Reform: The Paradigm of German Orthodoxy," in: Daniel Frank/Oliver Leaman (eds.), *History of Jewish Philosophy*, London: Routledge, 1997.

Farber, Zev, "Torah Min ha-Shamayim. A Guide to the Four Questions," published online: torah.com, https://www.thetorah.com/article/torah-from-heaven-a-guide-to-the-four-questions (03.04.2025).

Feldmann-Kaye, Miriam, *Jewish Theology for a Postmodern Age*, London: Littman Library of Jewish Civilization, 2019.
Ferziger, Adam, "From Demonic Deviant to Drowning Brother: Reform Judaism in the Eyes of American Orthodoxy," *Jewish Social Studies: History, Culture, Society* 15, no. 3 (2009), 56–88.
Ferziger, Adam, "The Role of Reform in Israeli Orthodoxy," in: Michael/David Myers Meyer (eds.), *Between Jewish Tradition and Modernity*, 51–66. Detroit: Wayne State University Press, 2014.
Ferziger, Adam, "Religion for the Secular: The New Israeli Rabbinate," *Journal of Modern Jewish Studies* 7, no. 1 (2008), 67–90.
Ferziger, Adam, *Beyond Sectarianism: The Realignment of American Orthodox Judaism*, Detroit: Wayne State University Press, 2015.
Freudenthal, Gad, "The Biological Foundations of Intellectual Elitism. Maimonides vs. al-Farabi," *Maimonidean Studies* 5 (2008), 293–324.
Frimer, Dov, "Israel, the Noahide Laws and Maimonides. Jewish-Gentile Legal Relations in Maimonidean Thought," in: Yamin Levy/Shalom Carmy (eds.), *The Legacy of Maimonides. Religion, Reason, and Community*, 96–110, New York: Yashar Books, 2006.
Funkenstein, Amos, "'Scripture Speaks the Language of Man.' The Uses and Abuses of the Medieval Principle of Accommodation," *Philosophes Medievaux* 26 (1986), 92–101.
Gellman, Jerome (Yehudah), "Jewish Mysticism and Morality. Kabbalah and its Ontological Dualities," *Archiv fuer Religionsgeschichte* 9 (2008), 23–35.
Gellman, Jerome (Yehudah), *God's Kindness Has Overwhelmed Us. A Contemporary Doctrine of the Jews as the Chosen People*, Boston: Academic Studies Press, 2013.
Gellman, Jerome (Yehudah), *This Was from God. A Contemporary Theology of Torah and History*, Boston: Academic Studies Press, 2016.
Gibbon, Edward, *The History of the Decline and Fall of the Roman Empire* (abridged edition), London: Penguin Books, 2000.
Goldin, Joshua L., "On the Limits of Non-Literal Interpretation of Scripture from an Orthodox Perspective," *Torah u-Madda Journal* 10 (2001), 37–59.
Haidt, Jonathan, *The Righteous Mind: Why Good People are Divided by Politics and Religion*, New York, Pantheon Books, 2012.
Halbertal, Moshe, *Maimonides*, Princeton: Princeton University Press, 2014.
Halevi, Judah, *Kuzari*, trans. Michael Schwarz, Be'er Sheva: Ben Gurion University Press, 2017.
Harvey, Zev, "The Question of God's Incorporeality in Maimonides, Rabad, Crescas, and Spinoza," in: S. Rosenberg et al. (eds.), *Minḥah Le-Sarah*, 63–78, Jerusalem: Magnes, 1994.
Hayes, Christine, "The Torah was not Given to Ministering Angels. Rabbinic Aspirationalism," in: Charlottes Fonrobert et al. (eds.), *Talmudic Transgressions. Engaging the Work of Daniel Boyarin*, Supplements to the Journal for the Study of Judaism 181, 123–60, Leiden: Brill, 2017.
Heilman, Samuel C., *Sliding to the Right. The Contest for the Future of American Jewish Orthodoxy*, Berkeley: University of California Press, 2006.
Herberg, Will, *Protestant – Catholic – Jew. An Essay in Religious Sociology*, Chicago: University of Chicago Press, 1955.
Herzog, Isaac, "Zekhuyot Miutim le-fi ha-Halakhah," *Tehumin* 2 (1981), 169–99.
Heschel, Abraham Joshua, "No Religion is an Island," *Union Seminary Quarterly Review* 21, no. 2 (1966), 117–34.
Hirshman, Menachem, "Election and Rejection in the Midrash," *Jewish Studies Quarterly* 16 (2009), 71–82.

Hirshman, Menachem, "Rabbinic Universalism in the Second and Third Centuries," *Harvard Theological Review* 93 (2000), 101–15.

Hirshman, Menachem, *Torah Lekhol Ba'ei Olam. Zerem Universali be-Sifrut ha-Tana'im ve-Yaḥaso le-Ḥokhmat ha-'Amim*, Tel Aviv: Ha-Kibbutz ha-Meuhad, 1999.

Ivry, Alfred, "The Image of Moses in Maimonides' Thought," in: Aviezer Ravitzky (ed.), *Rambam. Shamranut, Meḳoriut, Mahapkhanut*, 481–99, Jerusalem: Merkaz Zalman Shazar, 2008.

Jospe, Raphael, "Moses Mendelssohn: A Medieval Modernist," in: Andrea Schatz/Irene Zwiep/Resianne Fontaine (eds.), *Sepharad in Ashkenaz: Medieval Knowledge and Eighteenth-Century Enlightened Jewish Discourse*, 107–40, Amsterdam: Royal Netherlands Academy of Arts and Sciences, 2007.

Kaminsky, Joel S., *Yet I Loved Jacob. Reclaiming the Biblical Concept of Election*, Nashville: Abingdon, 2007.

Kasher, Hannah, *'Al ha-Minim, ha-Kofrim, ve-ha-Epiḳorsim be-Mishnat ha-Rambam*, Tel Aviv: Ha-Kibbutz ha-Meuhad, 2011.

Kasher, Hannah, *'Elyon Al Kol Ha-Goyyim. Tsiyyunei Derekh Ba-Philosophia Ha-Yehudit Be-Sugiyat Ha-'Am Ha-Nivḥar*, Tel Aviv: Idra, 2018.

Kasher, Hannah, "Maimonides' Interpretation of the Story of the Divine Revelation in the Cleft of the Rock," *Da'at* 35 (1995), 29–66.

Kasher, Hanna, "Maimonides on the Intellects of Women and Gentiles," in: Charles Manekin/Daniel Davies (eds.), *Interpreting Maimonides*, 46–64, Cambridge: Cambridge University Press, 2018.

Kasher, Hannah, "Three Punishments Which are One, According to Maimonides," *Sidra* 14 (1988), 39–58.

Katz, Jacob, "The Vicissitudes of Three Apologetic Statements," *Zion* 23–24 (1958–59), 174–93 (Hebrew).

Katz, Jacob, *Exclusivism and Tolerance*, New York: Schocken, 1962.

Kellner, Menachem, "The Convert as the Most Jewish of Jews? On the Centrality of Belief (the Opposite of Heresy) in Maimonidean Judaism," *Jewish Thought* 1 (2019), 33–52.

Kellner, Menachem, *Dogma in Medieval Jewish Thought*, Oxford: Oxford University Press, 1986.

Kellner, Menachem, "*Farteitcht un Farbessert* (On 'Correcting' Maimonides)," *Me'orot* [=*Edah Journal*] 6, no. 2 (2007), 2–13.

Kellner, Menachem, *Gam Hem Ḳeruyim Adam. Ha-Nokhri be-'Eynei ha-Rambam*, Ramat-Gan: Bar-Ilan University Press, 2016.

Kellner, Menachem, *Maimonides' Confrontation with Mysticism*, Oxford: Littman Library of Jewish Civilization, 2006.

Kellner, Menachem, *Maimonides on Judaism and the Jewish People*, Albany: SUNY press, 1991.

Kellner, Menachem, *Maimonides on the "Decline of the Generations" and the Nature of Rabbinic Authority*, Albany: SUNY Press, 1996.

Kellner, Menachem, "Maimonides on the Science of the *Mishneh Torah*. Provisional or Permanent," *AJS Review* 18 (1993), 169–94.

Kellner, Menachem/Gillis, David, *Maimonides the Universalist. The Ethical Horizons of Mishneh Torah*, London: The Littman Library of Jewish Civilization, 2020.

Kellner, Menachem, "Maimonides' *True Religion* – for Jews, or All Humanity?" *Me'orot* [=*Edah Journal*] 7.1 (2008), 1–24.

Kellner, Menachem, "Misogyny. Gersonides vs. Maimonides," in: Menachem Kellner (ed.), *Torah in the Observatory. Gersonides, Maimonides, Song of Songs*, 283–304, Boston: Academic Studies Press, 2010.

Kellner, Menachem, *Must a Jew Believe Anything?*, Oxford: Littman Library of Jewish Civilization, 2006².

Kellner, Menachem, "A New and Unanticipated Textual Witness to the Reading, 'All Who Kills a Single Person – it is as if He Destroyed an Entire World'," *Tarbiz* 57 (2007), 565–66 (Hebrew).

Kellner, Menachem, "On Universalism and Particularism in Judaism," *Da'at* 36 (1996), v–xv.

Kellner, Menachem, *Science in the Bet Midrash. Studies in Maimonides*, Brighton, MA: Academic Studies Press, 2009.

Kellner, Menachem. "Steven Schwarzschild, Moses Maimonides, and 'Jewish Non-Jews'," in: Görge K. Hasselhoff/Otfried Fraise (eds.), *Moses Maimonides (1138–1204). His Religious, Scientific, and Philosophical Wirkungsgeschichte in Different Cultural Contexts*, 587–606, Wuerzburg: Ergon, 2004.

Kellner, Menachem, "Thinking Idolatry With/Against Maimonides. The Case of Christianity," (in press).

Kellner, Menachem, "We Are Not Alone," in: Michael J. Harris/Daniel Rynhold/Tamra Wright (eds.), *Radical Responsibility. Celebrating the Thought of Chief Rabbi Lord Jonathan Sacks*, 139–54, Jerusalem: Maggid Books, 2012.

Kellner, Menachem, "We Are Not Alone," in: Hava Tirosh-Samuelson/Aaron Hughes (eds.), *Menachem Kellner. Jewish Universalism*, 107–18, Library of Contemporary Jewish Philosophers 12, Leiden: Brill, 2015.

Kimelman, Reuven, "Irving Greenberg, For the Sake of Heaven and Earth. The New Encounter Between Judaism and Christianity," *Modern Judaism* 27 (2007), 103–25.

Kimelman, Reuven, "Judaism and Pluralism," *Modern Judaism* 7, no. 2 (1987), 131–50.

Kimelman, Reuven, *"Lekha Dodi" ve-Ḳabalat Shabat. Ha-Mashma'ut ha-Mistit.* Jerusalem: Magnes, 2003.

Kimelman, Reuven, "Rabbis Joseph B. Soloveitchik and Abraham Joshua Heschel on Jewish-Christian Relations," *Edah Journal* 4, no. 2 (2004), 1–21.

Klein-Braslavy, Sara, "The Philosophical Exegesis," in: Magne Saebo (ed.), *Hebrew Bible / Old Testament. The History of its Interpretation*, 302–20, Goettingen: Vandenhoeck and Ruprecht, 2000.

Korn, Eugene, "Extra Synagogam Sallus Est? Judaism and the Religious Other," in: Robert McKim (ed.), *Religious Perspectives on Religious Diversity*, 37–62, Leiden: Brill, 2016.

Korn, Eugene, "Gentiles, the World to Come, and Judaism. The Odyssey of a Rabbinic Text," *Modern Judaism* 14 (1994), 265–87.

Korn, Eugene, "Idolatry and the Covenantal Pluralism of Irving Greenberg," in: Shmuly Yanklowitz (ed.), *A Torah Giant. The Intellectual Legacy of Rabbi Dr. Irving (Yitz) Greenberg*, 59–70, Jerusalem: Urim Publications, 2018.

Korn, Eugene, "One God, Many Faiths: A Jewish Theology of Covenantal Pluralism," in: Eugene Korn/John T. Pawlikowsky (eds.), *Two Faiths, One Covenant?*, 147–54, Lanham, MD: Rowman and Littlefield, 2005.

Korn, Eugene, "The Man of Faith and Religious Dialogue. Revisiting 'Confrontation'," *Modern Judaism* 25, no. 3 (2005), 290–315.

Korn, Eugene, "The People Israel, Christianity, and the Covenantal Responsibility to History," in: Robert W. Jensen/Eugene Korn (eds.), *Covenant and Hope*, 145–72, Grand Rapids, MI: Eerdmans, 2012

Korn, Eugene, "Religious Violence, Sacred Texts and Theological Values," in: Robert W. Jensen/Eugene Korn (eds.), *Plowshares into Swords? Reflections on Religion and Violence*, 61–99, Jerusalem: Center for Jewish Christian Understanding and Cooperation, 2014.

Korn, Eugene, "Rethinking Christianity. Rabbinic Positions and Possibilities," in: Alon Goshen-Gottstein/Eugene Korn (eds.), *Jewish Theology and World Religions*, Littman Library of Jewish Civilization, 189–215, Liverpool: Liverpool University Press, 2012.

Kraemer, Joel, *Maimonides. The Life and World of One of Civilization's Greatest Minds*, New York: Doubleday, 2008.

Kreisel, Howard, "Maimonides on Divine Religion," in: Jay Harris (ed.), *Maimonides after 800 Years. Essays on Maimonides and His Influence*, 151–66, Cambridge: Harvard University Press, 2007.

Kymlicka, Will, "Two Models of Pluralism and Tolerance," in: David Heyd (ed.), *Toleration. An Elusive Virtue*, 81–105, Princeton: Princeton University Press, 1996.

Lachter, Hartley, "Israel as a Holy People in Medieval Kabbalah," in: Alan Mittleman (ed.), *Holiness in Jewish Thought*, 137–59, Oxford: Oxford University Press, 2018.

Lasker, Daniel J., *Jewish Philosophical Polemics against Christianity in the Middle Ages*, Oxford: Littman Library of Jewish Civilization, 2007^2.

Lasker, Daniel J., "Popular Polemics and Philosophical Truth in the Medieval Jewish Critique of Christianity," *Journal of Jewish Thought and Philosophy* 8 (1999), 243–59.

Lasker, Daniel J., "Proselyte Judaism, Christianity, and Islam in the Thought of Judah Halevi," *Jewish Quarterly Review* 81 (1990), 75–91.

Lasker, Daniel J., "Tradition and Innovation in Maimonides' Attitude toward Other Religions," in: Jay Harris (ed.), *Maimonides after 800 Years. Essays on Maimonides and His Influence*, 167–82, Cambridge: Harvard University Press, 2007.

Levenson Jon D., "The Universal Horizon of Biblical Particularism," in: Mark G. Brett (ed.), *Ethnicity and the Bible*, 143–69, Leiden: Brill, 1996.

Lubitch, Ronen, "The Righteous among the Nations of the Earth in the Thought of R. Hayyim David Halevi. Kabbalah and Natural Justice in the Question of the Attitude Towards Gentiles," in: Zvi Zohar/Avi Sag (eds.), *Yahadut Shel Ḥayyim. ʿIyyunim be-Yetsirato ha-Hagutit-Hilkhatit Shel ha-Rav Ḥayyim David Halevi*, 215–34, Jerusalem: Keter, 2007 (Hebrew).

Luria, Maxwell, "Rabbi Eliyahu Benamozegh. Israel and Humanity," published online: Institute for Jewish Ideas and Ideals, https://www.jewishideas.org/article/rabbi-eliyahu-benamozegh-israel-and-humanity (accessed on 03.04.2025).

Maimonides, *Book of Commandments*, trans. Charles B. Chavel, London: Soncino, 1967.

Maimonides, "Epistle on Martyrdom," in: S. Halkin/David Hartman (eds.), *Crisis and Leadership. Epistles of Maimonides*, 15–33, Philadelphia: Jewish Publication Society, 1985.

Maimonides, "The Epistle to Yemen," trans. A. S. Halkin, in: A. S. Halkin/David Hartman (eds.), *Crisis and Leadership. Epistles of Maimonides*, 93–131, Philadelphia: Jewish Publication Society, 1985.

Maimonides, *Guide of the Perplexed*, trans. Shlomo Pines, Chicago: University of Chicago Press, 1963.

Maimonides, "Introduction to His Commentary on the Tractate Avot," trans. Raymond Weiss/Charles Butterworth, *Ethical Writings of Maimonides*, New York: Dover, 1983.

Maimonides, *Mishneh Torah*, Yohai Makbili (ed.), Haifa, 2008 (Hebrew).

Melamed, Abraham, *Dat. Me-Ḥoḳ le-Emuna. Ḳorotav Shel Minuʾaḥ Mekhonen*, Tel Aviv: Ha-Kibbutz Ha-Meʾuhad, 2014.

Mendes-Flohr, Paul, "Israel. In Pursuit of Normalcy – Zionism's Ambivalence Towards Israel's Election," in :William R. Hutchison/Hatrmut Lehman (eds.), *Many Are Chosen. Divine Election and Western Nationalism*, 201–24, Minneapolis: Fortress Press, 1994.

Mendus, Susan, *Toleration and the Limits of Liberalism*, Atlantic Highlands, NJ: Humanities Press International, 1989.

Nehorai, Michael Zvi, "A Portion in the World to Come for the Righteous/Sages of the Nations," *Da'at* 50–52 (2003), 97–105 (Hebrew).

Nehorai, Michael Zvi, "'Righteous Gentiles Have a Share in the World to Come'," *Tarbiz* 61 (1992), 465–87 (Hebrew).

Nelson, Cary, *Israel Denial. Anti-Zionism, Anti-Semitism, & the Faculty Campaign against the Jewish State*, Bloomington: Indiana University Press, 2019.

Novak, David, *The Image of the Non-Jew in Judaism. An Historical and Constructive Study of the Noahide Laws*, New York: E. Mellen Press, 1983.

Novak, David, "Maimonides and Aquinas on Natural Law," in: David Novak et al. (eds.), *Talking with Christians. Musings of a Jewish Theologian*, 67–88, Grand Rapids, MI: Eerdmans, 2005.

Rabinovitch, Nachum, *Melumadei Milḥamah*, Ma'aleh Adumim: Ma'aliyot, 1992.

Ravitsky, Aviezer, "The Question of Tolerance. Between Pluralism and Paternalism," in: *Ḥarut Al ha-Luḥot*, 114–38, Tel Aviv: Am Oved, 1999 (Hebrew).

Ravitzky, Aviezer, "The Question of Tolerance in the Jewish Religious Tradition," in: Yaakov Elman/Jeffrey S. Gurock (eds.), *Hazon Nahum. Studies in Jewish Law, Thought, and History Presented to Dr. Norman Lamm on the Occasion of His Seventieth Birthday*, 359–91, New York: Michael Sharf Publication Trust of the Yeshiva University Press, 1997.

Ross, Tamar, *Expanding the Palace of Tora. Orthodoxy and Feminism*, Walthan, MA: Brandeis University Press, 2004.

Roth, Leon, "Moralization and Demoralization in Jewish Ethics," in: Leon Roth (ed.), *Is There a Jewish Philosophy?*, 128–43, London: Littman Library of Jewish Civilization, 1999.

Rynhold, Daniel/Harris, Michael J., *Nietzsche, Soloveitchik, and Contemporary Jewish Philosophy*, Cambridge: Cambridge University Press, 2018.

Sa'adia Gaon, *Book of Belief and Opinions*, trans. Samuel Rosenblatt, New Haven: Yale University Press, 1948.

Sand, Shlomo, *The Invention of the Jewish People*, London: Verso, 2008.

Schlossberg, Eliezer, "Maimonides' Attitude towards Islam," *Pe'amim* 42 (1990), 38–60 (Hebrew).

Schwartz, Dov, *Religion or Halakha. The Philosophy of Rabbi Joseph B. Soloveitchik*, Leiden: Brill, 2007.

Schwarzfuchs, Simon-Raymond, "Les Lois Royales De Maimonide," *Revue des etudes juives* 111 (1951–52), 63–86.

Schwarzschild, Steven, "Do Noachites Have to Believe in Revelation? (a Passage in Dispute Between Maimonides, Spinoza, Mendelssohn, and Herman Cohen) a Contribution to a Jewish View of Natural Law," in: Menachem Kellner (ed.), *The Pursuit of the Ideal. Jewish Writings of Steven Schwarzschild*, 29–59. Albany: SUNY Press, 1990.

Schwarzschild, Steven, "On Jewish Eschatology," in: Menachem Kellner (ed.), *The Pursuit of the Idea. Jewish Writings of Steven Schwarzschild*, 209–28, Albany: SUNY Press, 1990.

Schwarzschild, Steven, *The Pursuit of the Ideal*, Albany: SUNY Press, 1990.

Sha'arei Geulah, New York: Kehat, 1992.

Shapiro, David, *Studies in Jewish Thought*, vol. 2, New York: Yeshiva University Press, 1981, 272–75.

Shapiro, Marc, "Is It Permissible to Enter a Church? First Publication of a Responsum by Ha-Ga'on R. Eliezer Berkovitz on the Matter," *Milin Havivin* 4 (2011), 43–50.

Simon, Ernst, "The Neighbor (Re'a) Whom We Shall Love," in: Marvin Fox (ed.), *Modern Jewish Ethics. Theory and Practice*, 29–56, Columbus: Ohio State University Press, 1975.

Sklare, David, "Are the Gentiles Obligated to Observe the Torah? The Discussion Concerning the Universality of the Torah in the East in the Tenth and Eleventh Centuries," in: Jay Harris (ed.), *Be'erot Yitzhak. Studies in Memory of Isadore Twersky*, 311–46, Cambridge: Harvard University Press, 2005.

Smith, Anthony D., *Chosen Peoples*, Oxford: Oxford University Press, 2003.

Soloveitchik, Joseph B., "Confrontation," *Tradition* 6, no. 2 (1964), 5–29.

Stone, Suzanne, "Tolerance Versus Pluralism in Judaism," *Journal of Human Rights* 2, no. 1 (2003), 105–17.

Turkel, Eli, "Partial Bibliography of works by and about Rabbi Joseph B. Soloveitchik Zt"l," published online: Eli Turkel, http://www.cs.tau.ac.il/~turkel/ (accessed on 05.08.2019).

Twersky, Isadore, *Rabad of Posquieres. A Twelfth-Century Talmudist*, Philadelphia: Jewish Publication Society, 1980.

Urbach, Ephraim E., "'Whoever Saves One Soul… [mSan 4:5].' The History of a Recension," in: *Me-Olamam Shel Ḥakhamim. Ḳovets Meḥḳarim*, 561–77, Jerusalem: Magnes, 1988 (Hebrew).

Weiss, Raymond L., *Maimonides' Ethics. The Encounter of Philosophic and Religious Morality*, Chicago: University of Chicago Press, 1991.

Williams, Bernard, "Toleration. An Impossible Virtue?," in David Heyd (ed.), *Toleration. An Elusive Virtue*, 18–27, Princeton: Princeton University Press, 1996.

Wolfson, Elliot, *Venturing Beyond. Law and Morality in Kabbalistic Mysticism*, Oxford: Oxford University Press, 2006.

Suggestions for Further Reading

Ferziger, Adam S., "'And Who Even Knows What It Is': The Role of Reform in the Rulings of R. Yosef Eliyahu Henkin," in: Yitzhak Berger/Chaim Milikowsky (eds.), *'In the Dwelling of a Sage Lie Precious Treasures': Essays in Jewish Studies in Honor of Shnayer Z. Leiman*, 323–39, New York: Yeshiva University Press, 2020.

Ferziger, Adam S., "'The Road Not Taken' and 'The Road Less Traveled': The Greenberg-Lichtenstein Exchange and Contemporary Orthodoxy," in: Adam S. Ferziger et al. (eds.), *Yitz Greenberg and Modern Orthodoxy: The Road Not Taken*, 254–88, Boston: Academic Studies Press, 2019.

Jacobs, Jonathan A., "Judaism, Pluralism & Public Reason," *Daedalus* 149 (2020), 170–84.

Jospe, Raphael, *Accepting and Excepting: On Pluralism and Chosenness Out of the Sources of Judaism* (Boston Academic Studies Press, forthcoming).

Lehtipuu, Outi/Labahn, Michael (eds.), *Tolerance, Intolerance, and Recognition in Early Christianity and Early Judaism*, Amsterdam: Amsterdam University Press, 2021.

Christian Polke (1980–2023)
The Concept of Tolerance in Christianity

What is tolerance? While seemingly straightforward, the question resists easy answers. One common assumption is that, theologically, tolerance refers to a concept shaped by a specific framework. Yet even this definition invites skepticism. We speak of tolerant people and tolerant groups. We also associate tolerance with ideas like those of European Enlightenment. However, an idea does not inherently become a conceptual framework. In the first case, tolerance appears less as an abstract idea and more as a lived virtue. Therefore, it is important to note that in any attempt to develop tolerance as a concept, our cognitive preferences already resonate. Later sections will demonstrate how overlooking this leads to fundamental misunderstandings of tolerance itself. The problems which then arise lead to further complications in speaking of theological concepts and their justifications in favor of a Christian ethos of tolerance. But let us first discuss what is considered by talking about a Christian concept of tolerance.

There is no singular "Christian concept of tolerance," just as there is no monolithic Christianity. Instead, we as contemporaries in a global world and in our multicultural societies are aware of *Multiple Christianities* or *Christendoms* with their different histories, confessional und denominational backgrounds and their varieties of liturgies, organizational structures and cultural heritages. Therefore, it requires sincerity in disclosing one's own confessional standpoint. My analysis emerges from a Protestant European context, specifically from a bi-confessional cultural mentality shaped by Reformation and Counter-Reformation legacies. This environment intertwines religious and secular voices, influencing contemporary understandings of tolerance. Thus, the question of tolerance is by these socio-cultural conditions not only shaped but also — to a large extent — a result of them.[1]

---

[1] For an overview of political regimes of tolerance cf. Walzer, Michael, *On Toleration*, New Haven: Yale University Press, 1997.

Editorial addition: With philosopher Rainer Forst, who has extensively studied the concept of tolerance in past and present, we can distinguish at least four types of conceptions of tolerance in general, which all became effective historically: Tolerance as 1) a permission of an authority or majority towards a minority, for example the Edict of Nantes 1598, which was supposed to end the disputes between Catholics and Huguenots; as 2) a peaceful coexistence of different, but roughly equal groups; as 3) mutual respect, which considers the other as morally or ethically equal; and as 4) appreciation, which considers the views of the other as ethically valuable. (Forst, Rainer, *Toleranz im Konflikt. Geschichte, Gehalt und Gegenwart eines umstrittenen Begriffs*, Frankfurt/M.: Suhrkamp Verlag, 2003, 42–48). Multhammer points out, however, that even if in theory all four

In the following, after a brief look at biblical resources, the historical development in early Christianity and structural components of the concept or idea of tolerance (1.), I will shed light on the emergence of the problem in the early modern period (2.), in order to then discuss two exemplary and, for their time, innovative approaches to tolerance, those of Roger Williams (3.1.) and Pierre Bayle (3.2.). This is followed by a brief look at Roman Catholicism in modern times to put the Protestant focus into perspective (4.). Subsequently, I will present systematic reflections on the theological reconstruction of the idea of tolerance (5.), and finally by a discussion of the virtue of tolerance as an element of a Christian ethos (6.).

1 Biblical Resources, Historical Development in Early Christianity and Structural Components

Since modern and postmodern sensibilities shape today's concept of tolerance, it would be alien to biblical authors — demanding caution to avoid anachronistic readings.[2] Nevertheless, certain biblical passages have become particularly powerful in the course of history and have thus contributed significantly to develop the concept — although they were interpreted sometimes almost contradictory. We will go into more detail below.

Nor is the Christian worldview or church inherently linked to tolerance. Historically, it is more often tied to persecution (heresy trials, witch hunts), violence (crusades, religious wars), colonialism, forced missionary work, and suppression of free inquiry.[3]

---

types could be lived in societies at the same time, the historical context sets limits to this. Sometimes an impartial, neutral view of a case is only possible in retrospect, with a temporal distance, when the pressure to act or to react in a certain way no longer exists. Therefore, as we will see, the specific circumstances often determined which variant was preferred or omitted (Multhammer, Michael, "Johann Lorenz von Mosheims *Ketzergeschichte* oder der Sündenfall der Reformation. Ein Beitrag zur Toleranzdebatte in der Frühaufklärung," in: Friedrich Vollhardt et al. (eds.), *Toleranzdiskurse in der frühen Neuzeit*, 273–92, here 281f., Berlin: Walter de Gruyter, 2015.).

[2] This section, as well as the section "The Problem of Tolerance in the Confessional Age (Sixteenth–Seventeenth Century)", contain editorial additions.

[3] Barth, Hans-Martin, *Die Theologie Martin Luthers. Eine kritische Würdigung*, Munich: Gütersloher Verlagshaus, 2009, 383 f.

The Latin *tolerantia*, likely first used in Cicero's *Paradoxa Stoicorum* (46 BCE), denotes enduring pain or injustice. Its root, tol- ("to bear" or "carry"), underpins its meaning as a passive form of fortitude (*fortitudo*). This strength to endure something physically or mentally forms the passive part of the virtue of courage, *fortitudo*. Possibly it is a mere synonym for the much more frequently mentioned *patentia*, the capacity to suffer, or it is a neologism of Cicero himself. The term *intolerantia*, is much older and was used in reference to unbearable, intolerable arrogant individuals or tyrants.[4]

From there, the word finds its way into old Latin translations of the Bible[5] and some writings of the Church Fathers, where it is used in the sense of inner strength and patience (*patientia*) as well as — for the first time — endurance in relation to others. According to Tertullian (160–240) and Cyprian (d. 258), enduring evil, misfortune and persecution becomes a sign of faith and trust in God.[6] *Tolerantia* has been thus, quite differently from our present understanding, initially a virtue of the weak, of people who are at the mercy of powers.[7]

But even if the term "tolerance" does not explicitly appear in the Bible, we can ask whether there are episodes to which we now refer as questions of tolerance or for the phenomenon as such, as "[t]he quest for religious tolerance, respect, and recognition — albeit characteristic of modern and postmodern thought — is a human concern that runs throughout history, for coexistence and diversity are at the core of human culture."[8]

Then, different tendencies can be found in both the Hebrew Bible and the New Testament. For example, the prohibition to worship other gods may in historical terms have been directed at the Israelites in the first place, without the fact that it may even have involved a violent expulsion and suppression of foreign god cults: "But thus shall ye deal with them; ye shall destroy their altars, and break down their images, and cut down their groves, and burn their graven images with fire. For thou art a holy people unto the Lord thy God" (Dtn 7:5.6a, KJV). With the "Mosaic distinction" (Jan Assmann)[9] — enforced post-exile under

---

[4] Cf. Schubert, Christoph, "Toleranz in der römischen Antike," in: Dagmar Kiesel/Cleophea Ferrrari (eds.), *Toleranz*, 31–53, here 33 and 37, Frankfurt/M.: Klostermann, 2022.
[5] In the Vulgate, *tolarantia* is found today only in 2 Cor 1:6, the opposite of it, *intolerantia*, in 2 Macc 9:10. Ibid., 36.
[6] Cf. Forst, *Toleranz im Konflikt*, 54–57.
[7] Cf. Schubert, *Toleranz*, 50.
[8] Lehtipuu, Outi/Michael Labahn, "Introduction," in: Outi Lehtipuu/Michael Labahn (eds.), *Tolerance, Intolerance, and Recognition in Early Christianity and Early Judaism*, 9–16, here 11, Amsterdam: Amsterdam University Press, 2021.
[9] Cf. Assmann, Jan, *The Price of Monotheism*, trans. Robert Savage, Standford (Ca.): Stanford University Press, 2010.

Persian rule (Ezra, Nehemiah) — the rejection of foreign cults became central to preserving Israel's ethno-religious identity.[10]

Tolerance extends beyond periods of (perceived) stability to include religious outsiders. For minorities like early Christians, tolerance was less a priority than survival — its meaning diverging sharply from modern notions.

As minority groups, both Jews and Christians had to work out ways of coexisting with their Graeco-Roman neighbors. Relationships with those neighbors were often strained, but even within Jewish and Christian circles, issues of tolerance and intolerance surfaced regularly.[11]

Typical for this is the Pauline approach in connection with the question whether Christians are obliged to avoid the meat sacrificed to idols. Here religious commandments and social circumstances interlock, and the question arises in what strict way religious identity must also be recognizable in the (personal) way of life of the believers. The manner in which the strong interact with the weak is a recurring theme in the epistles of the Apostle Paul, particularly in *Romans* 14–15 and 1 *Corinthians* 8. This thematic focus advocates a fundamental tolerant attitude, which is further complemented by a sense of responsibility in matters that do not directly concern the religious identity of Christians. In this context, Paul emphasizes the importance of personal conscience, bringing a crucial element to later discourses on tolerance.[12]

We also find a precursor of the idea of tolerance in 1 Cor 13:7, the verse that contained the verb *tolerare* in the Old Latin translations (*caritas tolerat omnia*) and calls for enduring the faults of others, including false brothers (*falsi fratres*, 2 Cor 11:26), out of love.[13]

Nevertheless, Paul's worldview differs strongly from a liberal pluralistic consciousness, as Stephan C. Barton points out in his essay *Paul and the limits of tolerance*. In *Galatians,* Paul pronounced an "anathema" against dissenters, and he

---

[10] It must be noted, however, that such assessments of biblical texts are always reception-driven. What the historical reality looked like is still hardly ascertainable. Conversely, the post-exile motive of theological universalism (monotheism; Second and Third Jesaiah) in particular, results in an attitude towards foreign peoples that is not only tolerant but also inclusive, to whom JHWH's saving action is also directed. Cf. Fabry, Heinz-Josef, "Toleranz im Alten Testament? Ergebnisse einer Suchbewegung," in: Ingo Broer/Richard Schlüter (eds.), *Christentum und Toleranz*, 9–34, Darmstadt: Wissenschaftliche Buchgesellschaft, 1996.

[11] Stanton, Graham N., "Introduction," in: Graham N. Stanton/Guy G. Stroumsa (eds.), *Tolerance and Intolerance in Early Judaism and Christianity*, 1–6, here 1, Cambridge: Cambridge University Press, 1998.

[12] Cf. Forst, Rainer, *Toleranz im Konflikt*, 58.

[13] Cf. Angenendt, Arnold, *"Lasst beides wachsen bis zur Ernte": Toleranz in der Geschichte des Christentums*, Münster: Aschendorff Verlag, 2018, 44.

did not hope for tolerance from his opponents, but for their conversion to the truth.

Barton notes that there is a tendency to understand Jesus and Paul as two opposite poles: one as an example of intolerant fanaticism and the other as a figure of tolerance and love. This might be linked to the fact that Paul is often made responsible for the emergence of the church, while Jesus is seen as a teacher of universal love. He attributes this tendency to an anachronistic reading of the Bible: at the center of Paul's thinking, according to Barton, however, was love, zeal for God and apocalyptic hope, not the even-handed and neutral tolerance of modernity.[14]

Jesus, too, focuses on love, love for us and love for our neighbor, who can also be a stranger.[15] His demand for love of the enemy (Mt 5:44 par Lk 6:27) taught an appreciative recognition and an unconditional concern for the well-being of the threatening other, which goes much further than a mere endurance or simple indifference.[16]

Both, Jesus and Paul, set a new accent in this respect, in which they overcome their initially ethno-centric and particularistic approach and universally include people of all nations in their message (cf. especially Jesus encounter with the Syro-Phoenician woman, Mk 7:24–30; the conversion of the Roman centurion Cornelius, Acts 10; Paul's mission to the Gentiles and his speech of a new identity "in Christ", Gal. 3:28: "There is neither Jew nor Greek, there is neither bond nor free, there is neither male nor female: for ye are all one in Christ Jesus." KJV).[17]

In the history of ancient and medieval Christianity, the verses Mt. 13:29–30 have been particularly influential in dealing with heretics, deviants and apostates.

---

[14] Cf. Barton, Stephan C., "Paul and the limits of tolerance," in: Graham N. Stanton/Guy G. Stroumsa (eds.), *Tolerance and Intolerance in Early Judaism and Christianity*, 122–34, Cambridge: Cambridge University Press, 1998.
[15] Cf. the commandment to love one's neighbor (Lev 19:18); the double commandment of love (Lk 10,27) and the parable of the good Samaritan (Lk 10,30–37).
[16] Cf. Labahn, Michael, "Der geliebte ‚Feind'. Wahrnehmung des Anderen in Jesu Gebot der Feindesliebe und ihre Rezeption im Dokument Q – ein Beispiel antiker ‚Toleranz' und ‚Anerkennung'?," in: Outi Lehtipuu/Michael Labahn (eds.), *Tolerance, Intolerance, and Recognition in Early Christianity and Early Judaism*, 73–109, Amsterdam: Amsterdam University Press, 2021.
[17] But Paul's thinking is also marked by a certain ambivalence. For if one compares his insistence on the love commandment with the severity with which he opposes alternative interpretations of the (Jewish) Law in the congregation in Galatia, the tension can hardly be resolved. Cf. Broer, Ingo, "Toleranz im Neuen Testament? Ein Versuch zum Toleranzgedanken in den paulinischen Briefen," in: Ingo Broer/Richard Schlüter (eds.), *Christentum und Toleranz*, (fn. 3) 57–82, Darmstadt: Wissenschaftliche Buchgesellschaft, 1996. These results become even more difficult for the *Corpus Johanneum*, in which likewise a strong tension between the love commandment (in relation to the brethren in Christ) and the clear demarcation to the outside world can be shown, including antijudaistic tendencies.

They are part of the parable of the wheat and the tares (Mt. 13:24–30).[18] Arnold Angenendt, in his study of the impact of this text, points out that the punishment of the sacrilege against God — whether heresy, apostasy or pollution — has been a basic pattern in the history of religion to protect the community from the wrath of God or the gods. Mostly the commandment of Jesus was interpreted in such a way that, since God will punish the offence himself, he forbade the punishment by humans, in the form of physical coercive measures or even death penalty. This related to the eschatological caveat, which should prevent a hasty judgment about what was wheat and what was tares.[19]

Angenendt argues that this interpretation prevented widespread heretic executions in the first millennium — until the revival of ancient practices targeting sacrilege. After that the parable was interpreted in the opposite way, as if it were possible to identify and necessary to pull out the weeds.[20] Pope Gregory IX (d. 1241) first advocated burning heretics at the stake.[21]

This new evaluation was decisively prepared already by the work of Augustine (354–430). On the one hand, Augustine used the term *tolerantia* in the sense of a Christian social virtue, which consisted in tolerating even bad people (*mali*) and being patient towards them. Augustine also framed Jews as "compulsory witnesses" to Christian truth, a concept later used in the Middle Ages to justify sparing them from violence.[22] On the other hand, long and intense conflicts as a bishop with the Donatists let his arguments for tolerance turn into those for intol-

---

[18] "Another parable put he forth unto them, saying, The kingdom of heaven is likened unto a man which sowed good seed in his field:

But while men slept, his enemy came and sowed tares among the wheat, and went his way.
But when the blade was sprung up, and brought forth fruit, then appeared the tares also.
So the servants of the householder came and said unto him, Sir, didst not thou sow good seed in thy field? from whence then hath it tares? He said unto them, An enemy hath done this. The servants said unto him, Wilt thou then that we go and gather them up?

But he said, Nay; lest while ye gather up the tares, ye root up also the wheat with them.
Let both grow together until the harvest: and in the time of harvest I will say to the reapers, Gather ye together first the tares, and bind them in bundles to burn them: but gather the wheat into my barn." (KJV)

[19] Cf. Angenendt, *"Lasst beides wachsen bis zur Ernte"*, 9–11, 16 and 35.

[20] Cf. Ibid., 72.

[21] Cf. Ragg, Sascha, *Ketzer und Recht: die weltliche Ketzergesetzgebung des Hochmittelalters unter dem Einfluß des römischen und kanonischen Rechts*, Hannover: Hahnsche Buchhandlung, 2006, 151.

[22] Schreiner, Klaus, "'Tolerantia': Begriffs- und wirkungsgeschichtliche Studien zur Toleranzauffassung des Kirchenvaters Augustinus," in: Alexander Patschovsky (ed.), *Toleranz im Mittelalter*, 355–89, here 338 and 369f., Sigmaringen: Thorbecke Verlag, 1998.

erance in relation to heretics and schismatics, towards whom he considered the use of force and coercion to be justified.[23]

Even more decisive was finally Thomas Aquinas (1224/5–1274), the most prominent representative of scholasticism, who in his *Summa Theologica* argued that, because theologians could identify the weeds, killing heretics was justified for the common good. By the High Middle Ages, this logic formalized the Inquisition: the Church tried heretics, while secular authorities carried out executions.[24]

The second verse with a strong impact in history has been the passage of Luke 14:23 "Compel them to come in" (KJV). At the latest from Augustine on it is hereby argued that even compulsion to true faith represents a service to one's neighbor, in so far as salvation is at least still possible. Although he did not justify the death penalty with it, he advocated other coercive measures towards the Donatists that continued to have an effect in the West until the modern times, such as the burning of writings, banishment, fines, deprivation of property, and the like.[25] The argument for the use of force here is a conditional love, which serves the salvation of the soul of the other. Since this salvation is seen as an objective thing that is independent of the respective person and can be determined according to the doctrine of the church, the human soul can and must be saved from damnation by God even against the will of the person. Despite the fact that the coercion did not result in a change in attitude, it was regarded as beneficial in terms of protecting others from the spread of heresy.[26]

So, power relations obviously played an important role in the interpretation of the biblical passages: Things change once you get in the majority position. In this regard Christianity went through a history from one extreme to the other: From persecution to toleration to privilege. At first, Christians were those who requested religious freedom — which was granted to them rather rarely at first. from the middle of the third century, Christians were persecuted throughout the empire. But with the conversion of the Emperor Constantine (d. 337) to Christianity the tide changed: in the year 380, Christianity became the state religion. At this juncture, the others had to hope for tolerance on the part of the representatives of Christianity. The emperors increasingly turned against the pagan cults with their decrees: under Justinian I (482–565), the pagans were largely disenfranchised. However, this also considerably increased the pressure to conformism in doctrinal as well as disciplinary terms: disputes within the church increased and the unity of the empire was to be founded in a homogeneous unity of faith

---

23 Cf. Forst, *Toleranz im Konflikt*, 69–78.
24 Cf. Angenendt, *"Lasst beides wachsen bis zur Ernte"*, 100–4.
25 Cf. Ibid., 60 ff.
26 Cf. Forst, *Toleranz im Konflikt*, 78–81.

and church — which increased the persecution of heresies and schisms. Therefore, at numerous synods convened by the emperor, disputes about the generally binding dogmas were held since 325.[27] The "Codex Theodosius" and "Codex Iustinianus" from the fifth and sixth centuries enumerate all the measures they envisaged against heretical movements such as the Arians, Donatists and Manichaeans: prohibition of assembly, destruction of churches, burning of scriptures, loss of civil rights, banishment, confiscation of goods, and physical punishments ranging from torture to forced labor and the death penalty.[28]

Furthermore, the biblical concept of two realms — or two kingdoms — one earthly and secular, the other spiritual and ecclesiastical, has had a significant impact throughout history.[29] Building on this idea, Pope Gelasius in the fifth century developed what became known as the "doctrine of the two powers." According to this doctrine, the world was governed by two distinct authorities: the spiritual and the secular. Although each had its own responsibilities, they were not equal in status — the secular power was ultimately understood as subordinate, being a component of the Church, the Body of Christ. The secular power was considered essential for maintaining peace and restraining evil, while the spiritual power was dedicated to the salvation of souls. Heresy, therefore, became a public crime that threatened the unity and stability of the state. This argumentation determined the social order until modernity. Thus, it was the church that decided what — and who — was to be tolerated. Apostates and heretics were often treated more harshly than Jews or pagans, as they posed an internal threat to the Church and directly challenged its authority.[30] Initially, heresy was dealt with solely by the Church, with excommunication serving as the principal form of punishment. This changed in the middle of the twelfth century, when a paradigmatic shift occurred: state authorities began to take an active role in religious matters. As part of this process, the legal codes of the late antique emperors were revisited and reapplied to address religious dissent.[31]

A major contribution to this discussion is the groundbreaking study of the social teachings of the Christian churches and groups by Ernst Troeltsch (1865–1923). His study highlights to what extent the social status of the Christian communities (churches) and their political influence is related to the formulation of clear

---

[27] Cf. Andresen, Carl/Ritter, Adolf Martin: *Geschichte des Christentums I/1. Altertum*, Stuttgart: Kohlhammer, 1993, 176 und 184 f.
[28] Cf. Ragg, *Ketzer und Recht*, 7–9.
[29] Cf. Forst, *Toleranz im Konflikt*, 58.
[30] Cf. Ibid., 83, 85 and 89 f.
[31] Cf. Ragg, *Ketzer und Recht*, 58 f.

dogmas and the claim to possess the truth.[32] According to Troeltsch, the way Christian communities relate to tolerance, error, and apostasy is closely tied to their structural form and theological self-understanding. He famously distinguished between three types of Christian association: church, sect, and mysticism, each fostering distinct mentalities and attitudes toward religious dissent. Institutional churches often permit internal diversity to retain their majority status, while sects and denominations prioritize doctrinal clarity and lifestyle conformity (discipleship). Even if the violent contact with heretics always rather falls back negatively on the official churches,[33] it is mentally rather the sect type that urges to avoid internal deviations and dissonances. The mystical type, in contrast to both, represents a paradigm of religious individualism. Its very structure leans toward a high degree of tolerance and recognition of divergent beliefs and experiences — though this openness may risk slipping into indifferentism. Basically, all these constellations of truth claims and tolerance commandments, which are organizationally structured and formed by the lifeworld, continue to influence the modern landscape of Christian pluralism. This applies both to sectarian fundamentalisms in the sphere of religious literalism (biblicism), and to the more syncretistic forms of Christian spirituality. Moreover, with this typology different strategies in dealing with (inner confessional and religious) plurality and tolerance can be diagnosed, as they can be found in and beyond the so-called mainline and established churches.

However, in the history of Christianity, the first groups whom a Christian majority had to tolerate and articulate were always dissenters. This includes the so-called heretics of the twelfth and thirteenth centuries — such as the Waldensians — as well as the radical wings of the Reformation in the sixteenth century. For these and similar reasons, the question of tolerance has always been inherently linked to claims for religious freedom in European history. These groups, regardless of their specific beliefs, were consistently labeled as heretical — typically by the dominant majority.

This dynamic mirrors modern debates about integrating conservative Muslim minorities into liberal democracies, highlighting enduring tensions between ma-

---

[32] Cf. especially his systematic considerations in his conclusion: Troeltsch, Ernst, *The Social Teachings of the Christian Churches*, vol. II, trans. Olive Wyon, Louisville (Ky.), London: Westminster John Knox Press, 1992, 997–99.

[33] Cf. Angenendt, Arnold, *Toleranz und Gewalt. Das Christentum zwischen Bibel und Schwert*, Münster: Aschendorff Verlag, 2008. This book by one of the most renowned medieval historians in the field of church history shows the different forms, arguments and strategies that have been formed and handed down in dealing with heretics, with questions of pluralism, but also with dissidents within the church.

jority norms and religious dissent. In consequence, Christian concepts of tolerance must hermeneutically refer to these social, political and cultural conditions by making the idea of religious freedom a subject of discussion.

2 The Problem of Tolerance in the Confessional Age (Sixteenth–Seventeenth Century)

Religious diversity is central to modern pluralistic societies, though confessional distinctions emerged earlier, rooted in the sixteenth- and seventeenth-century Western church schism following the Reformation. It is basically a product of the Western church schism in the wake of the Reformation. At latest after the Thirty Year's War (1618–1648) not only intellectuals, churchmen and political rulers but also ordinary people had realized that questions of (religious) truth about God and salvation can lead into dangerous consequences — at least for dissenters, and especially when they tried to play a crucial role in politics. In this precarious constellation, the idea of religious tolerance together with the idea of religious freedom arose and was quickly spread among intellectual and political circles around Europe. Of course, the established elites, church officials no less than political rulers, were suspicious of such discourses. They feared times of political and institutional destabilization because of an overly critical and even public debate on religious affairs. In any case, social and political cohesion, peace and security were at both sides of the story the guiding values for one's own action. However, if there is one lesson we can learn from this incubation period of the idea of religious tolerance, it is the following: where religious communities, or to be more precise: where churches have entered strategic or even worse ideological alliance with leading political powers, the claim for tolerance as well as the idea of a religiously legitimated idea of tolerance can only arise and be convincing when they come from "outside", namely from the side of the dissenting parties and oppressed groups.

It is therefore not surprising that the first conceptions of religious tolerance in the early modern period did not come from those who considered themselves to be in the tradition of the classical reformers, particularly Martin Luther (1483–1546) and John Calvin (1509–1564). Although Luthers's writings — especially of his early and middle years right up to the peasant's revolts[34] — contain elements that can be interpreted as Christian conceptions of tolerance, neither he nor his

---

[34] A brilliant analysis of Martin Luther's idea of tolerance is given by Heckel, Martin, *Martin Luthers Reformation und das Recht*, Tübingen: Mohr Siebeck, 2016, 662–98.

fellow Reformers articulated a consistent or inclusive doctrine of religious tolerance. Their frameworks largely excluded Catholics, heretics, Muslims (referred to as "Turks" or "Muselmanns"), unconverted Jews, and non-believers, such as atheists or so-called "Epicureans." The same general attitude is reflected in Calvin's thought.

The case of Michael Servet, an Antitrinitarian who was burned at the stake in Geneva in 1553 due to his writings, became particularly famous and controversial. The historian Johann Lorenz von Mosheim (1693–1755), who researched the case extensively in the eighteenth century, even referred to it as the "Fall of the Reformation", by which the movement had lost its innocence. No less insightful is the story of the Antitrinitarian Adam Neuser (1530–1576), who, to avoid execution, saw himself forced to flee to the Ottoman Empire and convert to Islam.[35] While Luther, Zwingli (1484–1531) and Calvin all advocated the death penalty for heresy, many in the left wing of the Reformation, the Anabaptists and Pietists opposed it.[36] Thus, the impression arises that it was the dissenters who contributed most to the emergence of the modern idea of tolerance.

The first strategies dealing with confessional plurality were put forward by political leaders and due to reasons of power in times of instability. By the Peace of Augsburg in 1555, the official maxim in religious politics was: *cuius regio, eius religio*; a rule that was in the meantime extensively enforced by the political rulers all over Europe. Thus, in the seventeenth century, Western Europe was mainly a bi-confessionally divided continent. Michel Foucault's concept of "pastoral power"[37] and Gerhard Oestreich's "social disciplining"[38] describe regimes that homogenized territories, regions, and mentalities — often more rigidly than ever before. For religious dissenters who did not belong to any of the so-called official or established religions and confessions, only few options remained. The two most familiar were either to go into inner exile or to emigrate from one's own homeland, like the famous Pilgrim fathers did by going to the still British New England territories.

Franco Buzzi draws attention to the fact that some of the first modern treatises on religious freedom were written in the regions of Eastern Europe, where Anabaptists and Antitrinitarians briefly found asylum: Poland and Transylvania. In 1632, Johannes Crellius (1590–1633), a Socinian theologian and professor in

---

35 Multhammer, Mosheims *Ketzergeschichte*, 273–92.
36 Angenendt, *"Lasst beides wachsen bis zur Ernte"*, 117–20, 128 f.
37 Cf. Foucault, Michel, *Security, Territory, Population: Lectures at the Collège de France, 1977–1978*, trans. Graham Burchell, New York & Basingstoke: Palgrave Macmillan, 2007.
38 Cf. Oestreich, "Gerhard, Strukturprobleme des europäischen Absolutismus," *Vierteljahresschrift für Sozial- und Wirtschaftsgeschichte* 55 (1969), 329–47.

Raków, addressed both the state and the Catholic Church in his treatise *Vindiciae pro religionis libertate* ("A Defense of Religious Liberty"). In it, he argued that divergent views in matters of faith need not disrupt peaceful civil coexistence. In this way, he opposed the long-held principle that only one religion could prevail in each region.[39]

3 Tolerance in the Spirit of Christianity: Two Examples from the (Protestant) History of Ideas

3.1 Tolerance in the Light of Liberty of Conscience: Roger Williams (1603–1683)

In the early modern period, under the conditions of intensified social and religious disciplining, two thinkers stand out in their struggle for the idea of religious tolerance. Both had a profound influence on the intellectual debates that have persisted for centuries. Each came from a confessional, mainly Protestant background, and each was also viewed with suspicion by many of their contemporaries and later thinkers: on one hand was the French philosopher Pierre Bayle (1647–1706); on the other, Roger Williams (1603–1683), an English-born theologian and preacher who later founded the first Baptist congregation in Rhode Island — though he never formally became a Baptist himself. In their writings, both Bayle and Williams articulated concepts of religious tolerance that reached far beyond the common assumptions of their age. By examining key elements of their thought, I aim to identify those aspects that remain essential for any constructive Christian — though firmly Protestant — approach to religious tolerance, including in the context of our own time.

I begin with Roger Williams. Williams' Treatise *The Bloudy Tenent of Persecution for Cause of Conscience*, published in 1644, still is a "historical landmark" in the debates on religious tolerance. No Puritan, congregationalist, Lutheran or Catholic thinker, no one before Williams has in such a clear, consequent and distinctive way outspoken and argued for the religious idea of tolerance, even towards so-called pagans. Williams was a sharp critic of the colonial occupation of Native American lands, and equally outspoken in his opposition to public dis-

---

[39] Cf. Buzzi, Franco/Krienke, Markus, *Toleranz und Religionsfreiheit in der Moderne*, Stuttgart: Kohlhammer, 2017, 63–67.

crimination and persecution of heretics, Catholics, Jews, Muslims, and even so-called pagans. It is revealing thereby that his treatise mainly takes the form of a dialogue between two allegorical figures, "Peace" and "Truth," offering early insight into his nuanced understanding of the worth and value of tolerance. In a dual sense, tolerance is crucial for society's harmonious coexistence. First, it is necessary because religious differences occur even among fellow Christians, which become evident through debates on the nature of church and ministry, of sin and justification or of right worship, and the essence of sacraments. Second, tolerance is indispensable for civil life: without it, lasting peace among citizens would be impossible in pluralistic societies. Thereby, for Williams, an irreducible tension between peace and truth must be recognized. It is evident that the phenomenon will persist over the course of time due to the fact that earthly peace cannot be guaranteed without the denial of any absolute truth-regime in civil and even in spiritual domains. In a world where individuals choose to pursue their own paths, and within different cultural and religious traditions there would be no way of overcoming this structural pluralism of belief-systems, worldviews, and religious attitudes. However, that does not mean — especially for the Protestant theologian Williams — to deny the nature and duty of mission for the church, and the articulation of truth-claims in debates between believers of different confessions (and religions). Nevertheless, it rejects traditional positions that subordinate peace to enforcing absolute religious truth — whether by the Church alone or in collusion with political powers. At least on earth we will not find the land of promise in which peace and truth will be completely in harmony. Therefore, a first element of any Christian concept of tolerance can be identified as an acknowledgment of the ambiguity of both peace and truth. This ambiguity irreducibly and irreconcilable roots in the inner and mutual tension that exists between these two poles: both, "truth and peace, their meetings are seldom and short,"[40] as Williams once wrote.

Considering the preceding discussion, the basic question arises whether and how the demands of peace and truth can be reconciled. Are there good reasons for any "reflective equilibrium"[41] between peace and truth, to use a famous phrase of John Rawls? For Williams, any answer to this question must begin with two foundational principles. Firstly, he affirms a version of the *Doctrine of*

---

[40] Williams, Roger, "The Bloudy Tenent Yet More Bloudy (1652)," in: Perry Miller (ed.), *The Complete Writings of Roger Williams*, Vol. IV, New York: Russel and Russel, 1963, 501.
[41] Cf. Rawls, John, *A Theory of Justice: Revised Edition*, Cambridge (Ma.): The Belknap Press of Harvard University Press, 1999, 42–44.

the Two Kingdoms[42] — namely the separation of church and state; and secondly, he defines the *idea of personal conscience* as the locus of God's spiritual work on men in which claims for truth and peace usually meet. For Williams, tolerance arises from two principles: the separation of civil-political and religious-spiritual domains, and the pneumatological reconstruction of the Holy Spirit's inner testimony within personal conscience. For Williams, religious homogeneity is in no way needed for any functioning civil life if the Rule of Law is guaranteed. In his interpretation of the famous *Parable of the Tares* (*Matthew* 13:30–38) he does *not* compare the tares or weeds with heretics and false worshippers *within* the true church, but with all non-faithful believers *outside* the church in the "field of the world", who have to be left alone and thereby tolerated regarding their own belief until the Day of the Last Judgement, until the time of the eschatological harvest has come — to speak in the metaphorical way of the *Parables*.

In the end, for Williams, the relation between the "Garden of the Church" and the "Field of the World" — as he again metaphorically frames the relationship between church and world, and between the true faith and its wrong opponents — is not simply a negative one. Instead, his plea for separation of church and city does not only guarantee disputes about the right understanding of faith within the church. It also clarifies why the *pax civitatis* (a civil way of union) operates independently of a "spiritual union". "[S]pirituall oppositions in point of […] Religion" must not lead to breach of civil peace if all "men keep but the bond of Civilitie."[43] And they can do that because according to Williams, spiritual virtues are distinct from civil and moral virtues, though both can interpenetrate. Therefore, all civil states, with their officers of justice in their respective constitutions and administrations, are proved essentially civil, and are therefore not judges, governors, or defenders of the spiritual or Christian state and worship.[44] So, value pluralism — in the sense of ambiguous relations of peace and truth — represents Williams' initial criterion for a concept of religious tolerance. A second one pertains to his insistence on the separation of spiritual unions on the one hand

---

[42] Cf. Luther, Martin, "Von weltlicher Obrigkeit, wie weit man ihr Gehorsam schuldig sei (1523)," in: Karin Bornkamm/Georg Ebeling (eds.), *Martin Luther. Ausgewählte Schriften*, vol. IV, 36–84, Frankfurt/M.: Insel Verlag, ²1983. The English version can easily be found in: Luther, Martin, "Temporal Authority: To What Extent It Should Be Obeyed (1523)," in: Walther I. Brandt/Helmut T. Lehmann (eds.), *Luther's Works: The Christian in Society II*, 81–129, Philadelphia: Fortress Press, 1962.

[43] Williams, Roger, *The Bloody Tenent of Persecution for Cause of Conscience*, London, 1644, 74.

[44] Williams, Roger, "The Bloody Tenent of Persecution for Cause of Conscience (1644)," in: *On Religious Liberty. Selections from the Works of Roger Williams*, ed. and with an Introduction by James Calvin Davis, Cambridge (Ma.)/London: The Belknap Press of Harvard University Press, 2008, 86.

and a (common) civil union on the other hand. But only a third criterion as a basic component completes his conception of religious tolerance. Williams fiercely advocated "Liberty of Conscience," grounding his case in pneumatology (tolerance as divinely ordained) and ethics (religious freedom as a moral imperative for protecting minorities).[45] The latter aspect results in Williams' idea that "this conscience" as "holy light" is "found in all mankind [...] in Jewes, Turkes, Papists, Protestants, Pagans, etc."[46] This is why protection of personal conscience requires that no worship is disturbed and must even be permitted "for public peace and quiet sake." Especially the second aspect of his theory of religious freedom indicates a crucial test case for every community regarding its duty of respecting religious "others". It is the guarantee of rights for religious or spiritual minorities, even of atheists, in which religious freedom receives its full reality. Nevertheless, his main theological argument for this is rooted in the first aspect, namely that "Toleration gives God Time to Bring an Erroneous Conscience to Faith." "Time in peace" therefore is needed "until God may be pleased to reveal his truth to him,"[47] that is the still non-believer. In other words, toleration is an earthly tool for God's saving will, not *directissme* but in a profound indirect way. Again, in using metaphorical images of the New Testament's parables, Williams insists: "Wherease he that is a briar — that is, a Jew, a Turk, a pagan, or an Antichristian— today, may be (when the Word of the Lord runs freely) a member of Jesus Christ tomorrow cut out of the wild olive, and planted into the true."[48]

Williams does not deny the absolute truth of his own faith. But he is willing to see that any persecution or simply constraint in questions of faith corrupts and destroys not only the faith of others but one's own faith. Any legitimation of violence in the name even of the true religion and against — what he calls — the "arrogance of religious dissent" in consequence "falls heaviest upon the most godly persons."[49] Conversely, this means that religious tolerance and religious freedom ultimately serve the spread of the true religion.

---

[45] For a deeper understanding of Roger Williams' ideas: Cf. Nussbaum, Martha C., *Liberty of Conscience. In Defense of America's Tradition of Religious Equality*, New York: Basic Books, 2008, chap. 2. Cf. also my own considerations on Nussbaum's concept of religious equality: Polke, Christian, "Gewissensfreiheit als Dissidentenschutz. Martha C. Nussbaums Verteidigung der amerikanischen Verfassungstradition," *Evangelische Theologie* 70 (2010), 268–83.
[46] Williams, Roger, *The Correspondence of Roger Williams*, vol. I. 1629–1653, Glenn La Fantasie (ed.), Hannover: Brown University Press/University Press of New England 1988, *supra* note 4, 340.
[47] Cf. Williams, Roger, *On Religious Liberty* (fn. 9), 105.
[48] Ibid., 106.
[49] Cf. Ibid., 96–102.

3.2 Tolerance Within Faith and (Finite) Reason: Pierre Bayle (1647–1706)

Like Williams, Pierre Bayle was a defender of the right of religious freedom, or in his own words, of the right of the erroneous conscience.[50] Bayle grew up in a family of Huguenots who later suffered repressions since Louis XIV had repealed the *Edict of Nantes* (1598) which guaranteed non-Catholic French Christians some (private) rights in practicing their own religion and faith. Again, like Williams, Bayle later — in his exile in Rotterdam — came into trouble with the Reformed elites, especially with his former friend Pierre Jurieu (1637–1713) due to his ideas on toleration.

For Bayle, as articulated in his 1686 work, *A Philosophical Commentary on These Words of the Gospel, Luke 14:23, "Compel Them to Come In, That My House May Be Full,"* the case for tolerance is twofold: First, there is an *epistemological* argument for tolerance. Regarding religious questions, no absolute truth can be reached on earth. Therefore, God has only commanded man's search for his (God's absolute) truth. Religion, as understood by Bayle, is man's quest for God and his truth. Thus, it is because of human reason's finitude and fallibility that we must accept religious diversity and differences in our belief-systems. And this is true not only for our current period but through human history in general. Nevertheless, Bayle is no fideist, though he was clearly influenced by Michel de Montaigne (1533–1592) and his mild skepticism. Instead, the importance of human conscience, which he has elaborated, is based precisely on the fact that absolute truth cannot be proven in an abstract and objective way. It is the *personal* conscience where people get convinced of the truth of the Gospel, and that must happen *without any force* or *violence*. I will come back to this argument shortly.

But before, we must focus on the second line of argument which I call the *moral* argument. For Bayle, human beings inhere "the natural right" that helps them to act morally. In other words, humans could examine their deeds in the light of reciprocity to overcome basic iniquities. And again, this is true universally. Against this background, Bayle refutes any literal interpretation of the famous words of Jesus "Compel them to come in" (Luke 14,23) in his treatise mentioned above. Otherwise it would be allowed for every religious party to force non-believers and heretics to accept their own faith with violence: "I have the Truth on my side, therefore my Violence are good Works: Such a one is an Error, therefore his

---

[50] For an instructive interpretation of Bayle cf. Forst, Reiner, *Toleration in Conflict: Past and Present*, trans. C. Cronin, Cambridge et al.: Cambridge University Press, 2013, chap. V, § 18, 237–65 [German version 312–51].

Violences are criminal."⁵¹ Moreover, as Bayle has argued, if violence is allowed to force people to believe or accept the truth, then the principles of morality are overruled by metaphysical convictions. Consequently, actions would become righteous only if carried out in the name of true religion. Bayle argues that the Gospel would contradict itself if taken as a literal justification for coercion. He rejects the Augustinian tradition of Luke 14:23⁵² which prioritizes saving souls through coercion over reasoned dialogue with dissenters. Coercion is better than the threat of hell, and this is understood as an act of loving one's enemies.

Returning to Bayle's insistence on the right of "erroneous conscience", an insoluble problem has been frequently pointed out by critics, namely the "reciprocity of the argument." In Bayle's theology, God is perceived as engaging in a dialogue with humanity through the medium of conscience. However, this detail can lead to dangerous consequences because the erroneous conscience — as the binding voice of God — could legitimate violence against non-believers or people of other religious beliefs. However, Bayle is aware of this dilemma. As he writes: "The [...] Difficulty props'd is, That my Doctrine does in its Consequences destroy what I wou'd endeavor to establish. My design is to shew, that Persecution is a horrible thing; and yet everyone who thinks himself oblig'd in Conscience to persecute, shall be oblig'd by my Doctrine to persecute, and sins if he does not."⁵³

Here, the dilemma of any religious argumentation is clearly outspoken. But Bayle is sensitive enough to avoid further problems. Therefore, he continues:

> I answer, That the Design of this *Commentary* upon these words, *Compel'em to come in*, being to convince Persecutors that Jesus Christ has not enjoin'd Constraint, I don't destroy my own Design, if I shew by solid Arguments that the literal Sense of these words is false, impious, and absurd. If I succeed this.

— by showing that violence against people of other faith is against Jesus Christ's commandments —

> "I have reason to hope that they who examine my Argument, may perceive those Errors of Conscience, which they may be under as to Persecution; and therefore, my Design is just. I don't deny but they who are actually persuaded that 'tis their Duty to extirpate Sects, are oblig'd to follow the Motions of their false Conscience; and that in not doing so, they are guilty of a Disobedience to God, because they persist in not obeying what they believe to be his

---

51 Bayle, Pierre, *A Philosophical Commentary on These Words of the Gospel, Luke 14:23, "Compel Them to Come In, That my House May Be Full*, ed. and intr. John Kilcullen/Chandran Kukathas, Indianapolis: Liberty Fund, Inc., 2005, 134.
52 Cf. his argumentation in: Ibid., 88–92.
53 Ibid., 242.

Will. But, 1. It does not follow, that they act without Sin, because they act by Conscience. 2. This ought not to hinder our crying out loudly against their false Maxims and endeavoring to enlighten their Understandings." (II,9)[54]

What is congenial in Bayle's argumentation is his relentless disclosing of the dilemma any kind of religious or secular metaphysical argumentation must face. Instead of giving up the Right of Conscience he argues for a two-fold critical engagement which leads in my view to a third kind of argument, namely the *hermeneutical* argument. The first kind of engagement refers to one's own conscience within the wider public, e.g. in debates with others, whereas the second form of critical engagement opens for a hermeneutical approach of the sources of one's own faith, of the holy texts and traditions from which the "erroneous conscience" gets his ideas. We should not forget: Acting according to one's own conscience does not automatically prevent from sin. Moreover, a tolerant faith must be interested in a critical understanding of its own tradition. So, for any Christian conception of tolerance, following Bayle, three aspects are crucial: first, recognizing the finiteness and fallibility of human reason; secondly, the distinction — not complete separation — of morals and faith (religion), grounded in reciprocal fairness evaluated through dialogue; and finally, the need of critical hermeneutics of holy texts and one's own self-understanding as faithful. In other words, an ethos of tolerance which can be articulated also in a conceptual understanding of tolerance as a (basic) Christian idea, results in and again must lead to a conduct in which tolerance has to be seen as one of its basic virtues.[55]

---

54 Ibid., 242.
55 What distinguished Bayle was his complex way of thinking, being able to take multiple perspectives simultaneously and to accept antinomies. Bayle's writings were widely noticed, received, and controversially discussed by German theologians, philosophers, historians, and jurists until the beginning of the nineteenth century. Christian Thomasius, an important pioneer of the German Enlightenment, was interested in him, Leibniz was inspired by him to write his "Théodicée," Herder and Lessing held him in high esteem, and even Frederick II, in his capacity as a ruler, was influenced by Bayle's thoughts, cf. Bizeul, Yves, "Pierre Bayles Kritik des Aberglaubens und Plädoyer für die Toleranz," in: Friedrich Vollhardt et al. (eds.), *Toleranzdiskurse in der frühen Neuzeit*, 177–216, here 203f.; 210–16, Berlin: Walter de Gruyter, 2015.

4 The Fate of Religious Tolerance in the Modern History of Christianity: Roman Catholicism

As far as we have seen, the idea of tolerance is by no means a simple one. It consists of different elements which together form a set of inferences from which conceptions of tolerance can be construed. What we have tried to reconstruct here from a Protestant perspective by referring to Roger Williams and Pierre Bayle finds its equivalent in the more recent Catholic tradition. Thereby, the different circumstances that helped lead to the gradual acceptance of foreign beliefs and thus to the idea of religious tolerance in Catholicism show the special nature of historical and cultural path dependencies. While particularly in the nineteenth century in the fights against modernism, laicism and *Kulturkampf* (e.g., the Anti-Modernist Oath, Syllabus of Errors) the papal magisterium strictly concentrated on a sole and absolute claim to the fullness of truth in questions of faith and morals (*Dogma of Infallibility*, Vatican I, 1871). Hence, after the Second World War, at the latest, moderate voices revived elements of Catholic theology and natural law thinking that had long acknowledged tolerance as a Christian imperative, aligning with Enlightenment-era Catholic thinkers.[56] It should not be overlooked that Vatican II was the first time that the universal Church was represented by the episcopate, as for the first time native bishops from the Global South were represented in large numbers. This also led to a broadening of horizons, just as the recognition of democracy was facilitated due to the negative experiences with totalitarianism and the persecutions of the Church. However, it remains controversial to what extent inner-church tolerance is lived by the magisterial authority. With regard to religious pluralism and inter-religious understanding, the groundbreaking declaration *Diginitatis Humanae* (1965) of Vatican II about freedom of religion — and thus the meaning of tolerance from the Christian point of view — is still valid:

> The declaration of this Vatican Council on the right of man to religious freedom has its foundation in the dignity of the person, whose exigencies have come to be fully known to human reason through centuries of experience. What is more, this doctrine of freedom has roots in divine revelation, and for this reason Christians are bound to respect it even more conscientiously. Revelation does not indeed affirm in so many words the right of man to immunity

---

[56] For a constructive understanding of religious freedom, pluralism and tolerance in the tradition of Catholic thought, the Frenchman Jacques Maritain and the American Jesuit John Courtney Murray have had a broader impact. For Maritain Cf.: Maritain, Jacques, *Christianity and Democracy, and The Rights of Man and the Natural Law.* Foreword by Raymond L. Dennehy. Introduction by Donald A. Gallagher, San Francisco: Ignatius Press, 1986.

> from external coercion in matters religious. It does, however, disclose the dignity of the human person in its full dimensions. It gives evidence of the respect which Christ showed toward the freedom with which man is to fulfill his duty of belief in the word of God and it gives us lessons in the spirit which disciples of such a Master ought to adopt and continually follow [...] God calls men to serve Him in spirit and in truth, hence they are bound in conscience but they stand under no compulsion. God has regard for the dignity of the human person whom He Himself created and man is to be guided by his own judgment, and he is to enjoy freedom. This truth appears at its height in Christ Jesus, in whom God manifested Himself and His ways with men. Christ is at once our Master and our Lord and meek and humble of heart. In attracting and inviting His disciples He used patience.[57]

This not only sounds like an official correction to long dominating misinterpretations of Luke 14:23, "Compel them to come in", but it is.

The history of Catholicism in the twentieth century shows in an exemplary way how different and antagonistic the paths towards tolerance from the spirit of Christianity and the recognition of religious freedom are. Alongside the official doctrine, which also became the political agenda (e.g. human rights) of the Vatican, especially under the pontificate of John Paul II, however, strong cracks can also be seen. Within the church, it is disputed how far freedom of faith can go. Tolerance in questions of truth is the keyword under which the struggles between not only Catholic conservatives and progressives can be subsumed. The same applies to all facets of Protestantism, especially regarding strongly fundamentalist currents and movements. And not to forget Orthodoxy, which, especially in the sphere of influence of the Moscow Patriarchate, always sees the question of tolerance as a problem of Western hegemony. A return to ethnoreligious denominationalism that plays tolerance off against firmness of faith (in combination with cultural hegemony) does not seem out of the question in many places in the world. Conversely — and this can also be illustrated in a particularly impressive way by worldwide Catholicism — the peaceful, tolerant encounter with other religions and under diverse cultural contexts is one of the most important contributions to social cohesion and peaceful development. It is not so much Western theology with its conceptions as the reflection on lived intercultural practice, especially in missionary contexts, that seems to anchor the idea of tolerance more than ever in the Christian cosmos of faith across all borders. Incidentally, the history of the missionary orders testifies to how important intercultural

---

[57] *Declaration on Religious Freedom Dignitatis Humanae on the Right of the Person and of Communities to Social and Civil Freedom in Matters Religious*, promulgated by his Holiness Pope Paul VI on December 7, 1965, No. 9 and 11. The text is easily accessible below: http://www.vatican.va/archive/hist_councils/ii_vatican_council/documents/vat-ii_decl_19651207_dignitatis-humanae_en.html (accessed on 05.05.2022).

and interreligious understanding has always been in practice. Otherwise, the inculturation of the Christian faith could not have been successful. A Catholic understanding of mission is still based on the latter today.

5 Towards a Christian Concept of Religious Tolerance

The role of practice, reflection, and experience will be addressed in more detail at the conclusion of the present considerations. Indeed, it must be acknowledged that tolerance, in essence, should be a virtue that has the potential to evolve into a habit. However, this does not absolve theology of the task to articulate — through its own tradition — arguments that make religious tolerance coherent and compelling within a Christian framework. The result of these argumentative strategies is the elaboration of an idea or concept of Christian tolerance. Nevertheless, this endeavor cannot be undertaken without acknowledging the history of problems, which has also been a history of violence, concerning religiously inspired intolerance, extending over many centuries until the present day. Theology is also predicated on theories derived from the (negative) experiences and contexts from which they arise.

Four points of view shall serve me as building blocks for a systematic hermeneutics of the idea of tolerance in the spirit of Christianity. The first two are directly linked to monotheism. On the one hand, it is about tolerance in the search for truth, wherein God is recognized as the only truth (5.1.). On the other hand, in soteriological terms, the question arises to what extent faith can be tolerant of its counterpart, namely disbelief (5.2.). In the age of global networking and cultural pluralism, it also deserves attention whether there are limits to tolerance in view of the relativism of values, convictions and world views. In a slightly different vein, it is thus a question of the scope of moral universalism in the face of radical indifference (5.3.). Finally, we will ask how a tolerant attitude can take shape in communication situations in which religious and non-religious voices are allowed to have their say and question each other. This is about the dialogical character of tolerance (5.4.).

5.1 Monotheism and Tolerance (I): The Quest of Truth

It seems to be a truism that monotheistic religions, because of their conviction of the exclusiveness of their own — the one and only — God, have a greater difficulty tolerating other beliefs than non-monotheistic ones. But this is far too simplistic. Apart from the fact that it cannot be empirically proven that monotheistic religions or their followers are more prone to violence than others, an additional precondition must first be added. It is the connection of the question of God with the question of truth. The concept of God as the absolute or ultimate truth, as articulated in Christian theology since the days of the early church, prominent in the thought of Augustine[58], implies the rejection of all other views of God, deeming them as false. Religion no longer becomes just a question of faith, but a question of truth. This connection, which Jan Assmann has repeatedly emphasized, and which does not apply to many ancient religions, is now at least a two-edged issue. Because of course the question of truth exacerbates the problem of tolerance. But conversely, it can also provoke tolerance in its very relevance. For where God alone — whether strictly monotheistic or trinitarian, the latter as in Christianity[59] — can be the truth, there is no one and nothing else that can claim absolute truth for itself. In the New Testament, especially in the Gospel of John, it is the Logos incarnate himself who names God alone as truth (Cf. John 4:8; KJV) and claims the same of himself, in the triad of the metaphors of way, truth and life: "I am the way, the truth, and the life." (Joh 14:6; KJV) On the basis of these indications alone, both can apparently be read out hermeneutically: the claim of the absolute nature of the Christian faith together with the vanishing line of a radical intolerance towards others (as evinced in the Johannine corpus

---

[58] Already in *De vera religione* (390) Augustine argues for the unity of God and truth. About his dealings with disbelievers (Donatists, Pelagians, etc.), he initially relied on voluntary insight and persuasion, but then, due to failure, decided to confront them by force if necessary. He reports this himself: "For originally my opinion was, that no one should be coerced into the unity of Christ, that we must act by words, fight only by arguments, and prevail by force of reason, lest we should have those whom we knew as avowed heretics feigning themselves to be Catholics. But this opinion of mine was overcome not by the words of those who controverted it, but by the conclusive instances to which they could point." (Augustine, *Letter 93*, § 67, cited from: https://www.newadvent.org/fathers/1102093.htm, accessed on 11.04.2025). Behind this lies his insight, which is by no means meant as a rhetorical question: "'For what is more deadly to the soul than the freedom for error?'" (Augustine, Letter 105, § 10, quoted from: Augustine, *Political Writings*, trans. E.M. Atkins, Cambridge/New York et al.: Cambridge University Press, 2001, 168.) — It is important to note that his insight into the identity of God and truth did not change.

[59] For a Trinitarian-based understanding of tolerance, but oriented towards interreligious dialogue, cf. the studies by Schwöbel, Christoph, "The same God? The Perspective of Faith, the Identity of God, Tolerance, and Dialogue," in: Miroslav Volf (ed.), *Do We Worship the Same God? Jews, Christians, and Muslims in Dialogue*, 1–17, Grand Rapids/Cambridge: Eerdmans, 2012; Schwöbel Christoph, "Toleranz aus Glauben. Identität und Toleranz im Horizont religiöser Wahrheitsgewißheiten," in: Christpoh Schwöbel (ed.), *Christlicher Glaube im Pluralismus, Studien zu einer Theologie der Kultur*, 217–43, Tübingen: Mohr Siebeck, 2003.

towards both Jews and pagans, and early heretics). Alternatively, if one places a higher value on the personal character of truth, as exemplified by Jesus' call to discipleship, his life and his offer of the way to the Father, a processual understanding of knowledge of truth emerges. In this understanding, the necessity of tolerance is inherent, as truth can only be known and shared through love. God as truth is love — *Caritas in veritate*, as articulated by Pope Benedict XVI. This perspective is the strict opposite of violence and intolerance, at least towards the people who struggle for him, search for him, or have possibly forgotten him. Theologically, a correct decision can only be made between the two readings if two things are considered: first, even under the Trinitarian sign, the Christian faith in God is a radically monotheistic one. In this respect, truth is an exclusive predicate of God alone. It is more than knowledge insofar as it does not merge into sentences and convictions. Therefore, secondly, truth in the emphatic sense is always a communicative event. It communicates not by force, but by overcoming resistance, doubt, and unbelief. , In this light, the Gospel of John offers a decisive theological insight. When Jesus speaks with the Samaritan woman about the proper place of worship — whether on Mount Gerizim or in Jerusalem — he reframes the question entirely, pointing instead to the nature of true worship: "God is a Spirit: and they that worship him must worship him in spirit and in truth" (Joh 4:24; KJV). Tolerance, then, is the negative condition for not suppressing the work of God's spirit, which is a spirit of truth.[60]

There is therefore a double distortion of the concept of truth when it leads, as in the first reading, to assertions of Christianity's claim to absoluteness. Firstly, because truths are here reduced to doctrines instead of being understood as life-oriented certainties that owe their existence to a communicative event. Secondly, because the authority that decides on the truth or falsity of a way of life can only be God. In Christian terms, proof of truth is an eschatological event at the end of days. As we have seen, in church history, it was considered common knowledge to read the parable of the tares among the wheat (cf. Matt 13:24–30,36–42; KJV) in such a way that earthly authorities could not decide about a way of life or the existence or non-existence of true faith. Systematically, this explains why insight into the truth requires not only the absence of coercion, but also the freedom of conscience.

---

60 For Pope Benedict XVI, for example, the Christian understanding of tolerance is based on the conviction that God as truth is love (and *vice versa*). Cf. Ratzinger, Joseph Cardinal/Pope Emeritus Benedict XVI., *Truth and Tolerance: Christian Belief and World Religions*, San Francisco (Ca.): Ignatius Press, 2004, esp. 210–58.

"The theological argument is the tradition regarding the necessary freedom of act of faith ... This tenet [...] is held no less firmly by all who bear the name of Christian. In fact, even the atheist holds it. It is part of the human patrimony of truth, embedded in the common consciousness of mankind. The ethical argument is the immunity of conscience from coercion in its internal religious decisions. Even the Church, which has [or in Protestant opinion only may personally have; C.P.] authority to oblige conscience, has no power to coerce it. The political argument is the common conviction that the personal internal forum is immune from invasion by any powers resident in society and state. No external force may coerce the conscience of man to any form of belief or unbelief."[61]

Tolerance therefore respects the freedom of the conscience, because it knows that the individual cannot delegate his or her consent to recognized truth. This is only the same thing from another perspective as in the previous considerations. Truth as an eschatological reality and freedom of conscience as its earthly prerequisite are mutually dependent.

5.2 Monotheism and Tolerance (II): The Problem of Loyalty

The reference to freedom of conscience already alludes to the second aspect in the context of the monotheism-tolerance problem. Jan Assmann has modified his reflections on the cultural semantics of biblical monotheism in recent years, not least because of the criticism of his theorem of the "Mosaic distinction". In the meantime, he sees the proprium of biblical monotheism in its origins first in what he calls a "monotheism of loyalty".[62] It is the covenant figure that is central to describing the right God-man or God-people relationship. Not the cognitive conviction of truth, but first the right relationship of trust and loyalty[63] is decisive for the existence of true religion or true faith. From one point of view, this is a serious response to the fact that theologically, it is neither falsehood nor believing differently that ranks as the opposite of faith *strictissime*. Rather, the theological oppo-

---

[61] Murray, John Courtney, "The Problem of Religious Freedom," in: J. Leon Hooper, S.J. (ed.), *Religious Liberty. Catholic Struggles with Pluralism*, 127–97, 147–48, Louisville (Ky.)/Westminster: John Knox Press, 1993. The American Jesuit Murray can be considered a pioneer of newer Catholic thought, who knows how to affirmatively combine freedom of religion and freedom of knowledge with modern pluralism. Murray played an important role at Vatican II in persuading the bishops to adopt the ground-breaking Declaration on Religious Liberty, *Dignitatis humanae*,

[62] Cf. Assmann, Jan, *The Invention of Religion: Faith and Covenant in the Book of Exodus*, trans. by R. Savage, Princeton & Oxford: Princeton University Press, 2018, esp. 79–90.

[63] Cf. Niebuhr, H. Richard, *Faith on Earth. An Inquiry into the Structure of Human Faith*, New Haven & London: Yale University Press, 1989, esp. 46–50. For the biblical concept of faith, both Old and New Testament, has a covenantal structure.

site is defined as disbelief in soteriological terms. At first, this seems to amount to the same thing, not least because the monotheism of truth and the monotheism of loyalty are already intertwined for the late writings of the Old Testament (esp. for Second Isaiah, Jes 40–66).

Soteriological, however, it makes a difference whether a legitimate faith is founded in a loyal relationship with God or primarily in true beliefs. Sharply spoken that Jesus is the Christ, according to the New Testament, is especially acknowledged by Satan and the demons. But one cannot speak here of a true relationship with God. Not the true/false distinction, but the one between trust and betrayal characterizes the soteriological difference. In the tradition of Western Christianity in particular, despite all the differences between Catholicism and Protestantism, this explains the status of the idea of justification. For in this personal respect, believers and unbelievers cannot simply be divided into two kinds of people. Rather, the idea of grace, on which all human beings depend because they are all sinners, lives from the fact that we are always only on the way to faith, to loyalty towards God and fellow human beings. Martin Luther's use *of tolerantia Dei*[64] aims precisely at this. It applies to all people, because we are all sinners and not in a right relationship with God. Conversely, salvation as the newness of life lies in the forgiveness of sins, or better, in the restoration of the destroyed relationships of trust between God and human beings by reconstructing faithful relationships. Judas, the traitor, is the paradigmatic example of the unbelieving sinner.[65] But also Peter — an example for a follower of Christ — denies his Lord. In both figures of the Passion story, an anthropological characteristic is revealed: man is suspicious, disloyal and easily smells betrayal. Tolerance reckons with these human traits that endanger a successful community.

Tolerance requires acknowledging both our own flaws and others'. Recognizing humanity's shared propensity for betrayal — and refusing to let it destroy communities — fosters forgiveness and healthier relationships, both human and divine. This logic extends *a minore ad maius* to interfaith relations and interactions between believers and non-believers. The Christian understanding of religious freedom as a legal complement to the social virtue of tolerance must then also be shaped by such a view, that knows about its own limitations and allows others to be mistaken and imperfect. That's why religious freedom is only comprehensively guaranteed and understood when it also includes the radical rejection of religion and any religious way of life. Not the heretic or schismatic, but the

---

64 Luther rarely uses the word or the vocabulary tolerance. For this, cf. more fn. 45.
65 Cf. Gollwitzer, Helmut, *Krummes Holz – aufrechter Gang. Zur Frage nach dem Sinn des Lebens*, Munich: Christian Kaiser, 1970, esp. 271–83.

apostate must be protected in his right to live, and he must be respected or at least tolerated in his "view of faith."

Religious freedom is more than freedom of conscience. It does not exclusively respect the *forum internum* and the truth convictions of the individual but aims at the public right to dissent. Tolerance in the sense of putting up with dissenting, from one's own point of view erroneous and misguided views and ways of life, is something that Western Christianity, however, first had to learn with difficulty. Even the Reformers saw in the open activity of unbelievers or false believers the danger of invoking divine wrath on the community, which is why they had to be suppressed by force if necessary.[66] Catholicism, too, only dared to take the step towards a theologically qualified recognition of religious freedom as an implicit consequence of an ethos of tolerance and a monotheism that truly sees itself in the light of the Enlightenment.

However, respect for freedom of knowledge and religion of each individual and respect for his or her religious convictions does not mean that the dispute about the truth must be abandoned and the search for trust-based religious forms of life must be stopped. Tolerance means neither religious nor moral indifference, certainly not an absence of dispute with regard to the question of who God really is. Moreover, even if truth-oriented traditions harbor intolerance, this does not resolve whether a third, graver category exists alongside tolerance and intolerance: the intolerable.

5.3 Tolerance, Relativism and Indifference: The Problem of Moral Universalism

The history of the idea of tolerance is closely linked to occidental Christianity. This is since Christianity in its ecclesiastical organizational form has always also produced institutions of power. Churches have always been institutions with political power and public influence. It is therefore not surprising that the first treatises on tolerance, which bore this in their title, reflected experiences of religious wars (Locke, Spinoza). Lessing's famous Ring Parable in *Nathan the Wise* can also be understood as a product of a Christian-inspired enlightenment about the nature of tolerance. What all these efforts have in common, despite their differences, is that they are based on the distinction between the religious beliefs that a person

---

[66] Behind this is the reformers' theology of history, especially Luther's, which becomes more pessimistic with age. Therefore, even Melanchthon pleaded for the authorities to watch over the observance of the commandments of both tables — thus also of the right worship of God; for the sake of the *salus publicus*.

may hold on the one hand, and, on the other hand, the actions for which he or she is responsible, and which have an impact on others and the public good. It is therefore possible to treat a person with respect and at the same time be critical or even hostile towards his or her attitudes and behavior. This is the concept of tolerance in principle. But already Goethe knew that this was not enough. "Tolerance", he says, "should only be a passing attitude: it should lead to appreciation. To tolerate is to offend."[67] There is so much truth about this that one can hardly ever draw a sharp line between convictions on the one hand and actions or ways of life on the other. Outside of secular law and its norms, for which this distinction is necessary, one can state: attitudes and convictions are always expressed in ways of life. It is this insight, which then in the so-called postmodern era, including the steadily growing knowledge of cultural as well as religious diversity in the world, has become a dominant identity feature in the Western world, which provoked religious as well as secular fundamentalist and ideological counter-movements at an early stage. At its core is the suspicion that religious and cultural pluralism inevitably leads to radical relativism and indifferentism.

As absurd as such sweeping judgements may be, even they contain a kernel of truth that is important for the discourse on tolerance. Especially since Western Christianity and its churches fully came to terms with the religious-political regime of separation not only of state and church, but also of public and private spheres. Where faith has become primarily a personal, inward matter, it appears reasonable to conceptualize religious matters as matters of taste — analogous to aesthetic ones — rather than as matters of public concern, that is to say, politically and morally relevant.[68] Applied to the problem of tolerance, however, the following question arises: Must I tolerate not only everyone, but also everything? And can a coexistence of different religions and world views succeed without a minimal consensus on questions of values and social cohesion? What role does the state play and what contribution must its citizens and civil society institutions make? It is at this point that the French philosopher and Protestant Paul Ricoeur

---

[67] Goethe, Johann Wolfang, *Maxims and Reflecions*, P. Hutchinson (ed.), trans. E. Stopp, London: Penguin 1998, 116.
[68] Talal Asad has repeatedly emphasised that about Islam's assessment of the separation of state and religion, for example, and thus also of tolerance and pluralism, it is considered that these distinctions — ultimately above all those of public and private — already carry a specifically Christian, primarily Western Protestant (liberal) connotation. He speaks of the public/private binary. Cf. Asad, Talal, *Formations of the Secular: Christianity, Islam, Modernity*, Stanford (Ca.): Stanford University Press, 2003, esp. 181–87 (hereby critically commenting José Casanovas approach).

(1913–2005) injected the intolerable as a third variable into the discourse, alongside the virtue of tolerance and the vice of intolerance:

> The intolerable is that which one would not want to tolerate, although one could do so or even should do so. In this sense, the intolerable is the polar opposite of intolerance, the behavior of reprobation and of hindrance which tolerance sought to overcome. The intolerable is problematic only against the backdrop of tolerance, achieved or in the process of attainment.[69]

What at first glance sounds so harmless, however, basically represents the radical limit of any tolerance, which must be renegotiated again and again in terms of content.

> But while tolerance abstains from [...] the intolerable calls for suspending the abstention. This is why it is fully relevant only in culture that has been educated by and in tolerance. And it is for this precise reason that we can expect from it the effect of a wake-up call in a culture, lacking any clear points of reference, in which tolerance has already turned into indifference.[70]

But what is then to be thought of when one speaks of the intolerable? Ricoeur gives us two clues. The first leads to a hard limit of tolerance, namely violence. The intolerance is ultimately everything that humiliates, harms and destroys people, and does so without reason. The limit of tolerance is where violence destroys all respect for the dignity of the individual. In this sense, the idea of tolerance from the experience of violence over the centuries is combined with a "negative universalism of the suffering" (Johann Baptist Metz, 1928–2019) or a moral universalism as expressed in human rights. Within the Abrahamic religions, this moral universalism is rooted in the conviction that all human beings are God's unique creatures and children. In this context, figures like Spanish Dominicans Francesco Suárez (1548–1617) and Bartolomé de Las Casas (1484–1566) defended indigenous rights against colonizers — even challenging papal authorities in the sixteenth century. The Christian natural law tradition is a source for the ethos of human rights and for a Christian moral universalism based on the idea of the inalienable dignity of each human individual. In this sense, the idea of tolerance is not only related to freedom of knowledge and religion, but especially, where intolerance is concerned, to human rights themselves.

---

[69] Ricoeur, Paul, "The Erosion of Tolerance and the Resistance of the Intolerable (1995)," in: Pierre-Olivier Monteil *(ed.)*, *Paul Ricoeur, Politics, Economy, and Society* (Writings and Lectures, Vol. 4), 135–46, Cambridge (UK)/Medford (Ma.): Polity Press, 2021.
[70] Ibid., 142.

Open societies that constructively face up to religious pluralism must be able to transcend all particularistic loyalties in favor of the moral universalism embodied by human rights.[71] This has consequences for the form of government, insofar as it implies a plea for democratic structures. However, — and this is Ricoeur's second basic insight — a tolerant democracy that is committed to human rights can only be sustained in the long term if it lives from free, but controversial exchange and permanent understanding about the values of its coexistence at the level of civil society. In this process, the various religious and secular ideas and convictions must not be excluded. It is less about an "overlapping consensus" (John Rawls) than about a substantial, albeit always fragile, compromise. Democracies depend not only on security and welfare but on active civic participation. A culture of tolerance thus rejects radical indifference, which undermines these foundations.[72]

---

71 Editor's note: The Roman Catholic theologian Hans Küng (Global Ethic Project, Munich: Piper, 1990) founded the Weltethos Project based on moral universalism in the spirit of Immanuel Kant. Küng's starting point is the observation that living together in a pluralistic and globalised world requires a common ethos. Küng's operationalisation of tolerance consequently leads to a minimum consensus of values (non-violence, solidarity, tolerance, truthfulness, equality) based on the religious roots of cultures. Tolerance, however, is understood here as an implication of a comprehensive ecumenism, which should encompass all ethnicities, cultures and religions and implies constant forgiveness and renewal. This concept is undoubtedly to be commended as an approach that operationalises tolerance as the basis of interreligious dialogue. However, it is questionable whether this basis is sustainable. This can be seen at least from the following questions: In ethical terms, defining a kind of *minima moralia* seems extremely abstract in view of the ethical issues of the present to guarantee mutual understanding. In addition, values such as equality do not seem to be equally considered in the value horizon of all cultures and religions. In terms of the theory of religion, the strong moral perspective of the religious evokes the question of whether the religious is not merely a means of an abstract humanity. Finally, from an interreligious and ecumenical perspective, the fundamental question arises as to whether the goal of interreligious dialogue is a consensus at all. Christian theology from a Protestant perspective is traditionally critical of such a position, as such a consensus requires a comprehensive and profound change which, according to Protestant conviction, can only be brought about by God himself.

72 Karl Rahner sees the primacy of human freedom as the basis for tolerance and the willingness to engage in dialogue as essential to a truly humane society. Cf. Rahner, Karl, *Dialogue and Tolerance as the Foundation of a Humane Society*, trans. Cornelius Ernst, *Theological Investigations*, vol. XXII: *Humane Society and the Church of Tomorrow*, 14–25, Baltimore: Helicon Press, 1961.

5.4 Tolerance in (Inter-Faith-) Dialogues: Beyond the Secular and Religious Divide

Tolerance, one could say, is also a hermeneutic virtue. It lives from the insight that no human being can possess the truth, but at best, as Gabriel Marcel (1889–1973) has always emphasized, can hope to live in the truth on the long run. But this does not release us from the active search for truth, which can never be proven to be the ultimate truth. This search always consists of communicative or dialogical acts, however provisional and partial they may be. Truth is a social category and under finite, fallible conditions never fully given or recognized. Tolerance thus always lives from the spirit of compromise, and this also applies to the so-called ultimate, religious questions of humanity, to the search for God and salvation. The Inter-Faith Dialogue thus serves both purposes: the cultivation of cultural, religious and non-religious resources on the one hand, and learning in dialogue with others on the other. It is precisely because I am possibly trapped in my own perspective that the view and exchange with others helps me. Dialogicity is itself a structural feature of tolerance, precisely because it must not be linked to radical indifference or to false absolute claims to truth.

The problem of tolerance, especially in monotheistic religions with an emphatic claim to truth, thus also increasingly includes the question of interreligious dialogue and its goal, as well as the question of mission. In a certain sense, religions with a claim to salvation that is potentially valid for everybody, are prone to proselytize. This, however, exacerbates the situation because the cultivation of tolerance, in dealing with people of other faiths and non-believers, has to take this circumstance into account in such a way that secular and different religious voices are not patronized or even overwhelmed. It is no coincidence that a theology of religions with its models of exclusivism, inclusivism and pluralism has been developed in the context of occidental Christianity over the past decades and that the problem of inculturation as well as intercultural competences has been a concern of missiology for some time.[73]

---

[73] Editor's note: The distinction between inclusivism, exclusivism and pluralism was prominently represented by John Hick (Hick, John, *God and the universe of faiths*, London: Macmillan, 1973). Hick himself called for a Copernican turn in theology. According to him, theology should distance itself from an absolute claim to truth and instead seriously consider the possible fallibility of its own convictions. It is questionable whether such religious relativism can be regarded as a basis for tolerance at all, as the contradictory is always already cancelled out in the fundamental fallibility of all approaches. Hick's position is currently being taken up positively by Perry Schmidt-Leukel (Schmidt-Leukel, Perry, *Gott ohne Grenzen. Eine christliche und pluralistische Theologie der Religionen*, Gütersloh: Gütersloher Verlagshaus, 2005, 181f), who emphasises

Ernst Troeltsch already put Christianity's claim to absoluteness on the agenda of theology a hundred years ago, knowing fully well that the world was growing together and that the questions of intercultural and interreligious exchange and the comparison of religious world views were becoming more important. All of this becomes even more acute when postcolonial perspectives are considered, especially the inclusion of theologies from beyond the West. I refer to Troeltsch at this point because his theology emphasizes the idea of compromise even before all political and interreligious connotations. Troeltsch distinguishes, on the one hand, between a claim to truth, as it arises from the position of the individual believer, and the completely illusory concern to be able to provide proof of absoluteness, for example of Christianity, with the help of theology or even the sciences.[74] At the same time, he respects — as a liberal theologian — that every genuine religion cannot help but to promote its own faith, its own tradition, which is called proselytizing.

For dialogue between faiths, an ethos of tolerance is, of course, prior. It is not about mission, but about enlightenment and understanding, as well as about seeking the crucial points of dissent. In all of this, a dual attitude of compromise and consensus-seeking on the one hand, and recognition and respect for differences and mutual unfamiliarity on the other hand, is evident. This is perhaps even more true for dialogue between religious and secular people and groups. Christian theology, but also the churches, have increasingly taken on this dual task since the mid-1960s at the latest. On the one hand, the classic triad of exclusivism, inclusivism and pluralism in the theology of religions has given rise to approaches to what a comparative theology might look like — for example, in the wake of the late Paul Tillich's (1886–1965) reflections[75] — that also includes non-religious-

---

that a theologically pluralistic position on religion is not about tolerance, but about appreciation. By not disparaging other religions but viewing them as equal to one's own religious tradition, the demand for tolerance becomes superfluous (Cf. also 5.3 "Tolerance, Relativism and Indifference: The Problem of Moral Universalism").

74 Cf. Troeltsch, Ernst, *The Absoluteness of Christianity and the History of Religion*, trans. David Reid, London: SCM Press, 1972. According to Troeltsch, practical absoluteness as the certainty of life of faith must be strictly distinguished from the false claim to a theoretical proof of the unsurpassable religious tradition. It is precisely from this that religious tolerance concepts can be developed.

75 For Tillich cf. Tillich, Paul, *Christianity and the Encounter of the World Religions*, New York & London: Columbia University Press, 1963. In his *Bampton Lectures*, Tillich also drew attention to secular quasi-religions. In the third volume of his trilogy, Robert C. Neville, a representative of comparative theology, productively followed Tillich in developing a theory of religions based on understanding, plurality, openness and reflexive self-limitation in favor of the Ultimate. Cf. Ne-

ness and secular positions. On the other hand, even the Vatican deepened the cultural dialogue with agnostics and atheists in the wake of the last Council (1965) through the Pontifical Counsel for Dialogue with Non-Believers is today part of the Pontifical Council for Culture. Secular identities are now formed in all religiously influenced cultures but are no less plural in themselves than religious traditions and communities. Tolerance as a hermeneutic virtue of mutual dialogue and the desire to understand can therefore only take place between all chairs, beyond the religious-secular divides. It involves people making themselves "vulnerable" in their own convictions, attitudes and positions, insofar as they know that their faith, their own view of the last things can change, shift, radically transform, even convince them of the opposite. Tolerance does not exist without the danger of conversion, just as claims to truth cannot be represented — latently or openly — without mission.

Once again it becomes clear: dialogue presupposes openness, but it does not force agreement apart from convincing arguments, free consent, and shared experiences. Therefore, it presupposes at least an irritation, if not a preliminary rejection component, which it takes as the impetus for entering conversation into exchange. Furthermore, it requires at least acceptance of the dialogue partners, respect for their person and their convictions. And finally, every dialogue radically excludes violence. Therein lies the rejection of all coercion. In short: dialogue is itself a realization of tolerance.[76]

In contrast to negligent disregard of deep differences and a mere rhetoric of recognition, the idea of tolerance sharpens the awareness that we must constantly draw new boundaries to provide ourselves with orientation. In this, it itself has an

---

ville, Robert C., *Religion, Philosophical Theology Volume Three*, Albany: State University of New York Press, 2015.

76 Editor's note: Christian Polke did not specifically address the violent implications of communication. In this respect, the following comment is intended as an extension: new research into violence has drawn attention to various phenomena that fundamentally affect communication. Both forms of subtle (linguistic) violence and power imbalances within the tolerance discourse should not be underestimated. The fact that the violent naming of subtle violence in discourse may be discredited as violence in the sense of hyper morality is evidence of the complexity of this problem. Cf. on this Liebsch, Burkhard, *Verletztes Leben. Studien zur Affirmation von Schmerz und Gewalt im Gegenwärtigen Denken. Zwischen Hegel, Nietzsche, Bataille, Blanchot, Levinas, Ricoeur und Butler*, Zug: Die Graue Reihe, 2014. A greater awareness of the issue of violence within the question of tolerance is therefore also desirable from a Christian perspective. Ulrich Lincoln (Lincoln, Ulrich, *Precarious Creation. Contributions to the Theological Discourse on Violence*, Tübingen: Mohr Siebeck, 2023.) has presented one approach. What is remarkable in this approach is that expressions of violence are themselves to be understood as a form of communication in the sense of a "search". In our context: In intolerance and even in violence, a search for a right-wing understanding of tolerance can also be found.

almost religious-philosophical component, because, like all true religious ideas, it helps to distinguish between what is life-promoting and what is life-damaging. Tolerance does not hastily draw in differences, but respects them, even when they shift or transform into dialogue. This includes taking truth claims seriously as well as the insight that pluralism is not an enemy, but possibly even a friend of truth, at least of life. In his comprehensive study on the history and content of the concept of tolerance, Reiner Forst particularly emphasized the three components of acceptance, objection and rejection. "Against this background", he argues,

> it becomes clear that we should make a distinction between two boundaries. First, the boundary between (a) the normative domain of that which one agrees completely, in which there is affirmation and no objection — the domain of what is truly 'one's own', as it were — and (b) the domain of what can be tolerated in which there is normative objection and yet also acceptance which leads to toleration. The second boundary, the true limit of toleration, runs between the letter domain and (c) the domain of what cannot be tolerated, of what is strictly rejected and repudiated. As regards toleration, therefore, we must distinguish three normative domains, not just two.[77]

Forst has argued for his own concept and theory of tolerance by analyzing critically the Western — Christian, Jewish and secular — history of the idea of tolerance. Once again: because pluralism is not automatically an enemy, but possibly even a friend of truth, at least of life, it challenges traditional, but outdated ideas of truth, error and lie, of absoluteness, foundationalism and relativism. Because of these last considerations the basis for a Trinitarian concept on the Christian idea of tolerance can be developed. *E pluribus unum,* unity in plurality — are finally the structural components of a differentiated understanding of God, which includes the fact that — as Hannah Arendt aptly remarked — he intended plurality to be a characteristic of his (human) creatures.

Tolerance is thus on the one hand a meaningful concept for life-orientation, but moreover it roots in a set of practices, which opens its understanding as an individual attitude, a virtue. This is what shall be considered in conclusion.

6 Tolerance as Christian Virtue, Tolerance as Christian Practice — A Conclusion

However, besides all theories and conceptions of tolerance from a Christian point of view, even more important is this: conceptions of tolerance must be lived out,

---

[77] Forst, Rainer, *Tolerance in Conflict* (fn. 20), 24.

they must rely on forms of tolerant conduct and life-forms. Therefore, conceptions and ideas must really be "worked out" in moral habits. With the latter I come back to my opening statement that conceiving tolerance as a virtue is at least as important as conceptualizing tolerance as a religious idea. In my view, virtues form the (moral) *gestalt* of culturally rooted and developed habits. Thereby these habits must be sedimented in each person individually and in groups and milieus collectively. The essence of habits as such are,

> acquired predisposition[s] to ways or modes of response, not to acts except as, under special conditions, these express a way of behaving. Habits [therefore indicate] special sensitivity or accessibility to certain classes of stimuli, standing predilections and aversions, rather than bare recurrence of specific acts. It means will.[78]

Thus, virtues count in private and public life, they build up the moral web of every day's interactions for everyone.

In the end, I want to clarify the complexity of tolerance as a religious virtue, as an embodied and culturally embedded idea of religious tolerance. I go along the three levels of *civil* and *political sphere* (1), of *interreligious relations* (2), and of *personal* and *communal religious life* (3). Thereby, this shows that the elements of a Christian idea of tolerance are basically nothing more than attempts to interpret the attitude, the virtue of tolerance. This must be inscribed in people's lives and guide them if experiences of the success of peaceful coexistence are to be achieved. But the vigilant remembrance of suffering and violence can also help tolerance to become plausible. Both need not to be mutually exclusive.

On the first level, as we have seen in both Bayle and Williams, the separation of church and state goes hand in hand with the guarantee of religious freedom, even in its negative dimension as freedom from all religion. This institutional framework explicitly denies the view that without religion no moral or civil duties can be held up. So, what is needed to be tolerant in public debates and political discussions concerning deep life issues — not only of abortion and same sex-marriages but also of peace, justice or migration — is besides law-abiding behavior an attitude of political and sometimes even moral compromise. The *Will to Compromise* represents the basic (democratic) virtue for finding temporary results and decisions in conflicts.[79]

---

[78] Dewey, John, *Human Nature and Conduct. An Introduction to Social Psychology (1922)*, ed. Jo Ann Boydston, *The Middle Works of John Dewey, 1899–1924*, vol. 14, Carbondale: Southern Illinois University Press, 1983, 32.

[79] I have argued for the importance of compromise elsewhere. Cf. Polke, Christian, "Vom Kompromiss. Ein (kleiner) theologisch-politischer Traktat," in: Jörg Dierken/Dirk Evers (eds.),

As to the second level, the idea of tolerance is rooted in the double awareness of reasons and moreover human's basic finitude and fallibility on the hand and of value pluralism and value-ambiguity on the other side. Even more, we have our own religious faith only in "earthly vessels" (2Cor. 4:7; KJV). Our religious convictions are deeply embedded in and dependent on our cultural backgrounds, religious traditions and personal experiences. The courage to live one's own faith is inherently related to a willingness to hear and learn from "Others", co-fellow Christian and co-fellow non-Christians and of course vice versa. Only in a spirit of openness to dialogue can one be fully aware of the Otherness of the Other in their different beliefs. Then, tolerance as virtue can flourish, especially in interfaith-dialogue and thereby, personal conversion cannot be totally excluded. A tolerant attitude results from the awareness of the polymorphism of (religious) truth, which means something other than arbitrariness. It accepts the still greater mysteriousness of God and the finiteness of all human attempts to grasp, understand and understand him:

> A truth which, in the first instance, is a *truth for us* does not cease, because of this, to be very Truth and Life. What we learn daily through our live for our fellowmen, viz. That they are independent beings with standards of their own, we ought also to be able learn through our love for mankind as a whole — [...] In our earthly experience the Divine Life is not One, but Many. But to apprehend the One in the Many constitutes the special character of love.[80]

However, most elementary is the cultivation of tolerance as a religious virtue in religious practices and communities. Religious conduct must inhere tolerant attitudes. Otherwise talking about tolerant religions doesn't make sense any longer. On this third level religious forms of life and religious sorts of practices play the crucial role. I will only mention two of such practices by trying briefly to explain why they represent essential "en-acted" religious sources of and for tolerance: The first is what we Christians call the "confession of our own sins." Of course, "sin" is a controversial term for many, also Christian contemporaries. But in fact, there is no other religious word by which we can clearly articulate our own responsibilities for our being and doing. Christian tolerance has its arche-

---

Religion und Politik. Historische und aktuelle Konstellationen eines spannungsvollen Geflechts, 269–82, Frankfurt/M.: Peter Lang, 2016.
80 Troeltsch, Ernst, "The Place of Christianity among the World-Religions," in: Gangolf Hübinger/ Andreas Terwey (eds.), *Fünf Vorträge zu Religion und Geschichtsphilosophie für England und Schottland. Der Historismus und seine Überwindung (1924)/ Christian Thought. Its History and Application (1923)*, vol. 17, Kritische Gesamtausgabe, 134–48, Berlin/New York: de Gruyter 2006.

type — as already Luther knew — in God's toleration towards the sinner.[81] God does tolerate somehow sin not because it is sin but in respect of the sinner, who is His own creature and whom He wants to redeem. The practice of confessing sin therefore helps to cultivate a self-critical religious self-consciousness regarding one's own failures and the need for mutual and especially for divine forgiveness. Thereby, my neighbor whom I should forgive reminds me that it is me who also needs forgiveness. My second example is especially crucial for religious tradition with sacred texts. It aims at basic religious literacy, not only for clerics and intellectuals, but for all believers. We need a form of religious literacy that does not avoid critical engagement in reading and interpreting our holy books historically and contextually. By doing that we can deepen the understanding of our own beliefs. A faith who truly seeks understanding remains critical towards any naive assumptions of formulars and positions which historically arose in different contexts. That does not mean giving up our loyalty towards the history of our common faiths and their communities. But it reminds us that at any time our faith must be both, responsive towards and responsible for what God's will requires in our lifetime, temporally and self-critical. Thus, reading and interpreting scriptures basically leads to a dialogue with brothers and sisters in faith from different periods of time who had their own questions and challenges. In that respect, tolerance can only flourish when we are willing to be sensitive for this hermeneutical task in confessing our faith. In contrast, religious fundamentalism very often goes hand in hand with scriptural literalism — both frequently born out of fears of losing one's own identity. But then the door is again open for a culture of religious intolerance and constraints, which in turn lead to religious and political discrimination, even worse often also to religious violence. To prevent our societies from these disasters, Christian communities can help by creating and cultivating common atmospheres of tolerance in practicing — liturgically and spiritually — what Jesus Christ has taught us: "Why callest thou me good? None is good, save one, that is God." (Luke 18:19; KJV) "And why beholdest thou the mote that is in thy brother's eye, but considerest not the beam that is in thine own eye?" (Matt 7:3; KJV)

---

[81] Cf. Ebeling, Gerhard, *Die Toleranz Gottes und die Toleranz der Vernunft*, in: Gerhard Ebeling, *Umgang mit Luther*, 101–30, Tübingen: Mohr Siebeck, 1983. — The main textual source in Luther's works can be found in: Luther, Martin, *Martin Luther Werke*. Kritische Gesamtausgabe (Weimarer Ausgabe, WA), vol. 39,1, Weimar: Böhlau 1926, 82f. (Third series of disputation theses on Rome 3,28, = WA 39,1; 82f.).

Bibliography

Andresen, Carl/Ritter, Adolf Martin, *Geschichte des Christentums I/1. Altertum*, Stuttgart: Kohlhammer, 1993.
Angenendt, Arnold, *Toleranz und Gewalt. Das Christentum zwischen Bibel und Schwert*, Münster: Aschendorff Verlag, 2008.
Angenendt, Arnold, *"Lasst beides wachsen bis zur Ernte": Toleranz in der Geschichte des Christentums*, Münster: Aschendorff Verlag, 2018.
Asad, Talal, *Formations of the Secular: Christianity, Islam, Modernity*, Stanford (Ca.): Stanford University Press, 2003.
Assmann, Jan, *The Price of Monotheism*, trans. Robert Savage, Standford (Ca.): Stanford University Press, 2010.
Assmann, Jan, *The Invention of Religion: Faith and Covenant in the Book of Exodus*, trans. Robert Savage, Princeton/Oxford: Princeton University Press, 2018.
Augustine, *Letter 93*, § 67, published online: *New Advent*, https://www.newadvent.org/fathers/1102093.htm (accessed on 13.04.2025).
Augustine, *Political Writings*, trans. E.M. Atkins, Cambridge/New York: Cambridge University Press, 2001.
Barth, Hans-Martin, *Die Theologie Martin Luthers. Eine kritische Würdigung*, Munich: Gütersloher Verlagshaus, 2009, 383 f.
Barton, Stephan C., "Paul and the limits of tolerance," in: Graham N. Stanton/Guy G. Stroumsa (eds.), *Tolerance and Intolerance in Early Judaism and Christianity*, 122–34, Cambridge: Cambridge University Press, 1998.
Bayle, Pierre, *A Philosophical Commentary on These Words of the Gospel, Luke 14:23, "Compel Them to Come In, That my House May Be Full"*, ed. John Kilcullen/Chandran Kukathas, Indianapolis: Liberty Fund, 2005.
Bizeul, Yves, "Pierre Bayles Kritik des Aberglaubens und Plädoyer für die Toleranz," in: Friedrich Vollhardt et al. (eds.), *Toleranzdiskurse in der frühen Neuzeit*, 177–216, Berlin: Walter de Gruyter, 2015.
Buzzi, Franco/Krienke, Markus, *Toleranz und Religionsfreiheit in der Moderne*, Stuttgart: Kohlhammer, 2017.
Broer, Ingo, "Toleranz im Neuen Testament? Ein Versuch zum Toleranzgedanken in den paulinischen Briefen," in: Ingo Broer/Richard Schlüter (eds.), *Christentum und Toleranz*, 57–82, Darmstadt: Wissenschaftliche Buchgesellschaft, 1996.
Declaration on Religious Freedom Dignitatis Humanae on the Right of the Person and of Communities to Social and Civil Freedom in Matters Religious, promulgated by his Holiness Pope Paul VI on December 7, 1965, No. 9 and 11, published online: http://www.vatican.va/archive/hist_councils/ii_vatican_council/documents/vat-ii_decl_19651207_dignitatis-humanae_en.html (accessed on 05.05.2022).
Dewey, John, *Human Nature and Conduct. An Introduction to Social Psychology (1922)*, ed. Jo Ann Boydston, *The Middle Works of John Dewey, 1899–1924*, vol. 14, Carbondale: Southern Illinois University Press, 1983.
Ebeling, Gerhard, *Die Toleranz Gottes und die Toleranz der Vernunft*, in: Gerhard Ebeling, *Umgang mit Luther*, 101–30, Tübingen: Mohr Siebeck, 1983.

Fabry, Heinz-Josef, "Toleranz im Alten Testament? Ergebnisse einer Suchbewegung," in: Ingo Broer/Richard Schlüter (eds.), *Christentum und Toleranz*, 9–34, Darmstadt: Wissenschaftliche Buchgesellschaft, 1996.

Forst, Rainer, *Toleration in Conflict: Past and Present*, trans. C. Cronin, Cambridge et al.: Cambridge University Press 2013 [English version].

Forst, Rainer, *Toleranz im Konflikt. Geschichte, Gehalt und Gegenwart eines umstrittenen Begriffs*, Frankfurt/M.: Suhrkamp Verlag, 2003 [German version].

Foucault, Michel, *Security, Territory, Population: Lectures at the Collège de France, 1977–1978*, trans. Graham Burchell, New York & Basingstoke: Palgrave Macmillan, 2007.

Goethe, Johann Wolfgang, *Maxims and Reflecions*, ed. P. Hutchinson/trans. E. Stopp, London: Penguin 1998.

Gollwitzer, Helmut, *Krummes Holz – aufrechter Gang. Zur Frage nach dem Sinn des Lebens*, Munich: Christian Kaiser, 1970.

Heckel, Martin, *Martin Luthers Reformation und das Recht*, Tübingen: Mohr Siebeck, 2016.

Küng, Hans, *Projekt Weltethos*, Munich: Piper, 1990.

Hick, John, *God and the Universe of Faiths*, London: Macmillan, 1973.

Labahn, Michael, "Der geliebte ‚Feind'. Wahrnehmung des Anderen in Jesu Gebot der Feindesliebe und ihre Rezeption im Dokument Q – ein Beispiel antiker ‚Toleranz' und ‚Anerkennung'?," in: Outi Lehtipuu/Michael Labahn (eds.), *Tolerance, Intolerance, and Recognition in Early Christianity and Early Judaism*, 73–109, Amsterdam: Amsterdam University Press, 2021.

Lehtipuu, Outi/Michael Labahn, "Introduction," in: Outi Lehtipuu/Michael Labahn (eds.), *Tolerance, Intolerance, and Recognition in Early Christianity and Early Judaism*, 9–16, Amsterdam: Amsterdam University Press, 2021.

Liebsch, Burkhard, *Verletztes Leben. Studien zur Affirmation von Schmerz und Gewalt im Gegenwärtigen Denken. Zwischen Hegel, Nietzsche, Bataille, Blanchot, Levinas, Ricoeur und Butler*, Zug: Die Graue Reihe, 2014.

Lincoln, Ulrich, *Precarious Creation. Contributions to the Theological Discourse on Violence*, Tübingen: Mohr Siebeck, 2023.

Luther, Martin, "Temporal Authority: To What Extent It Should be Obeyed (1523)," in: Walther I. Brandt/Helmut T. Lehmann (eds.), *Luther's Works: The Christian in Society II*, 81–129, Philadelphia: Fortress Press, 1962.

Luther, Martin, "Von weltlicher Obrigkeit, wie weit man ihr Gehorsam schuldig sei (1523)," in: Karin Bornkamm/Georg Ebeling (eds.), *Martin Luther. Ausgewählte Schriften*, vol. IV, 36–84, Frankfurt/M.: Insel Verlag, ^{2}1983.

Luther, Martin, *Martin Luther Werke*. Kritische Gesamtausgabe (Weimarer Ausgabe, WA), vol. 39,1, Weimar: Böhlau 1926.

Maritain, Jacques, *Christianity and Democracy, and The Rights of Man and the Natural Law*, San Francisco: Ignatius Press, 1986.

Multhammer, Michael, "Johann Lorenz von Mosheims *Ketzergeschichte* oder der Sündenfall der Reformation. Ein Beitrag zur Toleranzdebatte in der Frühaufklärung," in: Friedrich Vollhardt et al. (eds.), *Toleranzdiskurse in der frühen Neuzeit*, 273–92, Berlin: Walter de Gruyter, 2015.

Murray, John Courtney, *Religious Liberty. Catholic Struggles with Pluralism*, ed. J. Leon Hooper S.J., Louisville (Ky.): Westminster John Knox Press, 1993.

Murray, John Courtney, "The Problem of Religious Freedom," in: J. Leon Hooper, S.J. (ed.), *Religious Liberty. Catholic Struggles with Pluralism*, 127–97, Louisville (Ky.)/Westminster: John Knox Press, 1993.

Neville, Robert C., *Religion*, Philosophical Theology Volume Three, Albany: State University of New York Press, 2015.

Niebuhr, H. Richard, *Faith on Earth. An Inquiry into the Structure of Human Faith*, New Haven/London: Yale University Press, 1989.

Nussbaum, Martha C., *Liberty of Conscience. In Defense of America's Tradition of Religious Equality*, New York: Basic Books, 2008.

Oestreich, Gerhard, "Strukturprobleme des europäischen Absolutismus," *Vierteljahresschrift für Sozial- und Wirtschaftsgeschichte* 55 (1969), 329–47.

Polke, Christian, "Gewissensfreiheit als Dissidentenschutz. Martha C. Nussbaums Verteidigung der amerikanischen Verfassungstradition," *Evangelische Theologie* 70 (2010), 268–83.

Polke, Christian, "Vom Kompromiss. Ein (kleiner) theologisch-politischer Traktat," in: Jörg Dierken/Dirk Evers (eds.), *Religion und Politik. Historische und aktuelle Konstellationen eines spannungsvollen Geflechts*, 269–82, Frankfurt/M.: Peter Lang, 2016.

Ragg, Sascha, *Ketzer und Recht: die weltliche Ketzergesetzgebung des Hochmittelalters unter dem Einfluß des römischen und kanonischen Rechts*, Hannover: Hahnsche Buchhandlung, 2006.

Rahner, Karl, *Dialogue and Tolerance as the Foundation of a Humane Society*, trans. Cornelius Ernst, Theological Investigations, vol. XXII: *Humane Society and the Church of Tomorrow*, 14–25, Baltimore: Helicon Press, 1961.

Rawls, John, *A Theory of Justice: Revised Edition*, Cambridge (Ma.): The Belknap Press of Harvard University Press, 1999.

Ratzinger, Joseph Cardinal/Pope Emeritus Benedict XVI., *Truth and Tolerance: Christian Belief and World Religions*, San Francisco (Ca.): Ignatius Press, 2004.

Ricoeur, Paul, "The Erosion of Tolerance and the Resistance of the Intolerable (1995)," in: Pierre-Olivier Monteil *(ed.)*, *Paul Ricoeur, Politics, Economy, and Society* (Writings and Lectures, Vol. 4), 135–46, Cambridge (UK)/Medford (Ma.): Polity Press, 2021.

Schubert, Christoph: "Toleranz in der römischen Antike," in: Dagmar Kiesel/Cleophea Ferrrari (eds.), *Toleranz*, 31–53, Frankfurt/M.: Klostermann, 2022.

Schreiner, Klaus, ",Tolerantia': Begriffs- und wirkungsgeschichtliche Studien zur Toleranzauffassung des Kirchenvaters Augustinus," in: Alexander Patschovsky (ed.), *Toleranz im Mittelalter*, 355–89, Sigmaringen: Thorbecke Verlag, 1998.

Schmidt-Leukel, Perry, *Gott ohne Grenzen. Eine christliche und pluralistische Theologie der Religionen*, Gütersloh: Gütersloher Verlagshaus, 2005.

Schwöbel, Christoph, "The same God? The Perspective of Faith, the Identity of God, Tolerance, and Dialogue," in: Miroslav Volf (ed.), *Do We Worship the Same God? Jews, Christians, and Muslims in Dialogue*, 1–17, Grand Rapids/Cambridge: Eerdmans, 2012.

Schwöbel, Christoph, "Toleranz aus Glauben. Identität und Toleranz im Horizont religiöser Wahrheitsgewißheiten," in: Christoph Schwöbel (ed.), *Christlicher Glaube im Pluralismus, Studien zu einer Theologie der Kultur*, 217–43, Tübingen: Mohr Siebeck, 2003.

Stanton, Graham N., "Introduction," in: Graham N. Stanton/Guy G. Stroumsa (eds.), *Tolerance and Intolerance in Early Judaism and Christianity*, 1–6, Cambridge: Cambridge University Press, 1998.

Streib, Heinz et al., "Categorizing People by Their Preference for Religious Styles: Four Types Derived from Evaluation of Faith Development Interviews," *The International Journal for the Psychology of Religion*, 30,2 (2020), 112–27, published online: DOI: https://doi.org/10.1080/10508619.2019.1664213 (accessed on 05.05.2023).

Tillich, Paul, *Christianity and the Encounter of the World Religions*, New York/London: Columbia University Press, 1963.

Troeltsch, Ernst, *The Social Teachings of the Christian Churches*, vol. II, trans. Olive Wyon, Louisville (Ky.), London: Westminster John Knox Press, 1992.
Troeltsch, Ernst, *The Absoluteness of Christianity and the History of Religion*, trans. David Reid, London: SCM Press, 1972.
Troeltsch, Ernst, "The Place of Christianity among the World-Religions," in: Gangolf Hübinger/Andreas Terwey (eds.), *Fünf Vorträge zu Religion und Geschichtsphilosophie für England und Schottland. Der Historismus und seine Überwindung (1924)/ Christian Thought. Its History and Application (1923)*, vol. 17, *Kritische Gesamtausgabe*, 134–48, Berlin/New York: de Gruyter 2006.
Walzer, Michael, *On Toleration*, New Haven: Yale University Press, 1997.
Williams, Roger, *The Bloudy Tenent Yet More Bloudy (1652)*, in: Perry Miller (ed.), *The Complete Writings of Roger Williams*, Vol. IV, New York: Russel and Russel, 1963.
Williams, Roger, *The Bloody Tenent of Persecution for Cause of Conscience*, London, 1644.
Williams, Roger, The Bloody Tenent of Persecution for Cause of Conscience (1644), in: *On Religious Liberty. Selections from the Works of Roger Williams*, ed. James Calvin Davis, Cambridge (Ma.)/London: The Belknap Press of Harvard University Press, 2008.
Williams, Roger, *The Correspondence of Roger Williams*, vol. I. 1629–1653, Glenn La Fantasie (ed.), Hanover: Brown University Press/University Press of New England, 1988.

Suggestions for Further Reading

Enders, Christoph/Kahlo, Michael (eds.), *Diversität und Toleranz. Toleranz als Ordnungsprinzip?*, Paderborn: Mentis Verlag, 2010.
Jürgen Habermas, "Religiöse Toleranz als Schrittmacher kultureller Rechte," in: Jürgen Habermas, *Zwischen Naturalismus und Religion. Philosophische Aufsätze*, 58–278, Frankfurt/M.: Suhrkamp, 2005.
Härle, Wilfried, "Der Toleranzgedanke im Verhältnis der Religionen," in: W.E. Müller/H.H.R. Schulz (eds.), *Theologie und Aufklärung. FS für G. Hornig*, 323–38, Würzburg: Königshausen & Neumann, 1992.
Locke, John, *Two Treatises of Fivernment and A Letter Concerning Toleration*, Ian Shapiro (ed.). New Haven: Yale University Press, 2003.
Nussbaum, Martha C., *Liberty of Conscience. In Defense of America's Tradition of Religious Equality*, New York: Basic Books, 2008.
Rendtorff, Trutz (ed.), *Glaube und Toleranz: Das theologische Erbe der Aufklärung*, Gütersloh: Gütersloher Verlagshaus, 1982.
Schwöbel, Christoph/von Tippelskirch, Dorothee (eds.), *Die religiösen Wurzeln der Toleranz*, Freiburg i.B./Basel/Vienna: Herder Verlag, 2002.
Sedmak, Clemens (ed.), *Toleranz. Vom Wert der Vielfalt*, Darmstadt: Wissenschaftliche Buchgesellschaft, 2015.
Voltaire, *Über die Toleranz*. Mit einem Vorwort von Lauren Joffrin, Berlin: Suhrkamp Verlag, 2015.
Zagorin, Perez, *How the Idea of Religious Tolerance Came to the West*, Princeton/Oxfordshire: Princeton University Press, 2003.

Anna Ayşe Akasoy
The Concept of Tolerance in Islam

1 Introduction

Tolerance occupies a prominent position in the widely conducted and contentious debates about the relationship between "Islam" and "the West" or "Islam" and "modernity". These debates often focus on Muslim life in secular Western societies, the status of religious minorities in Muslim-majority countries, and the treatment of LGBTQ+ communities. Tolerance is frequently framed as a benchmark — even a prerequisite — for compatibility with modernity. It is celebrated as a universal value, its presence in a culture's tradition serving as an open sesame to the global community of civilized nations. Conversely, acts of violence or oppression justified by Muslims in religious terms are often labeled as manifestations of intolerance. They typically concern freedom of speech, the presence of women in the public sphere, and freedom of religion, especially to leave Islam for another religion or atheism. As Vincent Cornell put it, "The image of Islamic intolerance has caused Muslims to be regarded as the most uncivil members of global civil society."[1] In this context, "intolerance" serves as an umbrella term for political violence, although violence on the part of governments in Muslim-majority countries that do not overtly present themselves as Islamic is more regularly framed as human right violations. The UAE's 2019 "Year of Tolerance" campaign exemplifies how tolerance is strategically promoted to counter Islam's global image of intolerance. This discursive phenomenon predates the twenty-first century. In his pioneering article of 1970, Rudi Paret used the partition as a starting point to explore the view that Hindus of secular India are more tolerant than Muslims of Pakistan.[2]

Not surprisingly thus, as public discourse around tolerance and Islam has focused on politically charged relationships and on situations which have emerged as emblematic instances of tolerance or intolerance, it has not paid much, if any attention to tolerance in a more abstract sense or as a factor of interpersonal relationships in general. The Danish cartoon protests became emblematic of Muslim intolerance, while medieval al-Andalus' religious diversity is often idealized as a

---

[1] Cornell, Vincent J., "Theologies of Difference and Ideologies of Intolerance in Islam," in: Jacob Neusner/Bruce Chilton (eds.), *Religious Tolerance in World Religions*, 274–96, 278, West Conshohocken: Templeton Foundation Press, 2008.
[2] Paret, Rudi, "Toleranz und Intoleranz im Islam," *Saeculum* 21 (1970), 344–65.

model of Muslim tolerance. The present chapter seeks to cast its net more widely. For this survey, tolerance will be understood as a deliberate and voluntary acceptance of ideas and practices which are deemed objectionable. The moral ambition of this form of tolerance can be modest and does not require the appreciation of opposed views or of the people who hold them *because* one is opposed to them, although it does imply some affirmative recognition of the diversity of views which typically emerges from such a situation.

There are many reasons why we find people, what they say, do and think objectionable. This is as true for Muslims as for anybody else. Our objections can be moral in nature, they can be political, social, religious, aesthetic, several of these, or rooted in other realms of human activity and consideration. We may object on principle, on a hunch or out of selfish interest. Our reasons for tolerating a person or what they say or do also need not always fall into the same category either. We may object to something for subjective, emotional reasons, but tolerate it on grounds of principle, or the other way around. In line with the general interest of this book in interreligious encounters, this chapter's perspective will replicate to some extent parameters of both public and scholarly discourse and focus on intercommunal tolerance in public life shaped by conditions of political power.[3] The circularity this entails needs to be acknowledged. If we take it for granted that tolerance is primarily an issue of religious diversity, the religious identity of a tolerant or intolerant person is indeed significant. And if we foreground the religious identity of the person who exercises tolerance or intolerance, then it makes a lot of sense to focus on contexts where religion is the potential source of conflict. Whether Islamic traditions thus encourage certain responses to neighbors playing loud music, to children insisting on questionable fashion statements or to friends whose taste in poetry we absolutely do not share remains largely beyond the scope of this discussion. Future research might explore how such cases of interpersonal tolerance are negotiated in Islamic contexts and how they might relate to interreligious tolerance.

This chapter will also typically deal with religion as manifest in normative thought (e.g., in theology or law) and thus concentrate on doctrinal disagreements in the wider realm of religion. It will focus on situations where the objection is grounded in principle, that is, that the beliefs of other religious communities are wrong, rather than social encounters where Muslims might object to other habits or traditions associated with different religious communities out of purity

---

[3] For the reverse perspective and the framing of religious diversity in terms of tolerance cf. Friedmann, Yohanan, *Tolerance and Coercion in Islam. Interfaith Religions in the Muslim Tradition*, Cambridge: Cambridge University Press, 2003.

concerns, for example, or for reasons of diverging social convention. The subject of apostasy will only be mentioned in passing. The structure of the discussion, shaped in part by its reliance on written sources, underscores the chapter's focus on tolerance as a discursive phenomenon. This reflects another reality of tolerance — that we know of people's objections and of their reasons for acceptance despite objections because they verbalize their thoughts. Behind every expression of tolerance lurks intolerance as an alternative.

That the concern with theological truth is central to many notions of tolerance which can be usefully classified as "Islamic" is one of the most important points in this chapter. The fundamental rationale behind the decision of those who choose to tolerate (or not) in this chapter is predicated on the premise that what they deem to be objectionable is, in accordance with their convictions, not true. These disagreements are assumed to be irresolvable by way of compromise. However, as previously indicated, the concept of tolerance should be addressed Tolerance serves as a conceptual and practical solution to such specific sets of issues. This framing requires further elaboration due to the significant methodological challenges associated with studying tolerance outside of those Western European contexts which have historically shaped the meaning of the term. These challenges will be addressed in conjunction with other issues at the beginning of this chapter; and will remain a prominent theme throughout this survey.

A final difficulty must also be acknowledged. In the absence of theoretical and explicit discussions of tolerance, it is often defined by default as the absence of intolerance. But what counts as intolerance is itself not always clear. Practical, especially violent interventions in other people's lives might qualify most obviously, but what about polemics and literary condemnations? The proposition that underlies the concept of hate speech is that words matter, but connections between written discourse and real-life interactions can be hard to ascertain in Islamic history. This challenge brings us to a critical paradox: if tolerance requires some form of rejection or objection, it becomes difficult to discern tolerance without intolerance, especially when the latter has a low threshold. In other words, the very fact that somebody objects to a principle or practice in the first place may already be taken to be a case of intolerance. Much depends as well on our expectations of what commonly constitutes a source of friction and how disagreement is normally expressed. If our expectation is that a certain disagreement typically involves violence, a purely discursive expression might already be taken to constitute tolerance. By different standards, however, such verbal expressions may still be judged as intolerance.

2 A Particular Solution for a Particular Problem: How to Universalize Tolerance

Many general discussions of tolerance devote considerable attention to situating the concept historically. Tolerance, understood as a political principle which allows for the peaceful coexistence of diverse — especially religiously diverse — communities is the product of Europe's religious wars and connected to the rise of liberalism and the modern state.[4] Seminal works of Western European political philosophy contain the word in the title, notably John Locke's (1632–1704) *Letter Concerning Toleration* (1689). Literary classics too such as Lessing's (1729–1781) *Nathan the Wise* (1779) feature the subject prominently. The deeper roots of the concept as a political model for religiously diverse societies are often traced back to medieval discussions of religious others, especially Jews and Muslims. The methodological challenge posed by the presence of history in our understanding of tolerance is that we need to determine whether and how concepts can be disentangled from the historical circumstances that produced them. In other words, can tolerance be understood and applied as a universal value in political and social ethics, independent of its European origins?

In the context of developments that are commonly regarded in scholarship as positive milestones in human history — especially since the early modern period — it has been noted that trajectories seen in Western Europe had no counterpart in other parts of the world. This phenomenon is also observed in the context of tolerance. For example, Locke and Lessing are regularly contrasted with an absence of similar treatises in the Islamic world, even though Locke himself regarded the Ottoman Empire as a paradigm for tolerance. Such comparisons are often terminological in nature and point out that the term for "tolerance" in modern Arabic, *tasāmuḥ*, only acquired this technical meaning comparatively recently.[5]

---

[4] For a detailed discussion cf. the chapter on tolerance and Christianity in this volume.

[5] For a discussion of terminology cf. especially Kokew, Stephan, *Annäherung an Toleranz. Ausgangspunkte, Kontexte und zeitgenössische Interpretationen des Toleranzbegriffs aus dem schiitischen Islam*, Würzburg: Ergon, 2014; "Toleranz im Islam," in: Michael Klöcker/Udo Tworuschka (eds.), *Handbuch der Religionen*, 50, Ergänzungslieferung, Munich: Mediengruppe Oberfranken, 2016. For recent surveys cf. also Hartmann, Angelika, "Pluralismus und Toleranz aus der Sicht des Islam," in: Christian Augustin/Johannes Wienand/Christiane Winkler (eds.), *Religiöser Pluralismus und Toleranz in Europa*, 123–86, Wiesbaden: VS Verlag für Sozialwissenschaften, 2006; Krämer, Gudrun, "Toleranz im Islam. Ein Blick in Geschichte und Gegenwart," in: Angelika Neuwirth/Günter Stock (eds), *Europa im Nahen Osten – Der Nahe Osten in Europa*, 39–52, Berlin: Akademie Verlag, 2010; Schulze, Reinhard, "Der Islam und die Toleranz," in: Romana Weiershausen/Insa Wilka/Nina Gülcher (eds.), *Aufgeklärte Zeiten? Religiöse Toleranz und Literatur*, 45–68, Berlin:

One may, of course, freely endorse a Eurocentric view of history and consider this a failure on the part of Muslims. However, most historians, including the present author, endeavor to avoid such paradigmatic notions of Western European history. While these approaches presuppose a Western European leadership in human achievements, they often downplay the violence of the crises that produced these commonly held political values. In other words, what is widely regarded as an achievement was a solution to a problem existing in the very same cultural and political sphere. The Reformation is an additional example that can be cited to demonstrate this point. On occasion, a "Reformation" has been declared to be lacking in Islamic history. And yet, it is worth considering that the Reformation — along with certain European concepts of tolerance or toleration — was a response to a specific constellation of problems such as the monopolizing position of the Catholic church or the inaccessibility of Latin scripture. In contrast, a religious institution as centralized and institutionally rigid as the Catholic Church never existed in Islamic history and the Qur'ān was translated into languages other than Arabic as early as the eighth century. The kinds of frictions which sparked Protestantism among Western Christians thus never existed among Muslims, certainly not at the same level and in the same form. Likewise, Muslims can hardly be faulted for their failure to engage in the same kind of religious warfare that devastated the European continent since the Reformation. Finally, it may be pointed out that in Europe, too, tolerance did not put an end to conflict. If blood was shed in the name of Christian sects during the periods of Reformation and Enlightenment, nationalism and racism provided the ideological underpinnings from the late nineteenth century onwards.

Thus, for two primary reasons, a notion of tolerance that is essentially and inextricably bound up with its Western European roots is inadequate for other cultural contexts. It may appear as a false universal, detached from the violent history that produced it. Universalizing the concept, however, is not a simple exercise, given that discussions conducted in Western European languages also reflect that

---

Erich Schmidt, 2011; Afsaruddin, Asma, "Tolerance and Pluralism in Islamic Thought and Practice," in: Vicki A. Spencer (ed.), *Toleration in Comparative Perspective*, 99–119, Lanham: Lexington Books, 2018. Cf. also Neusner, Jacob/Chilton, Bruce (eds.), *Religious Tolerance in World Religions*, West Conshohocken: Templeton Foundation Press, 2008, especially Kalin, Ibrahim, "Sources of Tolerance and Intolerance in Islam. The Case of the People of the Book," in: Jacob Neusner/Bruce Chilton (eds.), *Religious Tolerance in World Religions*, 239–73, West Conshohocken: Templeton Foundation Press, 2008; Cornell, "Theologies of Difference and Ideologies of Intolerance in Islam,"; Acar, Ismail, "Theological Foundations of Religious Tolerance in Islam: a Qur'ānic Perspective," in: Jacob Neusner/Bruce Chilton (eds.), *Religious Tolerance in World Religions*, 297–313, West Conshohocken: Templeton Foundation Press, 2008.

history, even if only unwittingly. When we speak of "tolerance" or "toleration" in English or of *Toleranz* in German, can we ever do so without the undercurrents of European history? A statement in a recent publication illustrates the resulting conundrum. In his monograph on Jewish and Christian life under Muslim rule, Jacob Lassner discusses the difficulty of relating "tolerance" to corresponding notions in Arabic. "Responsible scholars attuned to differences that are caused by time and place," Lassner writes, "are likely to note that current definitions of tolerance broaden considerably the semantic field of those Arabic words employed by medieval Muslims when they speak of tolerance."[6] While the current chapter as well as several surveys of tolerance in Islamic contexts basically concur with Lassner's statement, it is also the case that medieval Muslims did not speak of "tolerance" for the simple reason that they did not write in English. Our assumption here is not that "tolerance" is untranslatable, but that terminological and even conceptual discrepancies between Western European and various "Islamic" discourses need to be borne in mind.

The approach pursued in this chapter is not to perpetuate the discursive and indeed lexical parameters of Western European elaborations and seek out conceptual discussions among Muslims about principles which can be translated as "tolerance." The strategy is rather to focus on the nature of tolerance as a solution to a problem. After all, tolerance is not merely a theoretical achievement; rather, it is meant to make a difference for actual human interactions and the problems many of us face in dealing with people who challenge our habits and certainties. The religious wars that swept through early modern Europe are certainly a problem that can be universalized in several ways. Initially, the focus will be on problems of political ethics, namely, how to deal with the presence of individuals and communities that define themselves by way of ideas or practices that are deemed objectionable. As indicated above, the term "objectionable" here is broad. It comprises ideas and practices which are to some extent accepted, but in their particular shape considered ill-informed and mildly deviant. Additionally, it includes others which are deemed altogether false or even potentially corrosive. A somewhat artificial line needs to be drawn here between behavior that is uncontroversially criminalized and behavior that is only potentially criminalized. Slander, for example, is typically not considered a case for tolerance, whereas public preaching might be considered sedition or rebellion, but also be deemed acceptable. Such lines are admittedly ambiguous and subject to historical change. However, common sense gives us a clear idea which kinds of objectionable behavior and

---

[6] Lassner, Jacob, *Jews, Christians, and the Abode of Islam. Modern Scholarship, Medieval Realities*, Chicago: The University of Chicago Press, 2012, 177.

views are typically the subject of tolerance, which ones are not, and where we may find a gray area. The difficulty of drawing such lines is familiar from contemporary discussions about free speech, for example. In the following discussion, nothing is implied as to whether the present author considers the discussed objections valid or not.

In recent publications, tolerance is often coterminous with religious diversity. Albrecht Noth, for example, defined "Islamic tolerance" as "formal tolerance" and more specifically the space granted to non-Muslims to live under Muslim rule.[7] While this reflects the history of the concept in Western European thought, it is also not an inadequate association since across the world, religious diversity often provides fertile ground for conflict. In the context of Islamic history, it is useful to understand religious diversity both as inter- and as intrareligious, as will become obvious during this survey. It is usually easier to identify situations where tolerance seems absent and where views and behavior deemed objectionable are suppressed or eradicated. Where no or little evidence of such violent strategies is available, we often speak of tolerance. According to the understanding of tolerance applied in this chapter, such "tolerance" requires a somewhat deliberate choice, even if we only extrapolate such a choice from the broader historical circumstances. The person or community who exercises tolerance needs to be in a position where there is sufficient reason to assume that they also could have acted otherwise. This accounts for a focus on societies ruled by Muslims who sometimes intervened in the religious life of non-Muslims. That such interventions were not consistent already illustrates that there is no uniform "Islamic" attitude to tolerance. Indeed, the notion of an Islamic tradition of tolerance that requires all Muslims to be consistently tolerant is, by its very nature, an impossibly high bar to set. Likewise, not all forms of religious alterity have presumably been deemed objectionable or equally objectionable. To the extent of my knowledge, for example, there is no evidence that Muslim rulers in India suppressed vegetarianism even if Muslim theologians rejected metaphysical beliefs associated with the dietary practice. Vegetarianism may thus never have been an issue, whereas the figurative representation of multiple deities in Indian temples sometimes led to violent interventions. For the purposes of this chapter, the case of vegetarianism would not qualify as a case for tolerance, whereas allowing the presence of such objects would qualify. The extent to which such decisions are informed by moral rather than pragmatic considerations is often hard to determine, especially for the earlier periods, and will thus not receive much attention in this chapter.

---

7 Noth, Albrecht, "Möglichkeiten und Grenzen islamischer Toleranz," *Saeculum* 29 (1978), 190–204.

A final caveat requires elaboration. As noted earlier, this analysis is grounded in written sources, which are often products of educated, urban environments. The question of how Muslims truly acted across the centuries since Muḥammad's mission began in the seventh century CE — and across the vast and diverse territories of the Islamic world — remains largely unanswerable. Whether their tolerance (or lack thereof) reflected the intellectual debates found in the sources examined here lies beyond the scope of this inquiry and may ultimately be unknowable. It is, thus, worth reiterating that the following survey is one of written discourse and primarily of such discourse which can be classified as "Islamic." We will return to this aspect throughout the chapter.

3 Scripture: Approaches to Religious Diversity in the Qur'ān

A contrast is sometimes drawn between Christianity, in which God is believed to have manifested as a man, and Islam, where God is understood to have manifested as a book. In the Islamic tradition, the Qur'ān is the word of God, and it deeply permeates Islamic thought, literature, education, ethics, and aesthetics. It would be preposterous to deny its significance for Muslims. And yet, as this survey begins with scripture, a few notes of caution are necessary. When explanations are sought regarding attitudes of Muslims to a variety of issues, the Qur'ān often serves as a first reference point. While such answers may not be altogether inaccurate or irrelevant, they also remain markedly insufficient. Muslims do not simply embody doctrine, scriptural or otherwise. They are diverse human beings, shaped by individual experiences, embedded in social contexts, products of historical circumstances, and defined by a complex inner life. The way one Muslim relates to the Qur'ān may differ significantly from another, even if both share the same religious identity. Likewise, the extent to which one Muslim presents an Islamic theory of tolerance based on the Qur'ān may differ significantly from the interpretive choices of another. As will become clearer below, two Muslims might emphasize different Qur'ānic passages to justify either tolerant or intolerant positions — or interpret the same verses in divergent ways. The relationship between the Qur'ān and Islam is thus complicated. The overarching problem — namely, the explanatory power of Islam for the way that tolerance is theorized or practiced by individual Muslims or in Muslim-majority societies — will be addressed again further below. For now, it is sufficient to note that Qur'ānic references only constitute one aspect of religiously informed attitudes — they are neither exclusive nor exhaustive.

With these reservations in mind, one can recognize the great significance of the Qur'ān in Islamic history and thought, including for matters of tolerance. Two elements are especially relevant for the present discussion. First, there is the nature of the Qur'ān as a historical source and what it tells us about attitudes to religious diversity among the earliest Muslims. Secondly, there is the normative nature of the Qur'ān in classical Islamic law and beyond that in morality and ethics. Modern interpretations of pertinent Qur'ānic passages will be discussed again towards the very end of this chapter.

Surveys of tolerance in the Islamic tradition, whether descriptive or polemical, often point out that the Qur'ān does not contain a single term which would best be rendered as "tolerance". Some scholars write of the "tolerance verses" in the Qur'ān, but this label, in this precise form, is a modern construct. The absence of a clear term for tolerance shifts agency of interpretation to individual readers who make different determinations regarding the nature of tolerance, the area where it should or should not be applied, which passages of the Qur'ān are accordingly relevant and what exactly they imply. Among both insiders and outsiders to this religion, these determinations can vary considerably. The fact that both advocates of an innate Islamic value of tolerance and their discursive opponents adduce passages from the Qur'ān illustrates the difficulty of identifying relevant passages, the text's interpretive openness and the pivotal role of hermeneutic strategies in shaping meaning.

Nonetheless, several Qur'ānic verses are frequently cited. The *locus classicus* for discussions about a Qur'ānic notion of tolerance is verse 256 of sura 2 which states that "there is no compulsion in religion" (Arabic: *lā ikrāha fī d-dīn*).[8] Beyond signaling tolerance in religious matters, the verse is often adduced in contemporary scholarship as evidence of an Islamic principle of religious freedom: "It is undoubtedly as a timeless grant of universal tolerance that the vast majority of educated Muslims understand the verse today, especially when they write in English."[9] The verse is very commonly understood to refer to compulsion across religions, that is, to conversion, although historical interpretations varied between the emphasis on conversion *to* a religion, or conversion *from* a religion. Accord-

---

[8] Friedmann, Yohanan, "Tolerance and Coercion," in: Jane Dammen McAuliffe (ed.), *Encyclopaedia of the Qur'ān*, vol. 5, Leiden: Brill, 2005, 290–94. The translation of the Qur'ān quoted here is by M.A.S. Abdel Haleem.
[9] Crone, Patricia, "'No Compulsion in Religion'. Q. 2:256 in Mediaeval and Modern Interpretation," in: Mohammad Ali Amir-Moezzi/Meir M. Bar-Asher/Simon Hopkins (eds.), *Le Shī'isme Imāmite quarante ans après. Hommage à Etan Kohlberg*, 131–78, Turnhout: Brepols, 2009.

ingly, 2:256 is also crucial for the subject of apostasy.[10] Maha El Kaisy-Friemuth cites the verse as evidence that, following divine command, Muḥammad did not endorse contemporaneous practices of punishing apostates, instead viewing such punishment as reserved for the hereafter.[11] The extent to which attitudes to religious truth should have repercussions in this world is probably the most important variable in concepts of tolerance.

The openness of this verse to interpretation is evident in Patricia Crone's extensive survey of both historical and contemporary Muslim exegesis.[12] Crone argued that any implied religious freedom in the verse posed a challenge for commentators in societies where religion defined the public order. She distinguished three traditional interpretations which are still widely accepted. The first two interpretations consider the verse as outdated — because it was either abrogated by a later revelation (commonly known as the "sword verse"; see below), or tied to a specific historical context in which a group of converts during Muḥammad's lifetime were instructed not to compel their children to adopt Islam. The third reading is less restrictive and claims that the verse guarantees non-Muslims who pay the specially assigned poll tax (Arabic: *jizya*; see below) the right to continue practicing their religion.

Notably, in all the exegetical works surveyed by Crone, which were composed by members of very different Muslim religious communities, the verse was consistently taken to be prescriptive. The phrase "No compulsion" was understood as a negative command: Muslims *should not* compel others in matters of religion. It was not understood as descriptive, i.e., that compulsion in religion did not exist. Moreover, we can also find explanations why Muslims should refrain from compelling others.

Because, as the Qur'ān states, had God willed someone to believe, he would have made them a believer. Furthermore, because this world is a trial, humans are equipped to recognize the truth, but it is up to them whether they pass or fail (this is but one example of the important paradox of human freedom and re-

---

[10] For a travelogue concerned with Islamic law cf. Kadri, Sadakat, *Heaven on Earth. A Journey through Shari'a Law from the Deserts of Ancient Arabia to the Streets of the Modern Muslim World*, New York: Farrar Straus & Giroux, 2012. Chapter eleven ("'No Compulsion in Religion?' Apostasy, Blasphemy, and Tolerance") presents observations from Iran and Pakistan. Kadri criticizes the recent legal practice in both states as increasingly intolerant and contrasts this with the discursive affirmation of tolerance as well as a history of religious diversity.
[11] For this Cf. also El Kaisy-Friemuth, Maha, "The Concept of Freedom in Islam," in: Georges Tamer and Ursula Männle (eds.), *The Concept of Freedom in Judaism, Christianity and Islam*, 101–46, 133, Berlin: De Gruyter, 2019.
[12] Crone, "No Compulsion in Religion'".

sponsibility on the one hand and God's omnipotence and omniscience on the other). Medieval scholars distinguished human and divine agents in compulsion. Some brought forward the view that God did not compel people to believe, whereas others focused on humans who should not or could not do so. For some, the fact that God did not compel people to believe does not mean that Muslims should simply accept the unbelief of others. In fact, changing the external circumstances of a religious landscape might help individual non-Muslims to recognize for themselves the truth of Islam. Likewise, a difference was sometimes made between the inner and the outer individual; some interpreters emphasized that while inner faith could only result from someone's true and personal conviction and not from compulsion by other people, such a person was still obliged to follow the law. Thus, legal compliance was not exempt from compulsion.[13]

To modern readers, this law may appear infused with what we nowadays classify as religion. However, concepts of religion were neither homogeneous nor stable in the premodern period. What exactly constituted the category of "religion" in the context of the verse's declaration that there is no compulsion varied significantly across interpretations. On the level of religion in the sense of religious community, some exegetes saw in the verse a reference to non-Muslims who could not be compelled to convert and debated which religious communities were meant with this verse. Other interpreters argued that the verse referred in fact to Muslims who could not be compelled to accept falsehood. The two readings reflect two different concepts of religion as well. Both strands have a parallel history in Christian notions of religion. While "religion" — according to one understanding — is a universal category, the other understanding restricts it to what is considered a true religion. As Crone established, a consensus across centuries had it that the polytheists of Muḥammad's Western Arabia were not meant to enjoy freedom from compulsion.[14] As such, they were either viewed as exceptions to the principle of "no compulsion in religion," or deemed ineligible altogether, since their beliefs and practices were not recognized as religion. It was primarily Jews and Christians and, sometimes, other communities such as Zoroastrians, who occupied an intermediate position between the "true religion" and those beliefs that merely resembled it yet were regarded as falsehood. As distortions of the "true religion", they were considered to fall within the general category of religion, but clearly at a lower level than Islam.

It is only in recent times that the verse has been interpreted as a general statement in favor of freedom of religion and as a human right. This was in response to

---

13 Crone, "'No Compulsion in Religion'".
14 Ibid.

the rise of religious freedom as a political value and to rebut the accusation that Islam had been spread by the sword. Not unlike several modern Muslim intellectuals, Crone assigned the less liberal readings of the verse to an imperial, classical period, after Muḥammad, and illustrated how either an original meaning or a marginalized, more liberal interpretation could be recovered. She identified specifically a strand within the discursive rationalist theology of the Muʿtazilites, to be discussed further below. According to this interpretation, the verse states that humans are free from divine compulsion and that it is out of their own free will that they recognize the truth of Islam. At the same time, she emphasized that historical interpretations of the verse can indeed be different from modern views, thereby challenging modernist interpreters who frame their liberal readings as part of a longstanding exegetical tradition.[15] As much as a tradition of liberal views may validate such interpretations, history should not predetermine possibilities of later readings.

It is worth emphasizing the significance of the fact that verse 2:256 does not speak positively of tolerance, but rather negatively about its opposite to the extent that compulsion and intolerance overlap. The same is true of verses 99–100 of sura 10 which deal with the prophet Jonah and speak of compulsion. "Had your Lord willed, all the people on earth would have believed. So, can you [Prophet] compel people to believe? No soul can believe except by God's will, and He brings disgrace on those who do not use their reason." Exegetically applied to 2:256, 10:99–100 explicates that there is no compulsion in religion because a person's religious insight depends on God. Here, the reference more clearly designates humans, rather than God, as the agents of compulsion, whereas the differing interpretations reveal that 2:256 is ambiguous in that respect. The parallel between the two passages is thematic as well as lexical — the Arabic words translated as "compulsion" are derived from the same three root letters (k-r-h) and are thus closely related. Not uncharacteristically, the Qurʾān strikes a fine and complicated balance here between determination and free will, one of the main concerns of the Muslim theologians discussed below. While tolerance as a political and social principle is not necessarily the primary concern in the Qurʾānic passages which are commonly adduced to affirm the existence of such a principle, in theological debates, the treatment of those who do not share one's views receded even more into the background.

Another Qurʾānic passage which is frequently cited in discussions about tolerance is sura 109, which has the title *al-Kāfirūn* (The Disbelievers). As one of the last suras in the Qurʾān, it is typically short and theologically complex:

---

15 Crone, "'No Compulsion in Religion'".

> Say [Prophet], "Disbelievers:
> I do not worship what you worship,
> You do not worship what I worship,
> I will never worship what you worship,
> You will never worship what I worship:
> You have your religion and I have mine."

The sura operates with a powerful binary, a prominent stylistic feature of the Qur'ān in general. The text draws clear lines between God and the created world, but also between believers and unbelievers (who these people were meant to be historically and how these categories apply in later times is a different issue and subject of controversy). In this sura, the repetition, the reversal of perspectives, the extension into the future, and the concluding, somewhat summarizing verse leave no doubt concerning the essential, unbridgeable difference between Muḥammad and the disbelievers. His objection to their worship is presumably implied and provides one of the conditions of tolerance. That we are indeed dealing with a recommendation for tolerance, however, is not as obvious, for the implications of the two different religions are not spelled out. Those who read this verse as an expression of tolerance take the description of religious difference as an acceptance of this situation — the implication of the future tense being that there is no intention on the part of Muḥammad to change it, either out of respect for the disbelievers' preference or because such preference is ultimately considered a manifestation of God's plan, as 2:256 and especially 10:99–100 suggest. In a similar spirit, verses 118–119 of sura 11 state "If your Lord had pleased, He would have made all people a single community, but they continue to have their differences — except those on whom your Lord has mercy — for He created them to be this way, and the word of your Lord is final: 'I shall definitely fill Hell with both jinn and men.'" Likewise, the oft-quoted verse 13 of sura 49 declares that "People, We created you all from a single man and a single woman, and made you into races and tribes so that you should recognize one another. In God's eyes, the most honored of you are the ones most mindful of Him: God is all knowing, all aware." This verse is often taken as an expression that religious diversity is divinely ordained, but this is not the predominant theme of the context within the sura. The preceding and following verses exhort believers to treat each other with ethical integrity. Another critical variable in concepts of tolerance is thus how one perceives religious diversity — as a fact of life or as a problem that needs to be rectified.[16]

---

[16] Kalin, "Sources of Tolerance and Intolerance in Islam," 249.

It is not hard to see, however, that sura 109 could also be read very differently than as an acceptance, or even as an endorsement of religious diversity. The singer Yusuf Islam (formerly Cat Stevens) promotes tolerance as an Islamic virtue rooted in the Qur'ān but explains that "God Almighty is not pleased when some humans choose not to believe", referring to verse 39:7 which stresses again the dichotomy between believers and unbelievers.[17] Even more drastically, verse 8:39 belongs to a passage where similar contrasts are drawn, but with implications for the interaction between these groups in this world. It instructs believers to "fight them until there is no more persecution, and all worship is devoted to God alone: if they desist, then God sees all that they do." How all these statements are reconciled depends on one's exegetical methods, the extent to which the Qur'ān is adduced to explain itself or how much verses are interpreted in isolation. Most of the traditional interpretations Crone surveyed, for example, are derived from commentaries that proceed verse-by-verse and tend to conclude that 2:256 has been abrogated. It is only in modern times that the thematic commentary gained popularity and modernist interpreters argued in favor of an overall spirit of tolerance in the Qur'ān.

Some authors point to clusters of verses. Khaled Abou El Fadl speaks of the "tolerance verses" (Arabic: *āyāt at-tasāmuḥ*) which he describes as having "ignited one of the richest debates in human history regarding the moral value of tolerance,"[18] and lists several passages (2:109; 5:13; 15:85; 24:22; 43:89; 64:14). Abou El Fadl discussed this Qur'ānic evidence as part of a longer essay in which he made a case for an Islamic tradition of tolerance. As mentioned above, this presentation is slightly misleading in that "tolerance verses" is a modern designation and that to "ignite" a debate is not necessarily the same as making a constructive contribution. The word *tasāmuḥ* does not appear in any of these verses. Then again, there is a historical precedent for the exegetical idea that several verses in the Qur'ān recommend the gentle treatment of people Muslims disapprove of. Patricia Crone identifies the origins of the term "reconciliation verses" (Arabic: *āyāt al-muwāda'a*) among medieval commentators in the Muslim West, although she also points out that these verses were traditionally considered abrogated.[19] Of course, the difference in technical discourse and a certain looseness in the underlying concept of these "tolerance verses" need not affect the moral substance of Abou El Fadl's argument. A closer look at the corpus of "tolerance verses," how-

---

[17] Stevens, Cat, "Tolerance in Islam," published online: https://catstevens.com/think/spiritual-domain/tolerance-in-islam/ (accessed on 14.07.2024).
[18] Abou El Fadl, Khaled, *The Place of Tolerance in Islam*, ed. Joshua Cohen/Ian Lague for Boston Review, Boston: Beacon Press, 2002, 99.
[19] Crone, "'No Compulsion in Religion'", 149, note 109.

ever, reveals that the matter is not as straightforward as he implies. The common thread of the verses he lists is forgiveness, primarily God's. While there is some proximity between tolerance and forgiveness, these are also two different concepts. Forgiveness presupposes a moral certainty which pits an unambiguous transgressor against somebody with a negative view of the transgression. It also tends to capture a sequence where transgression is followed by forgiveness, where tolerance typically describes an ongoing situation. Furthermore, tolerance can at least be inspired by our lack of certainty in ways that do not extend to forgiveness. Not everything that we tolerate qualifies as a transgression or an offense. Finally, the diversity of views which results from tolerance can be regarded as a value in and of itself, whereas what is forgiven is more unambiguously negative and harder to be considered such a value. Both may operate with a proposition that individuals merit forgiveness or tolerance since their value as humans is greater than their transgressions and a spirit of forgiveness may inspire tolerance, but the underlying moral arguments differ in too much nuance to gloss over and subsume tolerance under forgiveness.

Furthermore, a single example serves to illustrate that the "tolerance verses" offer a rather mixed picture. Abou El Fadl lists 5:13 among them. In Abdel Haleem's translation, the verse reads as follows: "But they broke their pledge, so We distanced them [from Us] and hardened their hearts. They distort the meaning of [revealed] words and have forgotten some of what they were told to remember: you [Prophet] will always find treachery in all but a few of them. Overlook this and pardon them: God loves those who do good." The verse illustrates several difficulties. If cited without context, as Qur'ānic passages in discussions about tolerance usually are, verses can be very hard to read. Here, it is only the preceding verse which tells us that the people who broke the pledge are Jews. Furthermore, the translator has chosen to add his own clarifications, indicated by the square brackets. In general, such clarifications are not always obvious or consensual. That the person addressed here by the divine speech is the Prophet Muḥammad is consensual, as is that the Jews are being criticized in this passage for having distorted revealed words rather than other words, or words in general. It is less clear, however, to what extent Muslims should adopt the recommended attitude as a general disposition, and even less clear what exactly this might mean in practice. The context offered by the Prophet's biographers is that he had initially won Jews over for his mission, at least as political associates. The relationship soured when the Jews did not accept him as prophet and three Jewish tribes in Medina were enslaved, expelled and killed (more about these events below). These events are a narrative microcosm of the macrocosm in Islamic salvation history where Muḥammad was not the first, but the last prophet of Islam. God had sent revelations to earlier prophets, starting with Adam, including Moses and Jesus, but their messages were eventually distorted by subsequent generations of their followers. The accusation of "distortion" (Arabic: *taḥrīf*), directed by Muslim polemicists against Jews and Christians, constitutes the theological and polemical context for the accusation of distorting words in verse 5:13 as well. The flipside of the accusation of distortion, however, is a shared scriptural heritage. Referring to the Qur'ānic and Muḥammad's qualified recognition of the scriptures of Jews and Christians, Albrecht Noth argued that it was for this reason that Jewish and Christian material was adopted into the Islamic tradition rather than rejected.[20] This case, the recognition of commonalities, is another example of a very low threshold for tolerance, but it does not meet the criterion applied in the present chapter which requires some objection against the object of tolerance.

Finally, the tolerance granted to these Jews is very conditional, to say the least. The phrase "We distanced them [from Us]" is often translated as "We cursed them" and adduced as evidence of Muslim anti-Judaism. Whatever forgiveness and lenience Muḥammad is instructed to extend in this verse, it hardly serves as an unambiguous and comprehensive case of both divine and human tolerance. What the verse does suggest is that, despite the gravity of the transgression — so serious that it incurs divine curse — Muslims are not authorized to punish the offenders. That is in accordance with many classical notions of tolerance, which hold that there may very well be negative consequences for the mistaken views of the tolerated person, but such consequences are not the responsibility or prerogative of the person who tolerates them. Rather, they take place in the afterlife. Then again, there is little to indicate that this verse recommends a high moral standard for tolerance that involves any appreciation of Jews as being different. The Christian appreciation of Jews as testimonies to the past and protagonists of the last days, albeit very problematic ones, does not have an equivalent in Islamic attitudes.[21] While Abou El Fadl thus significantly understated the complexity of the verses he lists, he is right to identify them as texts with relevance regarding the subject of tolerance. Other authors who refer to "tolerance verses" simply mean verses that address religious diversity without advocating violence.[22] That

---

[20] Noth, "Möglichkeiten und Grenzen islamischer Toleranz," 193.
[21] For the Christian attitudes referred to here cf. Szpiech, Ryan, *Conversion and Narrative. Reading and Religious Authority in Medieval Polemic*, Philadelphia: University of Pennsylvania Press, 2013. For Jewish life under Muslim rule cf. Cohen, Mark R., *Under Crescent and Cross. The Jews in the Middle Ages*, Princeton: Princeton University Press, 1994; Angeles Gallego, María/Bleaney, Heather/García Suárez, Pablo, *Bibliography of Jews in the Islamic World*, Leiden: Brill, 2010; Lassner, *Jews, Christians, and the Abode of Islam*.
[22] Ismail Acar uses the phrase "tolerance verses" in such a way. He does not necessarily discuss what tolerance is, but rather principles which inspire tolerance, which allows him to consider a

assumes that violence rather than indifference is the default response of Muslims to non-Muslims.

The determination of which Qur'ānic passages one considers relevant is of critical importance for any subject, as are the specific interpretations of these individual verses and the contexts in which one interprets them. One additional variable shall be highlighted here, which is the historical *Sitz im Leben* of Qur'ānic verses. Although the Qur'ān is believed to be the sum of God's revelations for Muḥammad it does not take the shape of a prophetic biography. The verses do not even appear in the sequence in which they were revealed but are instead arranged according to the length of the sura they belong to. Both sequence and circumstances of revelation are recorded in other parts of the Islamic tradition. Anecdotes which record the occasions of revelation (Arabic: *asbāb an-nuzūl*) for specific verses allowed exegetes to argue about the extent to which a given verse may be considered universal or particular and its applicability to different contexts. The chronological sequence of revelations also indicated where God may have "abrogated" a verse. Not all medieval Muslim scholars endorsed this principle of "abrogation" (Arabic: *naskh*) which resolved apparent tensions between different verses of the Qur'ān or also between the Qur'ān and prophetic traditions (other scholars chose to harmonize what they considered only seemingly contradictory revelations and applied them to different contexts). As far as the relationship between Muslims and non-Muslims is concerned, historically, many Muslim scholars argued that the "sword verse" (9:5) abrogated earlier verses which recommended a more peaceful or tolerant attitude towards religious diversity. As Patricia Crone has illustrated, scholars who read 2:256 as an unqualified acceptance of the beliefs and practices of non-Muslims also thought that it had been abrogated by more hostile and violent verses. Those who did not consider it abrogated read it in a more restrictive sense as a reference to a very specific group of people. For instance, the Andalusi Ibn Ḥazm (994–1064/384–456) interpreted the verses as a reference only to non-Muslims living during the time of Muḥammad.[23] There was disagreement in traditional scholarship about when exactly 2:256 was revealed, the options ranging from the Meccan period, when Muslims were the victims of persecution, to the late Medinan period, when they clearly prevailed politically and militarily in the Hijaz and were in a position to compel others.

---

larger body of material. ("Theological Foundations of Religious Tolerance in Islam," 304 and 311). Yaser Ellethy distinguishes between "pro-tolerance" and "anti-tolerance" verses, using these phrases to capture the degree to which these verses recommend "kindness and peaceful dealing" with non-Muslims. Cf. Ellethy, Yaser, *Islam, Context, Pluralism and Democracy. Classical and Modern Interpretations*, New York: Routledge, 2015, 117 and 296.
23 Crone, Patricia, "'No Compulsion in Religion'," 141.

Accordingly, the term "no compulsion" can be understood as a reference to Muslims under pressure to abandon their religion or to various non-Muslims who should not be forced to convert. Depending on the timing of the verse's revelation, it is possible that it could have been abrogated by some verses, but not others.

Apart from taking a stance on such chronological relationships, modern Muslim scholars sometimes prefer an entire period of revelation as encapsulating an essence of Islam. They might prefer the earlier period when Muḥammad was still only preaching in Mecca as the "purer" period when religious principles were unadulterated by political power, whereas others saw in the later, Medinan period the principles of an ideal community, guided by their prophet without the interference of oppressors.

In addition to what the Qur'ān states, authors sometimes adduce what the Qur'ān does not state and make an argument from silence. Khaled Abou El Fadl, for example, does not find any evidence that the Qur'ān endorses Islamic expansionism.[24] As much as it may be true for many contexts that absence of evidence is not evidence of absence, if we understand the Qur'ān to be a comprehensive guide for Muslims, the absence of extensive exhortations to obvious intolerance may be taken as a sign that such intolerance is indeed not religiously validated. As the above has shown, however, some interpreters have extrapolated such extensive exhortations from select passages.

A final word is in place regarding more recent efforts to use the Qur'ān as a historical source independent of the centuries-old tradition of commentary which still shapes many interpretations in the present day. Among others, such efforts are undertaken by modernist Muslim intellectuals who seek to reestablish a more liberal, emancipatory, rationalist or egalitarian message of Muḥammad. They are also presented by scholars with no stake in the Islamic tradition as believers, although they often endorse the traditional internal dating of the Qur'ān to some extent. While concluding that the actual meaning of 2:256 in the era of Muḥammad could no longer be identified with certainty, Crone drew parallels between the verse and somewhat earlier and contemporaneous Christian criticism of religious compulsion. Consequently, she employed the historical context to establish what the verse may have meant. The verse thus appears as another reflection of the late antique religio-political climate of the Eastern Mediterranean and Near East with the violent suppression of religious others, both internal and external, in the Byzantine and Sassanian empires. This argument possesses significance that extends beyond the historical context of the Qur'ān, as the parallels demonstrate the extent to which conventions of religious diversity in one region

---

24 Abou El Fadl, *The Place of Tolerance in Islam*, 19.

can influence neighboring territories, independent of predominant religious affiliation.

Other Western historians use the Qur'ān as a witness to its own time without resorting as much to external contemporaneous evidence as Patricia Crone did. Adopting the traditional Islamic view of Muḥammad's biography, Rudi Paret cites several Qur'ānic verses to argue that especially in the early days Muḥammad was tolerant of Jews and Christians, but that he was intolerant towards polytheists.[25] In Paret's reconstruction, the prophet's attitudes to other religious communities was inspired by a combination of good will, resignation and disappointment, as well as strategic pragmatism. Verses 15:85 and 43:89, for example, are quoted to the effect that Muḥammad should be lenient towards the polytheists, but that they will be punished in the hereafter. In 43:89, Muḥammad is instructed to "turn away" from people he has recognized as unbelievers. "Say 'Peace': they will come to know." Intolerance only prevailed for defensive purposes, a view shared by several interpreters throughout Islamic history, as Crone has illustrated. Noth extended the explanatory force of history for the meaning of the Qur'ān into later periods. He assumed that the fact that the Arab-Muslim conquerors of the mid-seventh century did not systematically force all non-Muslims to convert to Islam reflected an original meaning and understanding of 2:256.

4 Prophetic Traditions

While the Qur'ān is considered the word of God, the Islamic—especially the Sunni tradition, recognizes a second source of revelation: the model of the Prophet Muḥammad as recorded in the so-called prophetic traditions (Arabic sing.: ḥadīth). These texts, which record actions and sayings of the Prophet, supplement Muḥammad's role as the primary recipient and transmitter of the Qur'ān. Since classical times, however, these traditions involved problems of certainty which did not affect the Qur'ān. In her study of the status of ḥadīth as scripture, Aisha Musa distinguishes between debates about authenticity and authority.[26] It was only in the eighth/ninth century CE that Muslim scholars compiled these tra-

---

25 Paret, Rudi, "Toleranz und Intoleranz im Islam," *Saeculum* 21 (1970), 344–65. For Muḥammad's criticism of polytheism, Paret lists 4:48, 4:116, 31:13, 7:71, 10:28f., 12:40, 53:23. 29:46 is quoted as sample affirmation that Jews, Christians and Muslims all believe in the one God. In 5:82, however, Christians are described as closer to Muslims than Jews or polytheists. Paret also surveys many references to Abraham and other Biblical characters.
26 Musa, Aisha Y., *Ḥadīth as Scripture. Discussions on the Authority of the Prophetic Traditions in Islam*, Basingstoke: Palgrave Macmillan, 2015.

ditions after they had examined them for authenticity. A "chain of transmitters" (Arabic: *isnād*) was meant to guarantee seamless preservation from the time of the Prophet himself to the time the report was committed to writing. During the classical period, these methods of verification were highly controversial. Rationalist theologians and legal scholars sometimes argued that since individual transmitters may very well have made mistakes, evaluating the *isnād* was ultimately an inadequate method of verifying the authenticity of *ḥadīths*. They rather insisted that an examination of the contents of the tradition, the actual text (Arabic: *matn*), provided the necessary certainty. Either way, scholars often made a distinction between matters of theology and the practical application of the law. On some level, the latter required a lower degree of certainty than the former. Scholars freely admitted the possibility of human error in legal judgment and made provisions accordingly. This is important for the present purposes since it illustrates that from the formative period of systematic Islamic law onward scholars allowed for a degree of uncertainty and ambiguity in their interpretation of religious regulations. Like other laws, those dealing with religious diversity are affected by such attitudes, but these attitudes are themselves expressions of a certain tolerance insofar as they grant objectionable legal interpretations the possibility of correctness. This acknowledgment of diversity in Islamic law will be discussed in further detail below.

Judging from recent discussions of Islamic notions of tolerance in general terms, the Qur'ān appears to be the more prominent reference point than prophetic traditions.[27] This might be somewhat surprising given that human relationships are often modeled after Muḥammad's ideal conduct. That "Islamic tolerance" is often framed as an issue of interreligious affairs and that it is so often associated with human freedom to believe or not to believe seems to be critical for this balance between the two sources, since both are important topics in the Qur'ān, as is the fact that the Qur'ān offers very succinct statements which are both relevant and open to a variety of interpretations.

There is no prophetic tradition as emblematic as 2:256. And yet, Muḥammad is credited with many statements on both religious alterity and personal conduct which are pertinent in the context of tolerance. Three areas might be singled out here. Among traditions frequently cited in the larger context of tolerance as a gen-

---

[27] Conventional surveys of Islamic attitudes to a given subject typically start with the Qur'ān, proceed with prophetic traditions and continue with the different intellectual traditions such as law, theology, philosophy and mysticism. This structure is chosen in the present chapter as well. Among scholars who have recently published survey articles on tolerance in Islamic contexts, Asma Afsaruddin devotes a long section to the Qur'ān, but no separate section to prophetic traditions. There is a similar balance in Stephan Kokew's publications listed in footnote 5.

eral ethical principle are those where Muḥammad recommends *tasāmuḥ* — the Arabic word currently translated as "tolerance" — as a general way of achieving peace among people.[28] In a similar spirit, the Islamic tradition contains a wealth of such recommendations of mildness, compromise and forgiveness which may not speak to any theoretical notion of tolerance, but support the overarching ethical incentive for tolerance as a condition of peace. In his survey of Arabic and Persian terminology related to tolerance, Stephan Kokew identified a similar field of values which have deep roots in the Islamic tradition.[29] In addition to *tasāmuḥ*, which might imply the intention of conciliation, he lists *ṣabr* (close to the Christian concept of *patientia*, this term suggests more passivity than modern notions of tolerance), the equally passive *taḥammul* (bearing or enduring) and *tasāhul* (mutual easy and generous treatment) among Arabic terms and *modārā* (a sense of magnanimity) and *shakībā'ī* (patience) among prominent Persian words (interestingly, the Persian terms derived from Arabic sometimes change connotations. Kokew describes the Arabic *tasāmuḥ* in Persian adaptation as negative). Cumulatively, these terms and underlying concepts and values suggest an ethically nuanced notion of tolerance as an individual disposition. While the selection of terms acknowledges the discomfort experienced by the person who tolerates, they also imply that this person exercises tolerance out of their own choice. There is a communal dimension to some of these words too. Both *tasāmuḥ* and *tasāhul* belong to a morphological type in Arabic which implies mutuality. To reconstruct a prophetic model of tolerance, other virtues such as forgiveness might thus be added. The second example where a prophetic tradition is critical for notions of tolerance is that Muḥammad is credited with an appreciation of a diversity of opinions (Arabic: *ikhtilāf*) within his community, which he called a blessing. We will return to the subject of diversity in the section about Islamic law where this became most relevant.

The reverse exercise, of course, was conducted as well. Muḥammad is also reported to have said that his community would divide into seventy-three groups, only one of which would be saved. Given the vast number of prophetic traditions, one can just as easily select examples which portray Muḥammad as much a model of intolerance as of tolerance. A case in point is our third example, which is that advocates of the death penalty for Muslims who abandon their religion often refer to a *ḥadīth* in which Muḥammad stated, "Whoever changes his religion, kill him." The statement is included in the collection of al-Bukhārī (810–870/194–256), one

---

28 Schulze, "Der Islam und die Toleranz", 56.
29 Cf. Kokew's publications listed in footnote 5 and Hartmann, "Pluralismus und Toleranz aus der Sicht des Islam," 128–29.

of six canonical collections in Sunni Islam.[30] What exactly this instruction entails is controversial. As followers of a proselytizing religions, it makes little sense for Muslims to kill those who change their religion *to* Islam. The common understanding of "religion" in this context pertains to the notion of "true religion", understood to mean Islam.[31]

Independent of the specific selection of prophetic traditions, any use of *ḥadīth* involves several hermeneutical issues which determine how one selects them and how they are employed. As mentioned above, medieval Muslim scholars disagreed about issues related to the authenticity of *ḥadīth*s. A similar range of disagreements affected the authority of these traditions. Scholars disagreed about methods of evaluating traditions, principles of certainty, the resulting body of authoritative texts, methods of interpretation, and the doctrines which could be extrapolated from these traditions. This is a common pattern in Islamic intellectual history where hermeneutics and doctrine, method and outcome of interpretation, are often deeply entangled and it is hard to decide whether scholars preferred certain methods because they led to the results they favored or whether they were primarily invested in these methods. This is especially true of passages from the Qur'ān or prophetic traditions cited in support of certain hermeneutic principles. A rationalist might use rationalist methods to argue for the authority of a text which speaks to the superiority of rationalist methods, for example. A literalist might do the same and so might a scholar who prefers allegorical interpretations. These variables account for the variety of views relevant for any Islamic notion of tolerance—but also for the difficulty of identifying the decisive variable.

Modern historians of early Islam tend to be somewhat more skeptical about the authenticity of prophetic traditions, just as much of the Islamic tradition that purports to explain the circumstances of the Qur'ānic revelation is increasingly seen as a product of later times. Since the late 1970s, a variety of theories have emerged to explain the origins of these traditions in the legal and to some extent theological scholarship of the subsequent two centuries.[32] It was only when the authority of prophetical traditions had been irreversibly established, and scholars

---

[30] Cf. also Philpott, Daniel, *Religious Freedom in Islam. The Fate of a Universal Human Right in the Muslim World Today*, Oxford: Oxford University Press, 2019, 181.
[31] Cf. also for this Saeed, Abdullah/Saeed, Hassan, *Freedom of Religion, Apostasy and Islam*, Aldershot: Ashgate, 2005; Schirrmacher, Christine, *"Let There Be No Compulsion in Religion" (Sura 2:256). Apostasy from Islam as Judged by Contemporary Islamic Theologians. Discourses on Apostasy, Religious Freedom, and Human Rights*, Eugene: Wipf & Stock, 2016.
[32] For an introduction cf. Brown, Jonathan A. C., *Hadith. Muhammad's Legacy in the Medieval and Modern World*, London: Oneworld, 2018² and Brown, Daniel W. (ed.), *The Wiley Blackwell Concise Companion to the Hadith*, Chichester: Wiley Blackwell, 2020.

capitalized on their expertise in this area that these texts were systematically recorded. Thus, as much as traditions tell us about their function in the ninth century, they do not provide the necessary certainty to serve as reliable sources for the time of the Prophet. Similar concerns apply to biographies of the Prophet.[33] This is critical for our context since Muslims of the eighth and ninth centuries wrote against the backdrop of religiously diverse empires with evolving models of political leadership and sectarian conflicts which constituted a very different environment than the proto state of the early Muslims.

Apart from the Qur'ān, which appears more securely dated than the prophetic traditions, historians can resort to other sources of Muḥammad's time for impressions of this period, notably the so-called *Constitution of Medina*.[34] According to the Islamic tradition, this document marked the alliance forged between the Prophet's followers, the "believers," who had emigrated from Mecca to Medina, and local Medinans, both Jews and "believers." It represented a pact of mutual military solidarity which maintained some autonomy of the participating groups. Insofar as the *Constitution of Medina* tells us of Muḥammad's choices it has been interpreted as an ideal model of a religiously diverse community under Muslim rule. But two important caveats remain. First, even within the Islamic tradition, this is not the full story of Muḥammad's interactions with Jewish communities, as discussed above. The *Constitution of Medina* can just as easily be read as a snapshot of a relationship in flux, of initial collaboration which did not prevail. Having said that, a survey of the conditions of Jewish life under Muslim rule in subsequent centuries suggests that if either the *Constitution* or the fallout with the three Jewish tribes was chosen as a paradigm, it was more the *Constitution* than the fallout which served as a model. The second caveat concerns the uncertainties surrounding early Islamic history and the nature of the early Muslim community. The *Constitution of Medina* suggests that a difference was made between "believers," that is proto-Muslims, and Jews, but how exactly these constituencies and their relationship were understood remains unclear and may very well have varied among the different protagonists. Finally, the conceptual problem remains: religious diversity, on its own, is not necessarily a sign of tolerance, even if it does not point to systematic and comprehensive intolerance. Likewise, the motivation to maintain such diversity may very well have been entirely pragmatic.

---

33 Peters, Francis E., *Muhammad and the Origins of Islam*, Albany: State University of New York Press, 1994; Motzki, Harald (ed.), *The Biography of Muhammad. The Issue of the Sources*, Leiden: Brill, 2000; Schoeler, Gregor, *The Biography of Muḥammad. Nature and Authenticity*, Milton Park: Routledge, 2011; Ali, Kecia, *The Lives of Muhammad*, Cambridge: Harvard University Press, 2014.
34 Lecker, Michael, *The "Constitution of Medina": Muhammad's First Legal Document*, Princeton: Darwin Press, 2004.

We encounter a similar situation with the contracts of the subsequent conquest period analyzed by Noth. Because the Arab-Muslim conquests of the seventh century, immediately after Muḥammad's death, often took the form of surrender, the contracts record conditions for peaceful takeover of power and Muslim rule over non-Muslims. They became normative for the treatment of non-Muslims in general and reflect the pragmatic interest of Muslim conquerors and rulers to govern a tax-paying population. Indeed, the fact that the Muslim conquerors did not systematically force non-Muslims to convert has been explained as reflecting their economic interest in the continuing payment of the *jizya*. However, it may just as well betray an early understanding of Islam as a kinship religion of Arabs. The fact that non-Arab converts to Islam had to be "adopted" into an Arab tribe supports the assumption that such a concept of Islam may have prevailed in the first decades of Islamic history.

5 Islamic law

As indicated above, Islamic law is relevant here in two key respects. It prescribed tolerant attitudes to diverse religious views and practices—especially those deemed objectionable—and the people who held them. Islamic law served itself as a platform for elaborating, theorizing and debating such principles of fruitful disagreement. While the first point speaks to interreligious tolerance, the latter illustrates intrareligious tolerance.

Islamic law regulates the relationship between Muslims and non-Muslims by identifying normative statements and extrapolating rules and thus formalizes the extent of tolerance. The Qur'ān and *ḥadīth* serve as its primary written sources. Just as in the case of Qur'ānic references to religious diversity, the very fact that relationships between Muslims and non-Muslims are regulated in Islamic law has been taken as a sign of tolerance. This applies especially to communities which were acknowledged as "People of the Book," that is, people with a textual or verbal revelation. Designated as *dhimmīs*, they were permitted to practice their religions with certain restrictions and were obliged to pay the *jizya*. Abou El Fadl highlights this tax as an example which illustrates that religious diversity was meant to endure under Muslim rule.[35] Detailed provisions are also recorded in surrender documents composed during the conquest period as well as in the canonized version, the *Pact of 'Umar*, so named after the caliph 'Umar (reg. 634–644/13–23), though the preserved version is of later origin. On the

---

35 Abou El Fadl, *The Place of Tolerance in Islam*, 21.

other hand, Milka Levy-Rubin has conducted extensive research into these sources and demonstrated that their prehistory in fact reaches back into the ancient Near East.[36] This reinforces the argument emphasized throughout this chapter that religiously validated policies of tolerance or intolerance in Islamic history are entangled with similar policies that non-Muslims signed responsible for. Significantly, Levy-Rubin emphasizes the active role of the surrendering population in composing these documents. It was only in the ninth century, under Abbasid rule, that the various agreements were harmonized and canonized in the more restrictive document which constitutes the *Pact of 'Umar*. Much like other expressions of governance in the early Islamic empire, the *Pact* adapted Byzantine regulations regarding non-Christians as well as Persian laws that clearly distinguished the ruling Zoroastrian elites from religious minorities.[37]

These documents illustrate that non-Muslims, excluding Arab polytheists were allowed to continue practicing their religion under Muslim rule. This fact alone is oftentimes presented as evidence of Islamic tolerance, whereas critics of this argument point out that non-Muslims did not enjoy the same degree of religious freedom enjoyed by Muslims. These two positions are hard to reconcile since they reflect different definitions, expectations, and standards of tolerance. Regardless of how these practices compare to modern conceptions, the restrictions imposed on religious practice — particularly those related to public exhibitions, which might be interpreted as a promotion of the religion — along with the embedded socio-political hierarchy, may, in fact, reflect a context shaped more by tolerance than indifference. They are expressions of objection, although not necessarily of a desire for homogeneity.

As the section on the Qur'ān suggested, there are two religious communities in particular that, as "People of the Book," enjoyed Islamic tolerance on doctrinal grounds: Jews and Christians. It is therefore unsurprising that these two groups came to represent religious tolerance under Islamic rule. In studies about the relationship between Islam and other religions in Western European languages, they are also the two most prominently discussed religions. Historical and indeed contemporary realities, however, are different. Very early in its history, Islam spread into regions where Christianity and Judaism did not constitute a significant presence. Zoroastrianism (Arabic: *Majūsīya*), likewise widely acknowledged as a religion of the book, served as a model to classify communities and individuals

---

[36] Levy-Rubin, Milka, *Non-Muslims in the Early Islamic Empire. From Surrender to Coexistence*, Cambridge: Cambridge University Press, 2011.

[37] For the latter cf. Levy-Rubin, Milka, "'Umar II's *ghiyār* Edict: Between Ideology and Practice," in: Antoine Borrut/Fred Donner (eds.), *Christians and Others in the Early Umayyad State*, 157–72, Chicago: Oriental Institute of the University of Chicago, 2016.

we have come to call Hindus as well as to describe people in sub-Saharan west Africa.[38] This was a legal as much as an ethnographic exercise. Muslim travelers and geographers wrote about religious rituals involving fire which may have been reminiscent of Zoroastrianism, but perhaps more importantly, the legal scholar ʿAbd ar-Raḥmān al-Awzāʿī (707–774/88–157) argued that anybody who did not belong to the "People of the Book" should be classified as *Majūs* and hence enjoy the privileges of the *dhimma* pact.[39] As critical as Judaism and Christianity have been theologically and historically for Islamic attitudes to religious diversity, tolerant or otherwise, it would be desirable for future scholarship to expand its scope to take other religious communities more fully into consideration. Examples of Islamic tolerance and intolerance are often cited from South and Southeast Asia, yet they remain underrepresented in broader surveys. Assessments of religious diversity under Islamic rule often focus on theological proximity as a condition for coexistence as well as a source of conflict. We will only get a better sense of the significance of shared traditions with greater comparative possibilities. As much as the privileges for the "People of the Book" in Islamic law suggest a more amicable relationship than with those who did not share this scriptural tradition, the Iraqi writer al-Jāḥiẓ (776–869/159–255) points out in his treatise about Christianity that "man indeed hates the one whom he knows, turns against the one whom he sees, opposes the one whom he resembles, and becomes observant of the faults of those with whom he mingles; the greater the love and intimacy, the greater the hatred and estrangement."[40]

Islamic law also allows insights into the regulations of conflicts between individuals in matters beyond religious alterity and doctrinal certainty—namely, personal behavior. Legal judgments, or *fatwas*, offer valuable insights into the balance Islamic legal scholars sought to strike between one person's freedom to act and another person's right to be protected from harm. Building regulations are particularly revealing, as proximity often gives rise to conflict. By defining what an individual was allowed to do we get a clear sense of the tolerance another individual, typically a neighbor, was required to extend. At least in Maliki law as

---

[38] Friedmann, Yohanan, "Classification of Unbelievers in Sunni Muslim Law and Tradition," *Jerusalem Studies in Arabic and Islam* 22 (1998), 163–95. Friedmann illustrates that early Muslim scholars considered genealogy critical to collective religious identity. For sub-Saharan Africa cf. Akasoy, Anna, "Paganism and Islam. Medieval Arabic Literature on Religions in West Africa," in: John Marenbon/Carlos Steel/Werner Verbeke (eds.), *Paganism in the Middle Ages. Threat and Fascination*, 207–38, Leuven: Leuven University Press, 2012.
[39] Friedmann, "Classification of Unbelievers," 166.
[40] Finkel, Joshua, "A Risāla of al-Jāḥiẓ," *Journal of the American Oriental Society* 47 (1927), 311–34, 323.

practiced in medieval North Africa, which modern scholarship has examined, individuals had wide-ranging rights, unless others suffered an unambiguous harm, for example damage to their own building.[41] Although unrelated to doctrinal disagreement, it nonetheless enriches our understanding of tolerance as an interpersonal principle.

Turning to the quality of Islamic law as an area of intrareligious tolerance in the case of conflicting truth claims, the practice and theory of Islamic law itself provide examples of tolerance — if tolerance is understood as the emphatic acceptance of divergent opinions. In the Arabic Islamic tradition, disagreement as a concept or principle is called *ikhtilāf* (see above). In Islamic law, it served as a technical term for variations in legal opinion. The appetite for such disagreements was not always equally great. While some historical contexts saw a rise of literalism and a preference for single interpretations, variety seems to have been preferred at other times. In the Almohad caliphate, for example, the subject of *ikhtilāf* appears to have been particularly prominent, especially the matter of the one truth which can be described in different ways. Ibn Rushd (1126–1198/ 520–595), expert in law, theology and philosophy alike, wrote on the subject, as did the Jewish scholar Maimonides (1138–1204), who may have picked up other legal concepts and debates from his Muslim peers at the time.[42] The Almohads' tolerance for divergent views of Islam, however, was limited, as will be discussed below.

Ikhtilāf is connected to another important hermeneutical concept in Islamic law, in Arabic *ijtihād*, the individual effort of a scholar to reach an accurate conclusion.[43] Such efforts were considered valid even when the conclusions proved incorrect, as is inevitably the case when the human mind is in operation. This principle reflects the classical Islamic emphasis on a believer's intention.[44] The room granted to this tool of establishing the law differs significantly between the individual legal schools and has gained support among rationalist and modernist thinkers, though not exclusively. There are certain conditions for this instrument. A *mujtahid*, that is, someone who practices *ijtihād*, requires the necessary

---

41 Kahera, Akel I./Benmira, Omar, "Damages in Islamic Law. Maghribī Muftīs and the Built Environment (9th–15th C.E.)," *Islamic Law and Society* 5 (1998), 131–64.
42 Stroumsa, Sarah, *Maimondes in his World. Portrait of a Mediterranean Thinker*, Princeton: Princeton University Press, 2009, 61–70.
43 For an extensive study in the context of tolerance cf. Poya, Abbas, *Anerkennung des Iğtihād – Legitimation der Toleranz. Möglichkeiten innerer und äußerer Toleranz im Islam am Beispiel der Iğtihād-Diskussion*, Berlin: Schwarz, 2003.
44 Powers, Paul R., *Intent in Islamic Law. Motive and Meaning in Medieval Sunnī Fiqh*, Leiden: Brill, 2006.

training and needs to make an honest effort. The results of this effort are affirmed in the principle *kull mujtahid muṣīb* — "every *mujtahid* is right" (Arabic: *taṣwīb*).⁴⁵

The idea that conflicting legal judgments could coexist was not merely theoretical. Two examples illustrate its significance. Islamic legal schools differ on various levels, with sectarian affiliation being just one factor. They were inspired by different scholars who typically served as their eponyms. They prioritized different hermeneutical principles and dealt differently with the various source texts of Islamic law. They also varied in how much weight they gave to sources like local customs. But they also differed in regional presence and sometimes became involved with ideologies and claims for legitimacy of individual dynasties. In the tenth century, for example, the Umayyads on the Iberian Peninsula used their support for the Maliki school of law to bolster their claims for authority. Remarkably, the geographer al-Muqaddasī (945–1000/333–390) stated about al-Andalus that "The Muslims here declare: 'We know nothing but the Book of God and the *Muwaṭṭa'* [*The Beaten Path* — a book of legal maxims taken from the Traditions, and the basis of Mālik's system of jurisprudence] of Mālik.' Should they detect a Hanafite or a Shāfi'ite they expel him; but if they light upon a Mu'tazilite or a Shī'a or anyone heterodox such as these, they may kill him."⁴⁶ (al-Muqaddasī may have exaggerated the degree of oppression.) While some regions of the Islamic world such as al-Andalus were clearly dominated by a single school, others were mixed. This was especially the case for Syria and Egypt which were located at the crossroads of different larger regions of the Islamic world. Since the Fatimid period, rulers in these legally diverse regions appointed judges from different Islamic communities. The tradition endured in later centuries after Fatimid rule was replaced by Sunni dynasties. This plurality of legal doctrines and opinions became institutionalized. Yossef Rapoport's work illustrates how this played out in practice, showing that when it came to divorce, Muslims selected legal scholars of certain legal schools to obtain a judgment most favorable to them.⁴⁷

---

45 For criticism of this principal cf. Fierro, Maribel, "The Legal Policies of the Almohad Caliphs and Ibn Rushd's *Bidāyat al-Mujtahid*," *Journal of Islamic Studies* 10/3 (1999), 226–48. Bernard Haykel relates the principle to tolerance: Haykel, Bernard, "Reforming Islam by Dissolving the Madhāhib: Shawkānī and his Zaydī Detractors in Yemen," in: Bernard G. Weiss (ed.), *Studies in Islamic Legal Theory*, 337–64, Leiden: Brill, 2002.

46 For the Umayyad strategy cf. Fierro, Maribel, *'Abd al-Rahman III. The First Cordoban Caliph*, Oxford: Oneworld, 2005. For al-Muqaddasī cf. *The Best Divisions for Knowledge of the Regions (Aḥsan al-Taqāsīm fī Ma'rifat al-Aqālīm)*, trans. Basil Collins, Reading: Garnet, 2001, 195.

47 Rapoport, Yossef, *Marriage, Money and Divorce in Medieval Islamic Society*, Cambridge: Cambridge University Press, 2005, 8–9 and note 28 on Ottoman parallels.

The variety of coexisting legal opinions in Islamic history can be astounding and frequently frustrates those who are looking for straightforward and unambiguous answers to the question what "Islam" has to say about this or that subject. To illustrate the shortcomings of such expectations, Thomas Bauer has extensively eplored this ambiguity which has long been embedded in Islamic thought and culture.[48] The religious validation of *ikhtilāf* is critical evidence of what Bauer describes as a high tolerance for ambiguity. However, not everything was permitted. The binaries present in the Qurʾān are mirrored in subsequent Islamic thought, law, theology and philosophy. While scholars defined what was right and permissible, they also outlined its limits.

6 Islamic Theology and Philosophy

The relationship between attitudes towards certainty, doubt and doctrinal disagreement in Islamic law extends to Islamic intellectual history in general. This is hardly surprising, as Muslim scholars distinguished in theology or philosophy were often trained in the legal sciences. Furthermore, these disciplines were interwoven to the extent that they sometimes addressed similar problems, but especially because they operated with similar sources and were concerned with similar hermeneutic challenges. Hermeneutic preferences in law often reflect a scholar's broader intellectual dispositions. Rationalists in law were more likely to engage with theology, while legal literalists might regard theological inquiries into the relationship between God and creation as insufficient in capturing divine realities.[49] Philosophers sometimes regarded legal scholars and theologians with disdain. al-Fārābī (c. 870–950/256–338) famously viewed revelation and the associated sciences as essential for the masses.

Since theologians and philosophers did not directly address religious tolerance, their views must be inferred from other debates they engaged in. Two topics

---

48 Bauer, Thomas, *Die Kultur der Ambiguität. Eine andere Geschichte des Islams*, Berlin: Verlag der Weltreligionen, 2011. Bauer's historical argument that this tolerance has been declining since the mid-nineteenth century remains more controversial than his point about the diversity that permeates Islamic history and culture. Cf. also Griffel, Frank, *Den Islam denken. Versuch, eine Religion zu verstehen*, Stuttgart: Reclam, 2019, 60–76.
49 In the context of Islam, "theology" conventionally designates a specific form of intellectual engagements with the divine and divinely created reality, the phrase "discursive" or "dialectical" theology reflecting the rationalist inflection of this tradition. If understood more generically, "theology" in Islamic history is more diverse. Likewise, "philosophy" is conventionally used to refer to a tradition of thought informed by Aristotelian and Neoplatonic literature.

of great interest to theologians, closely tied to Qur'ānic verses often cited in discussions about tolerance, are free will and the nature of faith. Where medieval Muslim scholars positioned themselves regarding these issues determined whether they participated in the exercise of dialectical theology (*kalām*) at all, and if they did, which school they became affiliated with. There are three main schools: Mu'tazilites, Ash'arites and Māturīdis. The first to emerge were the Mu'tazilites, who flourished in Basra and Baghdad from the mid-eighth to the eleventh century. The school developed at a time when Muslim sectarian identities were still in flux and shows a certain proximity to Shi'ism without being a Shi'ite sect. Recent publications have also shed light on the lasting legacies of Mu'tazilism among the Muslim communities of Ibadism and Zaydism and the Jewish theological school of the Karaites. In addition to confronting the traditionalists—scholars whose authority rested on mastering *ḥadīth*, typically interpreted literally—the Mu'tazilites distinguished themselves by five doctrinal principles: divine unity, divine justice, promise and threat regarding the afterlife, the intermediate status of the grave sinner in between believer und unbeliever, and the commanding of good and prohibiting of evil. al-Ash'arī (874–936/260–324), the eponym of the Ash'arī school of theology, had been a Mu'tazilite himself. Ash'arites tend to be more reluctant in assigning human reason the ability to approach the divine reality. The Ash'arī school became the predominant theological branch in the Middle East, while Māturidism — sometimes viewed as a middle ground between Mu'tazilism and Ash'arism — gained influence in Central Asia and among Turkic scholars. Wael Hallaq described the period which began with rising predominance of Ash'arism as the "great rationalist traditionalist synthesis."[50]

In the context of tolerance, it is crucial to note that the Mu'tazilites considered free will a central doctrinal tenet.[51] To their minds, given the reality of both God's justice and retribution in the afterlife, free will was the only logical option. Applied to the Qur'ānic passages mentioned above, this argument is significant in at least two ways: firstly, the verses can be read as speaking primarily to the subject of free will and faith rather than to the way believers should treat religious others. Interpreted in this way, the verses are less relevant to discussions of interreligious tolerance. Secondly, as much as they suggest that religious diversity is the

---

[50] Hallaq, Wael B., *The Origins and Evolution of Islamic Law*, Cambridge: Cambridge University Press, 2005, 122–28.
[51] For notions of human freedom in *kalām* cf. El Kaisy-Friemuth, "The Concept of Freedom", 107–12. For a general survey cf. Ess, Josef van, *Theology and Society in the Second and Third Centuries of the Hijra*, vol. 4, *A History of Religious Thought in Early Islam*, Leiden: Brill, 2017–2019.

result of God's plan, the proposition that humans have free will assigns some agency and hence responsibility to those who reject Muḥammad's message.

In recent times, Yusuf Islam, likely writing primarily for a Western audience, has combined the concept of God's justice with the call for Muslims to practice tolerance toward non-Muslims. "God loves justice and those who strive to practice it, especially toward people who are different from them in any way, including in matters of religious belief."[52] The Qur'ānic passages Stevens refers to read "You who believe, be steadfast in your devotion to God and bear witness impartially: do not let hatred of others lead you away from justice, but adhere to justice, for that is closer to awareness of God. Be mindful of God: God is well aware of all that you do." (5:8) and "[...] and He does not forbid you to deal kindly and justly with anyone who has not fought you for your faith or driven you out of your homes: God loves the just." (60:8) While both the Muʿtazilites and a modern, liberal and spiritualist Muslim like Stevens emphasize justice, what exactly justice means in practice can differ.

The theological principle of divine justice is closely connected to the reality of human fallibility, especially in connection with the human obligation to apprehend the truth. Some scholars have emphasized that the best way to accomplish this is to use our God-given rational faculty, imperfect as it may be. In his *Decisive Treatise*, Ibn Rushd distinguished metaphysical from practical questions about the certainty rational explorations could achieve. Metaphysical, difficult questions should only be tackled by those with the required education — Ibn Rushd refers to them as the "demonstrative class" since these scholars master the highest form of evidence, the "demonstrative proof." The following considerations sum up several of his distinctions:

> Texts of Scripture fall into three kinds with respect to the excusability of error. [1] Texts that must be taken in their apparent meaning by everyone. Since the meaning can be understood plainly by demonstrative, dialectical, and rhetorical methods alike, no one is excused for the error of interpreting these texts allegorically. [2] Texts that must be taken in their apparent meaning by the lower classes and interpreted allegorically by the demonstrative class. It is inexcusable for the lower classes to interpret them allegorically or for the demonstrative class to take them in their apparent meaning. [3] Texts whose classification under the previous headings is uncertain. Error in this matter by the demonstrative class is excused.[53]

As the above shows, Ibn Rushd holds everybody responsible according to their status in the socio-intellectual hierarchy. We are obliged to aim as high as we can,

---

52 Cf. note 14 above.
53 *Classical Arabic Philosophy. An Anthology of Sources*, trans. with introduction, notes, and glossary by Jon McGinnis/David C. Reisman, Indianapolis: Hackett, 2007, 319–20.

but not higher. The author offers a safety net for those who aim especially high — if they make mistakes, they are forgiven. Ibn Rushd's socio-intellectual elitism is a common feature of his period, as we have already seen with al-Fārābī, and presents a problem if we aim to read this as an expression of tolerance. The limitation of tolerance for mistakes to the elites does not sit well with modern advocates who tend to be egalitarians. Ibn Rushd has very little tolerance indeed for those who approach difficult matters without the right training. Once again, one of the thoughts expressed in this treatise can serve as an important precondition for tolerance, but it is not sufficient.

It is worth emphasizing that although Ibn Rushd has become mostly known for his expertise in philosophy, particularly in relation to Aristotle's works, he was also a distinguished legal scholar within the Maliki school of Islamic jurisprudence. As much as the *Decisive Treatise* relies on arguments that seem philosophical in nature, it is ultimately an answer to a legal question, i.e., whether Islamic law commands or prohibits the study of philosophy. In this sense, Ibn Rushd's treatise sits at the intersection of legal and philosophical discourse on tolerance.

Ibn Rushd is also known for his rebuttal of the earlier al-Ghazālī (1058–1111/ 450–555), legal scholar, philosopher, theologian and mystic, who had criticized the philosopher Ibn Sīnā (980–1037/370–428) for several of his convictions. Indeed, al-Ghazālī is one of the Muslim authors most frequently associated with the subject of tolerance. In his *Tahāfut al-falāsifa*, he condemned a range of views held by philosophers. It was only for endorsing three of these views, however, that according to al-Ghazālī, a Muslim could be declared an unbeliever: 1) that the world is eternal and uncreated in time, 2) that God only knows the universals, not the particulars, and 3) that a bodily resurrection does not take place.[54] In modern Western scholarship, al-Ghazālī became emblematic of a presumed Muslim intolerance towards philosophy to the extent that he was credited with ending this intellectual tradition altogether. This narrative has now undergone significant revision. Recent scholarship has explored al-Ghazālī's works more systematically, challenging the theory of a philosophical decline after Ibn Rushd's time.[55] If this shift in the as-

---

[54] Griffel, Frank, "Al-Ghazālī's (d. 1111) *Incoherence of the Philosophers*," in: Khaled El-Rouayheb/ Sabine Schmidtke (eds.), *The Oxford Handbook of Islamic Philosophy*, 191–209, Oxford: Oxford University Press, 2017.

[55] Griffel, Frank, *Apostasie und Toleranz im Islam. Die Entwicklung zu al-Ġazālīs Urteil gegen die Philosophie und die Reaktionen der Philosophen*, Leiden: Brill, 2000 and *Al-Ghazālī's Philosophical Theology*, Oxford: Oxford University Press, 2009. Cf. also ""[…] and the Killing of Someone who Upholds these Convictions is Obligatory!" Religious Law and the Assumed Disappearance of Philosophy in Islam," in: Andreas Speer/Guy Guldentops (eds.), *Das Gesetz – The Law – La Loi*, 214–26, Berlin: De Gruyter, 2014. For an English translation cf. also Jackson, Sherman A., *On the*

sessment of al-Ghazālī has affected his position in any history of Islamic tolerance at all, it has brought his example into sharper relief. Precisely the fact that he considered certain views wrong, but not sufficiently for those who hold them to qualify as disbelievers, can be considered an illustration of doctrinal tolerance in practice. That he argued against dismissing fellow Muslims too readily as unbelievers, and this in a context of great intrareligious violence makes a comparison with the religious wars of early modern Europe appropriate as well.

Apart from any debates they had with fellow Muslims, we can detect among both philosophers and theologians a certain interest in religions other than Islam. Indeed, the tradition of Islamic theology known as *kalām* may have emerged out of the religious debates between Christians and Muslims in early Abbasid Iraq. One theory of the origins of *kalām* presents it as an apologetic and polemical tradition in which discursive, rational methods provided a common tool of argumentation for members of different religions. Likewise, the analytical terms of ancient philosophy may have served as a universal language which allowed non-Muslim intellectuals to find a place in debates dominated, at least politically, by Muslims.[56] How significant these "foreign" traditions were for Islamic discursive theology remains controversial. But whatever the roots of *kalām*, its conceptual and technical terms, some of its practitioners were clearly interested in the beliefs of non-Muslims and determined to engage with them intellectually. The literary format of the religious dialogue in early Abbasid Iraq testifies to this disposition.[57]

Boundaries of Theological Tolerance in Islam. Abū Ḥāmid al-Ghazālī's Fayṣal al-Tafriqa, Oxford: Oxford University Press, 2002.

56 Along such lines cf. Watt, John W., "The Strategy of the Baghdad Philosophers. The Aristotelian Tradition as a Common Motif in Christian and Islamic Thought," in: J.J. van Ginkel et al (eds.), *Redefining Christian Identity. Cultural Interaction in the Middle East since the Rise of Islam*, 151–65, Leuven: Peeters, 2005. For theories concerning the origins of *kalām* and especially its roots in Christological debates cf. Schmidtke, Sabine (ed.), *The Oxford Handbook of Islamic Theology*, Oxford: Oxford University Press, 2016: Treiger, Alexander, "Origins of Kalām," 27–43, and Griffith, Sidney H., "Excursus I: Christian Theological Thought during the First ʿAbbāsid Century," 91–102.

57 Griffith, Sidney H., "The Monk in the Emir's Majlis. Reflections on a Popular Genre of Christian Literary Apologetics in Arabic in the Early Islamic Period," in: Hava Lazarus-Yafeh et al (eds.), *The Majlis. Interreligious Encounters in Medieval Islam*, 13–65, Wiesbaden: Harrassowitz, 1999, and *The Church in the Shadow of the Mosque. Christians and Muslims in the World of Islam*, Princeton: Princeton University Press, 2008. For an overview Thomas, David/Roggema, Barbara (eds.), *Christian-Muslim Relations. A Bibliographical History*, vol. 1 (600–900), Leiden: Brill, 2009 and the following volumes for later periods. Cf. also Janos, Damien (ed.), *Ideas in Motion in Baghdad and Beyond. Philosophical and Theological Exchanges between Christians and Muslims in the Third/Ninth and Fourth/Tenth Centuries*, Leiden: Brill, 2016.

The fact that Muslims refuted theological aspects of Christianity made their polemics to some degree a theological exercise as well.

The intellectual tradition known in Arabic as *falsafa*, "philosophy," emerged in a similar milieu of the Abbasid upper classes. It was more clearly inspired by Greek antecedents, which is obvious not only from the calque, but also because philosophers tended to engage with the works of Aristotle, Plato, Plotinus and others by way of Arabic translations. Fully aware of their cultural and religious alterity, medieval Muslim philosophers considered them great authorities. Is this a case of tolerance? The polytheism of Aristotle and other luminaries was nothing positive. They were imaginatively reworked into monotheists rather than celebrated for their belief in many deities. As al-Kindī (d. 873/ d. 259) argued in his *First Philosophy*, however, one should accept the truth wherever it came from, a phrase which can be easily recognized as a concession that these philosophical insights should be accepted not because of but despite their origins. His phrase suggests that al-Kindī is responding to opponents of *falsafa* because of its origins:

> We must not be ashamed to admire the truth or to acquire it, from wherever it comes. Even if it should come from far-flung nations and foreign peoples, there is for the student of truth nothing more important than the truth, nor is the truth demeaned or diminished by the one who states or conveys it; no one is demeaned by the truth, rather all are ennobled by it.[58]

Then again, cultural prestige is often connected to alterity and distance. The caliphs of Abbasid Baghdad valued scholarship and objects precisely because they came from far away.

These intellectual trends illustrate in one way or another a critical condition of tolerance: many authors put pen to paper because they deemed the tolerated views objectionable. It is reasonable to assume that *Mutakallimūn*, or practitioners of *kalām* who engaged in polemics, did not merely intend to allow others' views to remain unchallenged. They argued against them, at least on paper, since polemical texts are often primarily produced for internal audiences rather than the purported polemical targets. The fact that these theologians used weapons of logic may be seen as an acknowledgement of the other as a rational equal, but overall, never precluded the use of violence either. In public discourse, the binary of tolerance and intolerance is frequently correlated with another binary — that between rationalists, who appear to use the weapons of words and logic, and activists, who resort to violent means. Islamic history illustrates that while both

---

[58] For the quotation and a brief introduction to al-Kindī's philosophy Cf. Adamson, Peter, "Al-Kindi," in: *Stanford Encyclopedia of Philosophy*, https://plato.stanford.edu/entries/al-kindi/ (accessed online on 14 July 2024).

contrasts are in and of themselves more complicated, the association of tolerance with rationalism and intolerance with violence is even more problematic. To begin with the theologians, a prominent example is the Abbasid caliph al-Ma'mūn (reg. 813–833/197–218), the greatest champion of the Mu'tazilites, who also patronized philosophers. He forced Muslim scholars to accept the doctrine of the createdness of the Qur'ān, a hallmark of Mu'tazilite belief. Another example of violent rationalism is the already-mentioned Almohads who spread their doctrine in northwest Africa and the Iberian Peninsula in the twelfth and thirteenth centuries. The Almohads too patronized philosophy, notably the commentaries on Aristotle's works by Ibn Rushd, although the scholar fell out of favor later in his career.[59] The Almohads were also connected with Sufi movements who opposed the Almoravids whose rule preceded that of the Almohads (for the relationship between tolerance and Sufism, see below). In both examples, rationalism served to bolster the authority of a leader who, may have genuinely championed these views. These historical examples stand in contrast to representations of Islamic tolerance which emphasize the religion's rationalist and mystical branches as models.

Another, high-profile case may illustrate where such modern inclinations can be misleading. The multi-facetted scholar and polemicist Ibn Taymīya (1263–1328/661–728) is nowadays mostly known for his rigorous and militant vision of Islam. This impression is justified but can be complicated as well. Just in his written work, Ibn Taymīya polemicized extensively against beliefs and practices of other Muslims, from Ismailis to philosophers and Sufis of certain inclinations. He also targeted non-Muslims in his writings, notably Christians. He thus does not appear to have been a tolerant man, albeit one who invested in the power of words. Anecdotes also describe Ibn Taymīya as an activist who did not shy away from physical confrontations with fellow Muslims. It may thus come as a surprise that he assumed that the Prophet had only led defensive wars. The scholar who has become an icon of aggressive Islamism thus offers a rather mixed picture — critical of philosophers, he employed their own tools of rationalism and

---

[59] For this relationship cf. Dutton, Yasin, "The Introduction to Ibn Rushd's *Bidāyat al-Mujtahid*," *Islamic Law and Society* 1 (1994), 188–205; Fierro, "The Legal Policies of the Almohad Caliphs"; Akasoy, Anna, "Was Ibn Rushd an Averroist? The Problem, the Debate, and its Philosophical Implications," in: Anna Akasoy/Guido Giglioni (eds.), *Renaissance Averroism and its Aftermath*, 321–47, Dordrecht: Springer, 2013. For the two Berber movements and dynasties in general cf. Bennison, Amira K., *The Almoravid and Almohad Empires*, Edinburgh: Edinburgh University Press, 2016.

logic. Violent against others, he did not endorse doctrines of comprehensive military aggression.[60]

It was not only as a tool of political leaders that rationalism took on a militant shape. That people should be compelled to acknowledge the truth was not entirely alien to philosophical authors either. Like other writers under the influence of Aristotelian ethics, al-Fārābī regarded happiness as the ultimate human aim. Other authors framed this aim as salvation. To al-Fārābī, again along Aristotelian lines, happiness was the perfection of human nature. Since the distinctive feature of human nature is reason, the best way of achieving happiness and perfecting one's human nature was to be a philosopher. The ability to recognize the truth stands at the heart of philosophical activity, but like others too, al-Fārābī offered a holistic vision which entailed practical alongside theoretical, ethical and moral as much as epistemological components of the philosopher's lifestyle. Remarkably though, al-Fārābī also considered the obligation of the state to compel people to act in their own interest.[61] The philosopher was notably brief regarding the practical details of this compulsion to happiness. To modern readers, this may look like familiar and widely accepted policies of "nudging," but also brings more sinister options to mind like a dystopian tyranny of happiness. Other philosophers offered more pessimistic views of the state and its impact on the happiness of human beings. The Andalusi philosopher Ibn Bājja (d. 1138/d. 532), for example, spoke of "weeds" to describe the few individuals in a corrupt society who had superior knowledge.

The notion of a compulsion to salvation or happiness can be found more widely in Islamic history. The *amr bi-l-maʿrūf wa-n-nahy ʿan al-munkar* ("Commanding Right and Forbidding Wrong") is one of the most significant principles related to tolerance among Muslims.[62] It assumes an obligation on the part of Muslims to intervene if they see fellow Muslims not acting according to religious principle, such intervention benefitting both the potential sinner and those potentially affected by this person's actions. The principle often concerns matters of social ethics or etiquette, especially the consumption of alcohol, playing of music, clothing for women, or interactions across genders or religions. As Crone pointed out,

---

[60] Hoover, Jon, "Ibn Taymiyya Between Moderation and Radicalism," in: Elisabeth Kendall/ Ahmad Khan (eds.) *Reclaiming Islamic Tradition: Modern Interpretations of the Classical Heritage*, 177–203, Edinburgh: Edinburgh University Press, 2018; see also Vasalou, Sophia, *Ibn Taymiyya's Theological Ethics*, New York: Oxford University Press, 2016.
[61] Sweeney, Michael J., "Philosophy and *Jihād*: Al-Fārābī on Compulsion to Happiness," *The Review of Metaphysics* 60 (2007), 543–72.
[62] Cook, Michael, *Commanding Right and Forbidding Wrong in Islamic Thought*, Cambridge: Cambridge University Press, 2000.

traditional Muslim commentators very rarely connected the "no compulsion" principle with the *amr bi-l-ma'rūf*, typically reserving the former for interreligious matters and the latter for intrareligious issues.

The Almohads are but one striking example of doctrinally rigorous activism in Islamic history, rationalist or otherwise. Unlike the Abbasids, they condemned large numbers of Muslims as unbelievers which made it legitimate to kill and enslave them.[63] The practice of *takfīr*, that is to declare other Muslims unbelievers, goes back to the earliest days of Islamic sectarianism. The Kharijites emerged from the conflict surrounding the succession of Muḥammad. Unlike most Muslims, they assigned no significance to the ancestry of a political leader and put all emphasis on his piety. This demand for moral purity was extended to the entire community. The Kharijites became notorious for denying the status of believer to sinning Muslims and it is for this reason that modern militant Islamists are sometimes designated "neo-Kharijites." On the Shi'ite side, the Safavids may be mentioned as a movement and ultimately dynasty who imposed their beliefs on the local population they came to rule, both non-Muslim and Sunni. It was only under Safavid rule that the territory of modern-day Iran became majoritarian Shi'ite. Jewish authors such as Bābāī ibn Luṭf (d. after 1662) speak powerfully to the pressure exercised on his community.[64] This case is not unique in Islamic history, but it constitutes the exception rather than the rule. In the Safavid case, the backdrop for the violent oppression is at least in part the antagonism with the Ottoman Empire, which was under Sunni leadership. These cases demonstrate the pivotal role that political formations play in Islamic practices of tolerance, independent of and across particular doctrinal affiliations.

Muslim rationalists, whether philosophers or theologians, have long provided historical models for those advocating for a liberal and tolerant Islam. Such arguments have been made both within the Islamic community and outside of it. And yet, as the above examples have shown, these historical models involve their own complications. These provide a starting point for exploring the terms of discussions about Islamic tolerance in a critical manner, especially any assumptions shaped by viewing Western European history as the standard model for religious tolerance. Put differently, if we are interested in identifying traditions within Islamic history and culture that inspire tolerance, we should ask ourselves why it is

---

63 For the latter cf. Empey, Heather J., "The Mothers of the Caliph's Sons. Women as Spoils of War during the Early Almohad Period," in: Matthew S. Gordon/Kathryn A. Hain (eds.), *Concubines and Courtesans. Women and Slavery in Islamic History*, 143–62, Oxford: Oxford University Press, 2017.

64 *In Queen Esther's Garden. An Anthology of Judeo-Persian Literature*, trans. with an introduction and notes by Vera Basch Moreen, New Haven: Yale University Press, 2000, 223–32.

these traditions we have selected and whether our selection may rest on skewed expectations.

In his analysis of contemporary representations of Islam, Andrew Shryock recognized a character he labeled the "good Muslim."[65] This discursive figure is culturally distinct but embodies what are commonly claimed to be "Western" values, those that also commonly considered products of historical periods, notably the Enlightenment. This discursive figure has a long-standing presence in Western European perceptions of Islamic tolerance, dating back several centuries. As Frank Griffel has demonstrated, the French philosopher Jean Bodin (1530–1596) used the example of the contemporaneous Ottoman and Safavid empires to make a case for tolerance.[66] Griffel suggests that in addition to Western European travel reports, translations of Arabic philosophical and theological texts may have provided Bodin with a vague notion of how some Muslim authors dealt with religious diversity. His representation may thus have been more than a simple rhetorical exercise in which the purported virtues of an enemy were used to shame an internal addressee. Montesquieu's *Persian Letters* (1721) are a well-known example of this literary strategy. In this epistolary novel, two fictitious Persians, Usbek and Rica, visit Paris and comment in a satirical style on their experiences, including religious tolerance. Whatever familiarity with the Islamic world these authors thus had, their texts were shaped by distinctly Western European concerns.

Shryock's "good Muslim" and his discursive ancestors should make us wary of where in Islamic history we find cases of tolerance. This is also the case where modern affiliations with all their implications can be easily back projected into past times, whether by Muslims or non-Muslims. Liberal Muslim contemporary movements such as the neo-Muʿtazilites or the neo-Averroists may have identified intellectual ancestors in the medieval period, but these do not serve unambiguously as models of liberalism and tolerance. What the preceding reveals is rather that whether we are dealing with inter- or intra-religious diversity, the rationalism which shaped theology and philosophy was a neutral tool and could serve rulers and movements in their violent exercise of power. It was precisely their belief in the rational power of everyone that justified their intolerance — their subjects should have known better than to reject Abbasid or Almohad interpretations of

---

[65] Shryock, Andrew J., "Attack of the Islamophobes. Religious War (and Peace) in Arab/Muslim Detroit," in: Carl Ernst (ed.), *Islamophobia in America: The Anatomy of Intolerance*, 145–74, 162, New York: Palgrave Macmillan, 2013.

[66] Griffel, Frank, "Toleranzkonzepte im Islam und ihr Einfluß auf Jean Bodins *Colloquium Heptaplomeres*," in: Ralph Häfner (ed.), *Bodinus Polymeres. Neue Studien zu Jean Bodins Spätwerk*, 119–44, Wiesbaden: Harrassowitz, 1999.

Islam. This may serve as a note of caution regarding historical equivalents as well as a reminder that trends which have gained a positive reputation can have significant complications.

7 Sufism

Like mystical traditions of other religions and alongside rationalism, Sufism is often considered the most tolerant branch of Islam. Sufis are often seen as prioritizing the inner, spiritual life over strict adherence to external rules. This perception suggests greater flexibility and openness to diverse expressions of piety, even beyond Islam. The fact that Sufis have been systematically targeted by Islamists in modern times has added to this peaceful reputation since Sufis are primarily perceived as victims rather than perpetrators of violence.[67] Several aspects of this representation need to be critically revisited. First, the relationship between mysticism and Sufism is complicated since throughout Islamic history the two are not as coterminous as they are sometimes treated. Another important component of Sufism is asceticism which sometimes includes social and political censorship. In later periods, especially since about the eleventh century, Sufism also involved brotherhoods as an important form of social organization and religious leadership. In contemporary Western Europe and North America, spirituality may often present itself as non-confrontational, pluralist, and socially liberal, especially outside of conventional and organized religions. This is not necessarily the case for Sufism, however. On the contrary, as Mark Woodward and others have argued, the simplistic assumption that Sufism always represents peace and tolerance, while Salafism stands for violence, can lead to serious misinterpretations of real-world conflicts.[68] Surveying examples from Southeast Asia and West Africa, the authors illustrate that violence can be found among both sides.

Woodward and his co-authors attribute some of the misrepresentation of Sufism as generally tolerant to the selective attention paid to classical texts, especially by the early Iraqi Rābiʻa al-ʻAdawīya (d. 801/d. 185), the Andalusi Ibn ʻArabī (1165–1240/560–638) and the mystical Persian poet Rūmī (1207–1273/604–672). This observation certainly applies to many surveys on tolerance in Islamic contexts, although Rābiʻa is not granted much space in the literature reviewed for

---

[67] For a history of critical responses to certain kinds of Sufism cf. Jong, Frederick de/Radtke, Bernd (eds.), *Islamic Mysticism Contested. Thirteen Centuries of Controversies and Polemics*, Leiden: Brill, 1999.
[68] Woodward, Mark, et al, "Salafi Violence and Sufi Tolerance? Rethinking Conventional Wisdom," *Perspectives on Terrorism* 7/6 (2013), 58–78.

this chapter, whereas the modern Iranian reception of the poet Ḥāfeẓ (1315–1390/ 714–792) is more regularly discussed (more about this last aspect below). In addition to the disproportionate presence of these authors, however, another problem in this representation of Sufism requires discussion, which is the extent to which the selected texts are representative of the authors' attitude to religious diversity and tolerance. Taken at face value, these texts appear to endorse a mystical tradition within Islam that supports tolerance, diversity, and religious freedom. Just like the Qur'ān, however, a text which is also often quoted in small portions and without much context, these sources merit a more extensive theological, literary and historical analysis.

An example shall illustrate this point. One of the most frequently quoted statements regarding tolerance and religious pluralism in Islamic history was composed by a Sufi. Ibn 'Arabī wrote the following verses, here in Reynold Nicholson's translation:

> (13) My heart has become capable of every form: it is a pasture for gazelles and a convent for Christian monks,
> (14) And a temple for idols and the pilgrim's Ka'ba and the tables of the Tora and the book of the Koran.
> (15) I follow the religion of Love: whatever way Love's camels take, that is my religion and my faith.[69]

The popularity of these lines is hard to exaggerate. They are ubiquitous in the public domain, mostly in publications that are sympathetic to mysticism, particularly Ibn 'Arabī. The verses have become iconic of the author himself. The Moroccan calligrapher Nouréddine Daifallah, for example, selected them for his *Hommage à Ibn Arabi* (2014). It is not hard to account for this phenomenon. The fact that this passage was translated into English more than a century ago helped as did the popularity of Ibn 'Arabī among seekers in the West. That the mystic included a positive reference to the early Muslims' archenemy, idolatry, is remarkable. But, as suggested above, the verses require more comprehensive analysis. It is critical to consider what the point of the passage is and whether the references which are taken to be indicators of tolerance might be instrumental to conveying a different point. Given the complexity of Ibn 'Arabī's work, only a very modest glimpse can be offered here as an impression how such interpretations might be conducted.

---

[69] Ibn 'Arabī, *The Tarjumán al-Ashwáq. A Collection of Mystical Odes by Muḥyi'ddín Ibn al-'Arabí*, ed. and trans. Reynold A. Nicholson, London: Royal Asiatic Society, 1911, 66–67 for the complete poem.

At the most superficial level, it is worth reading the three lines in the context of the poem where they appear. The first third of this sixteen-line poem takes the listener into the imaginary world of pre-Islamic Arabic poetry. In line with literary convention, the poet presents himself as a lover who is longing for his beloved. After addressing doves and imploring them not to amplify his own lament, he writes:

> (3) I respond to her, at eve and morn, with the plaintive cry of a longing man and the moan of an impassioned lover.

Ibn 'Arabī is tapping here into an old poetic tradition, but like other mystical Arabic poets of his time, he merges the established tropes of love poetry with mystical themes. Remarkably, ash-Shushtarī (1212–1269/608–667), another mystical poet from al-Andalus, identified the iconic female beloved, Layla, with the divine Beloved. Such a seemingly radically subversive feminization of God may not have raised as many eyebrows among contemporaries as one might expect since it was part of a poetic exercise.[70] Likewise, it may have been critical that from the first line Ibn 'Arabī situated his poem discursively within a literary tradition. How exactly the poem was understood at the time is hard to establish, but it is worth bearing in mind the possibility often discussed for literary expressions of transgressive thoughts, which is that their distinctive format allowed for greater space or indeed tolerance. The assumption is that because such verses were perceived as poetic interventions and operating in a symbolic or allegorical register, they were not understood to be real-world challenges. This explanation is often adduced to explain why Muslim poets described their consumption of alcohol, forbidden by Islamic law.[71] Indeed, later sympathetic Muslim commentators of Ibn 'Arabī such as 'Abd al-Ghanī an-Nābulūsī (1641–1731/1050–1143) "decoded" what might be understood as transgressive references and offered a metaphysical explanation for elements from other religions.

Modern scholars, too, have explored along similar lines the theological dimension of Ibn 'Arabī's poem.[72] The verses can easily be read as suggesting that con-

---

[70] For an analysis of this literary strategy cf. Akasoy, Anna, "Gender and the Poetics of God's Alterity in Andalusi Mysticism," in: Megan Moore (ed.), *Gender in the Premodern Mediterranean*, 97–117, Tempe: Arizona Center for Medieval & Renaissance Studies, 2019, and "Imaginary Spaces of Devotion in Andalusi Mystical Poetry. Christian Monks and Monasteries in a *Qaṣīda* by al-Shushtarī," *The Maghreb Review* 45/4 (2020), 721–43.
[71] Bauer, *Die Kultur der Ambiguität*, 244–46.
[72] For relevant interpretations cf., for example, Chittick, William C., *Imaginal Worlds. Ibn al-'Arabī and the Problem of Religious Diversity*, Albany: State University of New York Press, 1994. Cf.

ventional forms of religious devotion are all inadequate because the ontological difference between God and humans is so fundamental that any human effort to approach the divine will always fall short. In that sense, they share a common limitation and can be seen as equally insufficient human attempts at approaching the divine. Furthermore, the variety of religious expression is a function of the diversity of the created world which sits opposed to the unity of God (this is a common thought in Neoplatonic models of cosmology and metaphysics). Such a sentiment has parallels in Islamic philosophy, theology and law, as illustrated above, but also in Christian thought, such as Nicholas of Cusa's (1401–1464) concept of *una religio in rituum varietate*. While these views may not in and of themselves be expressions of tolerance, they can predispose those who share them towards tolerance. Much again depends on how such concepts are applied in actual social interactions. Islam may share with other religions the fact that it is a human phenomenon and as such irredeemably inferior to God. This absolute description, however, can be turned into a relative one — one of these religions, albeit insufficient compared to God, may still be superior to other religions, for example. We have seen this with Ibn Rushd, who combined a general acknowledgment of human fallibility with a strict hierarchy of intellectual ambition. Conversely, there is no reason why someone who insists on the absolute or relative truth of their views needs to be intolerant towards those they consider wrong.

Further complications and indeed reservations emerge from the historical context of Ibn ʿArabī's life. Reading such verses as literal reflections of Ibn ʿArabī's life may be misleading, as his urban background contrasts with the symbolic desert imagery often used in mystical poetry. As will be discussed in additional detail below, Ibn ʿArabī's native region, al-Andalus, provides examples of both peaceful and violent interactions between Muslims, Christians and Jews. Ibn ʿArabī's lifetime coincides with Almohad rule over al-Andalus, which was a low point in the history of interreligious relations. As mentioned above, the Almohads exercised violence against Muslims and non-Muslims alike. This was also a period in which the Christian "Reconquista" gained momentum. Like many others, Ibn ʿArabī left the Muslim West and spent the second half of his life entirely in the eastern lands of the Arabic-speaking world, mostly present-day Egypt, Syria, Iraq and Turkey. The family of the Jewish scholar Maimonides too left al-Andalus at around the same time, fleeing from Almohad violence. Steven Wasserstrom suggested that independent of their religion, such émigrés from Iberia socialized in Egyptian and Syrian exiles, mystics à la Ibn ʿArabī being an important example.

---

also Alvarez, Lourdes, "The Mystical Language of Daily Life. Vernacular Sufi Poetry and the Songs of Abū al-Ḥasan al-Shushtarī," *Exemplaria* 17/1 (2005), 1–32.

The son of Moses Maimonides is sometimes even described as a Jewish Sufi. Their common origin and intellectual inclinations, whether their leanings were toward mysticism or rationalism, may have served as a stronger unifying factor than religious affiliation.[73] Wasserstrom's examples are plausible and constitute an important reminder that the identities of medieval individuals were complex and whatever may have separated a Muslim from a Jew, there was much that may have united them.

Historical evidence, however, also suggests that some of the Western animosities were in fact imported to the eastern Mediterranean. Ibn ʿArabī himself is a case in point.[74] In 1212, the Andalusi mystic was in Anatolia, where he wrote a letter to the Seljuk sultan Kaykāʾūs in which he complained about the public presence of Christians. The text deserves to be quoted in detail since it provides an impression of the lasting significance of the *Pact of ʿUmar* as well as which elements of other religions attracted the objection of Muslims. Ibn ʿArabī wrote to the sultan:

> The worst thing that Islam and Muslims suffer in your realm is the sound of bells, the manifestation of infidelity, the affirmation of an associate of God, and the disappearance of the rules instituted by the Prince of Believers, ʿUmar b. al-Khaṭṭāb, regarding *dhimmīs*: namely that neither in the city itself nor in the surrounding regions are they to build new churches, monasteries or hermitages, that they are not to repair any of these buildings if they become dilapidated, that they are not to prevent any Muslim from being given food and shelter in their churches for a period of up to three days, that they are not to hide spies, that they are not to conspire in secret against Muslims, that they are not to teach the Qurʾān to their children, and that they are not to make public show of their polytheism.

If we consider Ibn ʿArabī's biography, this statement may seem less surprising than if read against the backdrop of his "religion of love" which seems so open and flexible. As Claude Addas points out, 1212 was the year of the Almohad defeat at Las Navas de Tolosa, a decisive victory for the Christian *reconquistadores*. Addas challenged interpretations of the letter as an expression of Ibn ʿArabī's hatred of Christians but rather read it as an expression of concern about Christian aggression both on the Iberian Peninsula and with the lasting Crusader efforts in the Levant. Indeed, that Ibn ʿArabī would insist on the obligation of Christians under Muslim rule to keep the peace fits into this picture of concern. Even if

---

[73] Wasserstrom, Steven M., "Jewish-Muslim Relations in the Context of Andalusian Emigration," in: Mark D. Meyerson/Edward D. English (eds.), *Christians, Muslims and Jews in Medieval and Early Modern Spain*, 69–87, Notre Dame: University of Notre Dame Press, 2000.
[74] For the following cf. Addas, Claude, *Quest for the Red Sulphur. The Life of Ibn ʿArabī*, Cambridge: Islamic Texts Society, 1993, 235.

the mystic's attitude can be classified as defensive, however, the letter sheds a different light on the irenic picture which emerges from his poem. Nor might Ibn 'Arabī's objection have been entirely defensive. There are other examples of Western Muslims who visited the Eastern Mediterranean and found non-Muslims in social positions they considered too high. Their objection may have been rooted in social conventions in their homelands, but also the regulations of the Maliki school of Sunni law which was predominant in North Africa and al-Andalus. Compared to the three other Sunni legal schools, some Maliki jurists expressed heightened concerns about ritual impurity resulting from contact with non-Muslims.[75] Given the format and addressee of Ibn 'Arabī's letter there is little reason to believe that the reference to Christians is allegorical.

Woodward and his co-authors suggest replacing the dichotomy of Salafi violence and Sufi tolerance with another binary, which is between pacifists and activists, both of whom exist on either side. As a result, it is not only the axiomatic dichotomy between Salafis and Sufis that is broken up. Implicitly, violence is identified with activism and tolerance with pacifism. There are good reasons for this. As discussed above in the section on scripture, a principle of tolerance can be extrapolated from a recommendation of peace. However, not everybody who refrains from violence is necessarily a pacifist. Another complementary dichotomy which captures some of the contrast between different groups is that between activists and quietists. Anybody who finds their social environment too disagreeable to tolerate it has after all two options: one is to change that environment, the other to withdraw from it, physically or spiritually. Examples of such a withdrawal strategy can be found throughout Islamic history and among different movements.[76] What this illustrates is that the absence of violence should not be equated too rapidly with tolerance or intolerance with violence.

Activists, too, are not necessarily violent or violent against other people. In fact, Sufism provides good examples of non-violent activism. Some Sufis embraced antinomian principles and deliberately broke laws and socio-cultural conventions.

---

[75] For a discussion of different explanations for the Almohad persecution of Jews and Christians, their adherence to the Maliki school of law being one of them, cf. Fierro, Maribel, "A Muslim Land without Jews or Christians: Almohad Policies Regarding the 'Protected People'," in: Matthias M. Tischler/Alexander Fidora (eds.), *Christlicher Norden – Muslimischer Süden. Ansprüche und Wirklichkeiten von Christen, Juden und Muslimen auf der Iberischen Halbinsel im Hoch- und Spätmittelalter*, 231–47, Münster: Aschendorff, 2011.

[76] For Andalusi scholars who kept their distance from political leaders as a matter of principle cf. Marín, Manuela, "Inqibāḍ 'an al-sulṭān: 'ulamā' and Political Power in al-Andalus," in: *Saber religioso y poder político en el Islam*, 127–40, Madrid: Agencia Española de Cooperación Internacional, 1994.

The dervishes of the thirteenth to sixteenth century studied by Ahmet Karamustafa, for example, distinguished themselves with their unusual clothing, facial hair and body piercings.[77] Drunkenness as well as public singing and dancing are other common forms of social deviance. These deviant renunciants incurred the disdain of intellectual elites, both in their own time and for a long time in modern scholarship. That they framed their antinomianism as an act of piety may have increased the tolerance of authorities, just as the poetic promotion of wine drinking may have been accepted because of its literary format. But are these antinomian Sufis themselves tolerant or intolerant? The case can be made for either. They may have opened space in societies for a greater diversity of practices, but they also challenged the way others preferred to live their lives.

There are examples of Sufi martyrs too, long before the rise of modern political Islam. Some paid a high price because the authorities did not extend greater tolerance to them. al-Ḥallāj was spectacularly put to death in Baghdad in 922 for heresy. While al-Ḥallāj may have been deliberately provocative, Shihāb ad-Dīn as-Suhrawardī (1154–1191/548–587), knowledgeable in both Avicennian philosophy and mystical traditions, may have been put to death because the local religious elites of Aleppo considered him dangerous.[78] Like Ibn Rushd who experienced a similar downfall and ended up in exile late in life, as-Suhrawardī was closely connected to political leaders, a situation which involved great risks for any number of reasons from personal intrigue to ideological disagreement. The Andalusi Sufi Ibn Barrajān died in jail in 1141/535 under somewhat uncertain circumstances, perhaps because the Almoravid rulers recognized a pattern of charismatic authority in him and feared his rise as a rebel.[79] In addition to violence against their opponents, actual or perceived, governments chose the method of book burning to suppress ideas they considered dangerous or otherwise objectionable.[80]

Then again, it is not hard to detect a certain degree of tolerance for subversive arguments in Islamic history either, mystical or otherwise. A case in point is the so-called freethinkers who tend to be rationalists. Abū Bakr ar-Rāzī (d. ca. 925/ 313) believed in one God but rejected the concepts of prophecy and revelation.

---

77 Karamustafa, Ahmet T., *God's Unruly Friends. Dervish Groups in the Islamic Later Middle Period, 1200–1550*, Oxford: Oneworld, 1994.
78 For as-Suhrawardī cf. Marcotte, Roxanne D., "Suhrawardī al-Maqtūl, the Martyr of Aleppo," *Al-Qanṭara* 22/2 (2001), 395–419. For al-Ḥallāj cf. Massignon, Louis, *The Passion of al-Hallaj*, vol. 4, *Mystic and Martyr of Islam*, Princeton: Princeton University Press, 1982.
79 Casewit, Yousef, *The Mystics of al-Andalus. Ibn Barrajān and Islamic Thought in the Twelfth Century*, Cambridge: Cambridge University Press, 2017.
80 Safran, Janina M., "The Politics of Book Burning in al-Andalus," *Journal of Medieval Iberian Studies* 6/2 (2014), 148–68.

The fact that neither he nor other "radical" authors or "freethinkers" were punished suggests that the tolerance Muslim rulers had for such challenges depended on many variables such as the style of presentation and political circumstances.[81] As mentioned above, poetic or philosophical formats may have granted authors license to express views which may not have been taken at face value or as challenges to authorities. Furthermore, texts that circulated within limited scholarly or elite circles were less likely to provoke official retaliation than public preaching, as they did not reach or mobilize broader audiences.

Finally, among activist Sufis there are also those who acted as censors and followed the *amr bi-l-maʿrūf* principle.[82] This is not hard to reconcile with other prominent aspects of Sufism. As in the case of Ibn ʿArabī, censoring Sufis may have had a notion that human approaches to the Divine are all inadequate, but they considered other approaches inferior to their own. Furthermore, religious practice is critical to many forms of Sufis. Many focus on their own practice, whether compliant with general rules or their own rituals of piety and worship. Activist Sufis sometimes took the requirements of Islamic law very seriously indeed, a commitment which manifested itself in their asceticism, but also in the intervention in the lives of other Muslims. Recent scholarship has explored such tendencies especially among Andalusi and North African Sufis.[83]

To sum up, Sufism by popular reputation may be irenic, pacifist and pluralist, but the historical reality is considerably more complicated and there is evidence of Sufi militancy as well. Whatever tolerance they practiced, it is fair to assume that to their minds, acknowledgement of human limitations should not come at the expense of truth and justice.

8 Do Ideas Matter?

To begin a survey like this with the Qurʾān and *ḥadīth* implies that texts matter. Continuing with philosophers, theologians and mystics as intellectual communities implies that ideas matter. According to common wisdom, nothing matters

---

[81] For this group of authors cf. Stroumsa, Sarah, *Freethinkers of Medieval Islam. Ibn al-Rawāndī, Abū Bakr al-Rāzī and their Impact on Islamic Thought*, Leiden: Brill, 1999; reprint 2016.
[82] Cook, *Commanding Right and Forbidding Wrong*, 459–68.
[83] García-Arenal, Mercedes, "La práctica del precepto de *al-amr bi-l-maʿrūf wa-l-nahy ʿan al-munkar* en la hagiografía magrebí," *Al-Qanṭara* 13 (1992), 143–65; Cornell, Vincent, "Mystical Doctrine and Political Action in Moroccan Sufism. The Role of the Exemplar in the Ṭarīqa al-Jazūliyya," *Al-Qanṭara* 13 (1992), 201–31; Fierro, Maribel, "Spiritual Alienation and Political Activism", *Arabica* 47 (2000), 230–60.

more than ideas. A quotation attributed to anybody from Socrates to Eleanor Roosevelt has it that small minds discuss people, mediocre minds discuss events and great minds discuss ideas. The quotation presupposes that we can separate ideas from both the people and the historical contexts that produced them. In his autobiographical account of different paths to the truth, al-Ghazālī, too, dismissed the significance of people when he criticized others for rejecting ideas just because they were presented by certain people. One should not challenge the importance of logic, for example, just because metaphysical ideas embraced by the same philosophers were so wrong.

al-Ghazālī's words are poignant:

> This is the practice of those dim-witted men who know the truth by men, and not the men by the truth... The intelligent man, therefore, first knows the truth, then he considers what is actually said by someone. If it is true, he accepts it, whether the speaker be wrong or right in other matters. Indeed, such a man will often be intent on extracting what is true from the involved utterances of the erring, since he is aware that gold is usually found mixed with dirt.[84]

Incidentally, al-Ghazālī implicitly provides another important rationale for tolerance in this passage, that individuals should be assessed for all they contribute to society. What concerns us here, however, are the entanglements between ideas, people and historical contexts, especially when we put them in relationship to the present. Can we ever extract ideas of past philosophers, theologians and mystics and apply them effectively to new contexts, or do they cease to be the same ideas? Do they do more than provide a different vocabulary for us to negotiate our political and social conditions?

To contemporary readers, al-Ghazālī's words still ring true. We can agree with something even if we find the person who says it in other respects disagreeable. At the same time, in modern thought, both ideas and the people who promote them are often understood as products of their respective historical, cultural and socio-economic environments. The intimate entanglements between power and knowledge disclosed prominently by Michel Foucault shift our attention from ideas to people and their material environments. Just as little as we might disentangle ideas of past people from their historical environments, our ideas may be little less than a function of our contemporary contexts. Accordingly, when it comes to ideas and practices of tolerance, whether past or present or combinations of both, there is no consensus about the importance of tolerant ideas for tolerant

---

[84] Al-Ghazālī, *Deliverance from Error. Five Key Texts Including His Spiritual Autobiography, al-Munqidh min al-Dalal*, trans. Richard J. McCarthy, Louisville, 1980, 68.

practices. A good example are the responses to Khaled Abou El Fadl's essay on tolerance which reveal fundamental disagreements about the significance of ideas, especially religious ideas, but also a variety of approaches to the same ideas. The same questions which these authors raise for the present can be directed towards the past. They can help us understand the past on its own terms, but also in terms of how it is invoked in contemporary debates. In his critical response, for example, Tariq Ali argues that the situations Abou El Fadl mentions as potential cases of tolerance are political problems. Theological principles, Ali suggests, are insignificant in these contexts. Neither do they account for the emergence of these problems in the first place nor do they offer solutions.[85] Another critical respondent, Abid Ullah Jan, challenges Abou El Fadl by stating that calls to Muslims to be more tolerant conflict with what he identifies as an Islamic value of justice, although his support for the Taliban in this context strikes Abou El Fadl — and presumably other readers as well — as troubling. His challenge is an important reminder that ideas can look very different when seen in isolation from other ideas. The problem of tolerance for the intolerant is of course a more widely debated problem of tolerance. In his own case for Islamic tolerance, the Tunisian sociologist Abdelwahab Bouhdiba insists on the mutuality of tolerance on theological rather than pragmatic grounds:

> I do not deny my peer's conviction without ruining my own. My freedom is nurtured by his freedom, and his freedom is nurtured by mine. In matters of faith, my conviction justifies itself to the exact extent that freedom of conscience is an unconditional universal… Faith must be tolerant, or it ceases to be faith.[86]

At the same time, he recognizes that it is necessary to impose certain restrictions to maintain a social equilibrium. In this way, concepts of tolerance become part of a holistic and comprehensive exercise of theology rather than separate theological ideas planted into a non-theological context. Bouhdiba's approach invites questions about the nature of ideas inspired by distinctive intellectual and religious traditions if adopted into different milieus. For instance, how does a mystically inspired conception of tolerance function in a non-mystical setting? Stanley Kurtz takes Abou El Fadl to task for his subjective interpretation of the Qur'ān which can be as easily challenged as the puritan use of the Qur'ān. Kurtz points out that Abou El Fadl himself has stressed the fluidity of the sacred texts. In line

---

[85] Ali, Tariq, "Theological Distractions," in: Khaled Abou El Fadl (ed.), *The Place of Tolerance in Islam*, 37–41, Boston: Beacon Press, 2002.
[86] Bouhdiba, Abdelwahab, "On Islamic Tolerance," *Diogenes* 176, vol. 44/4 (Winter 1996), 121–36, 128.

with several other critics, he identifies the root causes of violence in social stress rather than in putative immutable doctrine. These arguments point in two directions. They point towards the past and help us assess the nature of historical theological ideas, but they also point towards the present to discuss whether religious ideas ever have a real-life impact, what that impact is and what that means for present conflicts. One may also reconcile Tariq Ali's point that theological ideas are not the root cause of intolerance and violence with Rudi Paret's expectation that theology can provide a solution.[87] Theologians might at least provide some leadership and intervene on a discursive level to counter those who perpetuate calls for continuous agendas of mission and conquest (the former, according to Paret, a Christian obstacle to tolerance, the latter a Muslim obstacle).

9 History and Its Discontents

How can we identify prevalent attitudes to religious diversity in a community? Canonical authoritative texts are one source, the scholarly discourse of social, political and intellectual elites another one. These sources may tell us as much about the ways in which historical communities articulated certain problems and thought about solutions as they allow insights into the ways members of these communities perceived the social reality that surrounded them. Especially when it comes to practical aspects of the actual interactions of human beings, however, one might argue that discourse matters little when compared to practice. Put differently, regardless of the ideals a society expresses in writing or the agency we attribute to ideas, it is ultimately practice that reveals the true nature of its values.

The principle that events reveal meaning is embedded in Qur'ānic hermeneutics in various ways, most notably through the Islamic tradition of *asbāb an-nuzūl* — the "occasions of revelation" that associate specific verses with historical contexts. While these hermeneutical traditions may have been critical at the time of their formation, to what extent should they shape our contemporary understanding of the Qur'ān or determine the essential meaning of its verses? Even when these traditions are set aside, and interpretation instead relies on general biographical knowledge of Muḥammad — as in the case of Rudi Paret—the question remains: should historical assumptions dictate the meaning of a verse? In the context of 2:256, Paret assumes that the verse is a sign of resignation, and that

---

[87] Paret, "Toleranz und Intoleranz,"

Muḥammad was not able to convince everybody of the truth of his mission.[88] The emphasis of the verse is that one *cannot* coerce rather than that one *should* not. However, Paret also states that this historically original meaning need not confine our interpretation today. If one is mindful of historical change, one should be able to accept religious freedom and tolerance as the present meaning.

The proposition that history matters more than literalist dogma informs several surveys of tolerance in Islamic contexts. Thus, Rudi Paret and Albrecht Noth approached the subject of Islamic notions of tolerance quite explicitly by treating Islamic history as a manifestation of such notions. As much as he pointed out that the historical situation of the Islamic conquests became normative for later Muslims, Paret treated the variety of historical interactions between Muslims and non-Muslims as expressions of a more abstract phenomenon of tolerance or intolerance. Like many others, he assumed that violence was the default condition, and thus interpreted the absence of violence as an indicator of tolerance. Noth based his exploration on a similar decision. Like many other religions, Islam had to be theologically intolerant, he assumed, since in theological respects it claims superiority over other religions. The historian contrasted this with the more complex historical reality of Islam where tolerance and intolerance coexist.

As a quick survey of historical references in contributions to debates about Islamic tolerance reveals, evidence can be easily adduced both for the proposition that Muslims are tolerant towards non-Muslims and that they are intolerant. What we have found in the sections about textual and intellectual traditions, thus, also applies to actual interactions. In the case of Islamic history, two cases especially have attracted interest as exemplary manifestations of an Islamic concept of tolerance: medieval Muslim Iberia and the early modern Ottoman Empire.

Al-Andalus i.e., the parts of the Iberian Peninsula which were under Muslim rule, has provided a historical imaginary for theories about both Muslim tolerance and intolerance. The significance of al-Andalus in this context partly stems from its status as a historical utopia in the collective memory of European Jews. For more than a century, "lachrymose" views of Andalusi history have been contrasted with "saccharine" narratives, the two visions promoting an image that represents al-Andalus as either a vale of tears or as a haven of equality for Jews. It is not hard to find evidence to support either, or indeed, both views. This is true of historical examples of discourse as well as cases of actual interaction, and it is as true of the popular Andalusi and Ottoman examples as it is of cases that have received attention more recently — South Asia and sub-Saharan

---

[88] Cf. also Paret, Rudi, "Sure 2,256: lā ikrāha fī d-dīni. Toleranz oder Resignation?," *Der Islam* 45 (1969), 299–300.

Africa. Given how heterogeneous the historical evidence is, is it possible to identify variables which account for the varying degrees of violence and intolerance? One of them might be sectarianism. As the Almohad example suggests, it might be that intrareligious conflicts had a negative impact on interreligious relations. Modern examples too would suggest such an assumption.

In both cases, al-Andalus and the Ottoman Empire, the quality of religious coexistence is as controversial as the suitability of the term "tolerance." María Rosa Menocal made a widely received case for Muslim Iberia as a culture of tolerance while Karen Barkey presented a similar case for the Ottomans.[89] Both historians offered evidence of autonomous and flourishing non-Muslim religious life under Muslim rule and both received critical responses which highlighted the reality of communities dependent on a ruler's good will. By today's standards, these historical examples are inadequate.

Independent of how persuasive these two examples are, their prominence in discussions about tolerance in Islamic history deserves critical evaluation. Religious diversity was the rule rather than the exception in territories under Muslim rule in the premodern period. Shared sacred spaces can be found all over the Islamic world. It was a common constellation for Muslim rulers to rule over non-Muslims, much more common than for Western European rulers before the European expansion to rule over non-Christians. Recent scholarship has advanced theories that Iberian Christian rulers adopted models of governance over religiously diverse subjects from Iberian Muslim predecessors.

That Iberia and the Ottoman lands would have attracted greater interest than other regions confirm once again the significance of European perspectives on Islamic history. This is true in two respects. On the one hand, Europeans were understandably concerned about the way Christians fared in neighboring territories under Muslim rule, especially in periods of Islamic expansion. Furthermore, Islam has a centuries-long history of serving as the Western European discursive other. As much as recent debates about Islamic "intolerance" function to define Western European societies positively as tolerant, authors who sought to make a case for

---

[89] Menocal, María Rosa, *The Ornament of the World. How Muslims, Jews, and Christians Created a Culture of Tolerance in Medieval Spain*, New York: Back Bay Books, 2012. For a response cf. Filios, Denise K., "Expulsion from Paradise: Exiled Intellectuals and Andalusian Tolerance," in: Simon R. Doubleday/David Coleman (eds.), *In the Light of Medieval Spain. Islam, the West, and the Relevance of the Past*, 91–113, New York: Palgrave Macmillan, 2008. For the later example cf. Barkey, Karen, *Empire of Difference. The Ottomans in Comparative Perspective*, Cambridge: Cambridge University Press, 2008 and, for a response, Baer, Marc/Makdisi, Ussama/Shryock, Andrew, "Tolerance and Conversion in the Ottoman Empire. A Conversation," *Comparative Studies in Society and History* 51 (2009), 927–40.

greater tolerance in Western Europe have for centuries presented Muslims, historical or contemporaneous, as a model. This contrast remains present in historical references.[90]

Representations of Muslim tolerance and intolerance are often selective in other ways too. Like many other surveys, most of this chapter has focused on Sunnis as the majority of Muslims. Two examples illustrate that examples of both tolerance and intolerance can be found outside this community in a comparable manner. The case of the Kharijites has already been briefly mentioned, but in significance they pale in contrast with the Shiʿites who constitute about 15% of today's Muslim population. For most of Islamic history and in most regions of the Islamic world, Shiʿites were not in positions of power. Their ability to exercise tolerance with inter- or intrareligious others was thus limited. The period from around the mid-tenth to the mid-eleventh century of the Common Era, however, is known as the " Shiʿite century." During this time, the Fatimids ruled over large parts of North Africa, the Eastern Mediterranean and the Arabian Peninsula, while the Buyids controlled modern-day Iraq and Iran. The Fatimids were Ismailis or Sevener Shiʿites who followed an esoteric doctrine, the Buyids may have started as Fiver Shiʿites but were mostly Imami or Twelver Shiʿites.[91] To some extent, both Fatimids and Buyids embraced activist principles — the fact that they assumed political power illustrates this. Neither movement, however, forced the population under their rule to convert to their interpretation to Islam, or in the case of non-Muslims to Islam (at the time of the Fatimid conquest of Egypt in 969, the region was still predominantly Christian). Both may have realized that, as new and possibly foreign rulers in these regions, imposing their theology risked alienating their subjects. The Buyids coopted the Abbasid caliphs in Baghdad and tried to maintain peace over an urban society plagued by sectarian conflicts. The Fatimids kept their esoteric rituals mostly to themselves and even set themselves apart

---

[90] Kadri, *Heaven on Earth*, 245, contrasts present-day practices in select Muslim-majority states and historical precedents in the Islamic world which are significantly more tolerant than contemporaneous European practices. Likewise, Amartya Sen in his *Identity and Violence. The Illusion of Destiny*, New York: W.W. Norton & Co., 2006 contrasted an intolerant medieval Europe and a tolerant medieval Middle East, his example Maimonides does not actually serve the purpose here. Rather than abandoning Europe, the Jewish scholar had moved from an intolerant part of the Islamic world to another part which allowed for more religious diversity.

[91] The numerical names indicate where in the genealogy of ʿAli's descendants the respective Shiʿite community recognizes the last Imam. For an introduction to Shiʿism cf. Halm, Heinz, *Shiʿism*, New York: Columbia University Press², 2014.

physically.⁹² An exception during this period and indeed in Islamic history more generally speaking is the sixth Fatimid caliph, al-Ḥākim bi-Amri-llāh (reg. 996– 1021/386–411), a critical figure for the Druze.⁹³ Al-Ḥākim infamously destroyed sacred buildings of Jews and Christians, including the Church of the Holy Sepulcher, which may have contributed to the rise of the Crusader movement. The above-mentioned Safavids also spread their doctrine violently. If their attitude to non-Shi'ites should be described as tolerant at all, their motivation was presumably pragmatic.

Another set of circumstances deserves mentioning. During the twelfth century, significant numbers of Muslims came under non-Muslim rule for the first time. This situation was to endure with the Christian conquests on the Iberian Peninsula and the Levant, but especially with the Mongol incursions into Iran and Iraq. Muslims had to ask themselves for the first time in their history whether it was possible to live under non-Muslim rule. The response to this challenge was in many parts an internalizing turn in which priority was given to intention and personal faith. Given that the balance of power did not favor Muslims, it is hard to explore Islamic notions of tolerance in this context.

Additional complications must be considered. "Islam" is not an actor. When treated as an agent in discourse, it typically refers to Muslim rulers, states dominated by Muslims, or broader Muslim-majority societies. In this usage, "Islam" becomes a representation of what Muslims have historically done.⁹⁴ Of course, Muslim societies are not homogeneous, and within them, agents of tolerance and intolerance can frequently coexist. Moreover, identifying the principal actors behind acts of violence is often very difficult. Rudi Paret, for example, insinuates that throughout Islamic history, members of the lower social strata were less tolerant, more fanatical and more volatile than those who belonged to the upper, powerful strata.⁹⁵ The prominent presence of non-Muslim scholars and doctors at Muslim courts seems to support this observation, but need not automatically be taken as an expression of tolerance either. It is also important to bear in

---

92 Sanders, Paula, *Ritual, Politics, and the City in Fatimid Cairo*, Albany: State University of New York Press, 1994. For the Buyids cf. Kraemer, Joel L., *Humanism in the Renaissance of Islam. The Cultural Revival during the Buyid Age*, Leiden: Brill, 1993.
93 Walker, Paul E., *Caliph of Cairo. The Remarkable Story of the Ruler who Vanished. The Mysterious Case of Al-Hakim, Commander of the Believers*, London: I.B. Tauris, 2009.
94 In Albrecht Noth's survey, for example, "Islam" which is the agent of tolerance or intolerance, is often the state or ruler. This is a somewhat inevitable consequence of Noth's decision to prioritize history over theology.
95 Paret, "Toleranz und Intoleranz". Likewise, Noth, 203. The religious alterity of these men may have made them more vulnerable and hence dependent, but Muslim members of court were hardly immune to the vicissitudes of caliphal favor and court intrigue.

mind that lower social strata were not homogeneous either. In a revealing case study, for instance, Jessica Coope has demonstrated that the adoption of Muslim habits by non-Muslim men for the purposes of professional and hence social ascent did not extend to women who did not have such opportunities in the first place.[96] This question requires further research, but given the close relationship between tolerance, socio-economic opportunity and competition it may very well be the case that in the highly gendered societies of the premodern period interactions between religious communities differed more commonly according to gender. Coope's case study is revealing for another reason too. She explored which cultural habits were exclusively or predominantly associated with religious identities. Did learning Arabic involve a conversion to Islam, for example, and could one dress like a Muslim while remaining Christian? The historian's conclusions offer insights into conventional expressions of religious identity, but also which forms of cultural appropriation were tolerated despite objection, and which were considered unacceptable. This perspective allows us to expand the focus on religious truth considerably.

It is hardly surprising that Islamic history provides very heterogeneous evidence regarding the preponderance of tolerance. Apart from establishing any historical realities, what requires clarification in contemporary debate is whether history matters. As much as communities define themselves as historically rooted and as shaped by historical experience, the past does not comprehensively define who we are, nor does it determine how we put moral principles into practice. Nothing forces us to repeat the historical crimes of our ancestors and, sadly enough, the shining example of those who came before us does not save us from committing egregious acts of violence ourselves. In the use of historical examples in public discourse, this complication is oftentimes lost. History serves as a past manifestation of present essentials. If nothing else, however, Islamic history demonstrates variability and that the degree and shape of tolerance depends on a multitude of factors rather than a single doctrine.

10 Tolerance in the Twenty-First Century

As mentioned at the beginning of this chapter, many debates about the relationship between "Islam" and "the West" or "Islam" and "modernity" are framed in terms of tolerance. The relationship between these contemporary debates and

---

[96] Coope, Jessica A., "Religious and Cultural Conversion to Islam in Ninth-Century Umayyad Córdoba," *Journal of World History* 4/1 (1993), 47–68.

the exploration of notions of tolerance in Islamic history is dialectical: historical examples are very prominent in debates about the present, while concerns about the present often inform the representation of the past. In recent publications on tolerance and Islam, the line between scholarship and advocacy is sometimes hard to draw. Khaled Abou El Fadl, for example, as well as some of his interlocuters can be read as scholars and as contemporary representatives of Islam. His interpretation is in line with those of many other modernists or liberals, broadly speaking. Even when scholars produce balanced assessments —such as in the case of the Almohad persecutions — without any obvious advocacy agenda, they often reference the twenty-first century to explain the lasting relevance of their research.

A good example of the prominence of tolerance in more general political debates about Islam is a conversation between new atheist Sam Harris and Islamist-turned-reformer Maajid Nawaz. Published under the title "Islam and the Future of Tolerance," the exchange focuses on a critical assessment of violent Islamic extremism and the possibility of advocating for a secular and liberal Islam on the grounds of the Islamic tradition itself. In this discussion, tolerance primarily appears to evoke the possibility or describe the circumstances of peaceful and pluralistic coexistence in a globalized world as well as democratic egalitarian societies in compliance with universal human rights. Tolerance is mentioned only in passing and is never treated as a central subject. The choice to highlight tolerance in the title presumably reflects the expectation that readers will understand the issues debated in the conversations as problems of tolerance, that their understanding of tolerance allows for tolerance to be relevant in this context and that it might also offer a solution or at least a way of describing a desired outcome. Tolerance, however, remains a vague concept. It mostly appears in the negative as intolerance of right-wing extremists or as false tolerance of those who sacrifice liberal values in their campaigns against Islamophobia. Abou El Fadl's criticism clearly illustrates how difficult it is to disentangle tolerance from broader doctrinal agendas. For these "extremists," intolerance towards those who do not share their views, whether Muslim or non-Muslim, is part and parcel of a larger worldview.[97] It describes a general mode or attitude rather than a single doctrine.

Many recent authors emphasize that there is nothing intrinsically tolerant or intolerant in Islam and that references to the Islamic tradition can be mobilized to opposite ends. Still, there is a prominent tendency to make a case for greater tolerance in Muslim-majority societies than in historical Western Europe based on precedents which come from within Islamic history and culture. Just as represen-

---

97 Abou El Fadl, *The Place of Tolerance in Islam*, 4–5.

tations of the past serve as a stage on which ambitions for the present are negotiated, such examples from the past are selected to substantiate different cases for our own time. As the survey in this chapter indicates, three subcategories of "Islam" are more regularly highlighted as such models for tolerance: there are certain intellectual and spiritual strands, notably rationalism and Sufism, then there are historical periods, especially the Ottomans, Muslim rule over the Iberian Peninsula and the Mughals, and finally there are certain geographical areas of the Islamic world where tolerance is meant to have prevailed or does so currently. Sometimes, several of these categories overlap. As the example of Ibn ʿArabī illustrates, a Sufi from the Andalusi margins of the Islamic world enjoys the reputation of being especially tolerant.

Since historical examples and Sufism have been discussed above, a few more words are in order here about geographical areas. As already mentioned, Southeast Asia is regularly adduced as a model of peaceful religious coexistence in recent history and the present. Sub-Saharan Africa is another example. The volume *Tolerance, Democracy, and Sufis in Senegal* extrapolates from a case study to suggest that specific local examples may serve as broader models for the Islamic world.[98] Michael Frishkopf, too, came to the conclusion that in a comparison of Muslims in Ghana and in Egypt, the former were much more tolerant in matters of religious diversity than the latter.[99] Religious affiliations in Egypt were not a choice, he lists as an important argument. The quality of interreligious relationships in the Arab state were likewise modest by comparison. However, Frishkopf also stressed that when it comes to intrareligious relationships, Muslim communities in Ghana were much less tolerant since they had to compete for a comparatively small group of potential followers. Apart from illustrating the heterogeneity in religious diversity across the Islamic world, the ethnomusicologist thus identified key factors that help explain variations in Muslim expressions of tolerance. While their religious identity is clearly significant for the way these people interact with others, "Islam" as an abstract category or even "Sufism" in and of itself hardly explain anything in comparison with specific circumstances.

Contemporary Iran has proven to be a rich source for innovative notions of tolerance. Katajun Amirpur surveyed such views and their history, focusing on

---

[98] Diouf, Mamadou, (ed.), *Tolerance, Democracy, and Sufis in Senegal*, New York: Columbia University Press, 2013. Cf. especially the introduction, "The Public Role of the 'Good Islam': Sufi Islam and the Administration of Pluralism," 1–35.
[99] Frishkopf, Michael, "Muslims, Music, and Religious Tolerance in Egypt and Ghana. A Comparative Perspective on Difference," in: Karin van Nieuwkerk/Mark Levine/Martin Stokes (eds.), *Islam and Popular Culture*, 323–46, Austin: University of Texas Press, 2016.

Abdolkarim Soroush and his literary analysis of Ḥāfeẓ.[100] Inspired by the medieval poet, the philosopher emphasized the fallibility of humans, a common foundation for concepts of tolerance. Soroush is also widely associated with his phrase *sarāthā-ye mostaqim*, the "right paths." The significant feature here is the plural — the philosopher adapted the expression from the first sura of the Qurʾān, in which believers ask God to guide them to "the right path." Soroush substantiates the idea of the plurality of approaches to the truth with the Islamic tradition, notably Rūmī and the widespread Sufi idea that since God is ultimately unknowable to the human mind, a variety of expressions are possible — a notion we have already seen in Ibn ʿArabī's poem. The second example Amirpur discusses is the philosopher Mohammad Shabestari who insisted that the quality of the relationship between different religious communities and God should not determine their social relationships among each other. Both Soroush and Shabestari are prominent counterpoints to the high-profile examples of intolerance in Iran.

11 Conclusion

The discursive prominence of tolerance in discussions about "Islam" and "modernity" obscures some of the difficulties this concept involves. In historical research, a lot of progress has been made by those who analyze the changing quality of intercommunal relationships as well as conceptual-terminological aspects. To conclude, a few challenges shall be highlighted.

As Jonathan Israel and other historians of the Enlightenment have revealed in recent scholarship, Islam often served Western European intellectuals as a foil to articulate sociopolitical critiques and proposals for societal improvement in their respective contexts.[101] The history of Christian and of Western European representations of Islam is as old as Muḥammad's movement, and throughout this history such representations often tell us more about the agents than about the objects of the representation. It was when tolerance became a focus of Western European interest, that Islamic ideas and practices of tolerance became a subject

---

100 Amirpur, Katajun, "Gegenwärtige islamische Konzeptionen von religiöser Toleranz: das Beispiel Iran," in: Myriam Bienenstock/Pierre Bühler (eds.), *Religiöse Toleranz heute und gestern*, 169–91, Freiburg: Karl Alber, 2011.
101 Israel, Jonathan I., *Enlightenment Contested. Philosophy, Modernity, and the Emancipation of Man 1670–1752*, Oxford: Oxford University Press, 2008, 618. For the interesting case of eighteenth-century Western European appreciation of Wahhabism as pure monotheism without critical attention paid to the movement's intolerance cf. Falaky, Fayçal, "Radical Islam, Tolerance, and the Enlightenment," *Studies in Eighteenth-Century Culture* 47 (2018), 265–68.

of discussion and representation. Muslims were potential objects of tolerance, but they also served as models, whether positive or negative. It is worth bearing this history in mind whenever tolerance or intolerance in the Islamic world are debated and to consider what such debates reveal about the people who lead them and the interventions they make in their own societies.

Tolerance can be understood as a component of broader philosophical or ideological worldviews. It may be the case that it has been primarily in response to the prominence of tolerance in Western discourse that Muslim individuals or groups have been described in terms of tolerance or that they described themselves in such a way. That situation may well remain unchanged. This discursive difference, however, does not mean that tolerance as a problem or perhaps rather a solution for a problem is alien to Islamic contexts or that it cannot be discussed in terms derived from the Islamic tradition itself.

The parameters of this discussion must not be assumed and are themselves open to debate. Why are people sometimes tolerant and sometimes intolerant? Who determines which cases of conflict or collaboration are instances of tolerance or the absence thereof? How do concepts relate to social realities? How can we benefit from the experiences of our ancestors? The answers to these questions depend largely on where one stands regarding the grand methodological turns in the humanities and social sciences.

Does language matter? According to the Sapir-Whorf hypothesis, the way we speak has a critical impact on the way we see the world. Language plays a decisive role in articulating and constituting tolerance. An Arabic vocabulary thus offers a good impression of Islamic notions of pluralism, disagreement and tolerance (although, following that logic, attitudes of Arabic-speaking Christians or Jews would constitute interesting cases).

Do ideas matter? The historian Michael Cook faced a similar issue in a study in which he compared the presence of Islamic ideas in political discourse to other religious contexts.[102] While he might not go so far as attributing unambiguous agency to ideas, he grants them discursive significance. Propaganda would not work if words did not matter.

Does history matter? Are attitudes of historical Muslims a manifestation of a larger truth of Islam, or can we say that they have fallen short of the Qurʾān's ethical potential, as modernist thinkers often claim.[103] Conversely, does history reveal

---

[102] Cook, Michael, *Ancient Religions, Modern Politics. The Islamic Case in Comparative Perspective*, Princeton: Princeton University Press, 2014.
[103] Cf. Hashmi, Sohail, "A Conservative Legacy," in: Khaled Abou El Fadl (ed.), *The Place of Tolerance in Islam*, 31–36, Boston: Beacon Press, 2002.

the true meaning of a text? Vincent Cornell suggests they do. "Actions taken in response to scripture are interpretive statements."[104] The hermeneutic problem we are grappling with here is the fundamental question what texts mean outside the historical environment that produced them and to what extent authors or readers are constitutive for the meaning of a text.

Reframed in different terms, tolerance presents itself in the form of debates about our ability to reach certainty, how we can reach certainty, and what degree of certainty we can maximally achieve. The result of our efforts to gain certainty are inevitably different truth claims — either because we can only reach a modest level of certainty or because people make mistakes, even if the certainty we can gain about a matter is high. How much responsibility we have for our mistakes is controversial, but so is the question of what one person's mistake can mean for another person or the community at large. We may refrain from compulsion to truth in the realm of low certainty, but what are our obligations if we can have high certainty? There are obligations towards the person who is mistaken, but also towards people who may be influenced by that person. Frictions between tolerance and other values are thus obvious in Islamic history as well. The pursuit of truth is often intertwined with the pursuit of justice, reflecting the complex moral and ethical tenets that characterize Islamic thought. Freedom, a typical complementary or even foundational value of tolerance in modern discussions, is complicated in premodern Islamic literature since it wavers between being a fact (as in freedom vs. predestination) and being a value (as in freedom vs. slavery). Furthermore, we can recognize a classical precedent of epistemological justice in the principle that every human is meant to have ideal conditions for recognizing the truth. As much as an internalized view of the pursuit of religious truth which prioritizes honest effort and right intention thus furthers conditions of tolerance, it is not sufficient for such a disposition either.

Elaborating on the difficulty of insulating tolerance within a complex situation and returning to the observation that tolerance often takes the shape of a rejection of its opposite, politico-religious violence is regularly described as intolerance. There is certainly some justification in doing so. The reverse conclusion, however, is harder to draw. The absence of such violence is not necessarily a sign of tolerance. Even with a modest moral standard, tolerance presupposes an option, a temptation or inclination towards suppression. To assume that we are inclined towards such violence wherever we see diversity might involve a little too grim a notion of human nature.

---

[104] Cornell, "Theologies of Difference," 278.

If we recognize tolerance as a value, which traditions and authorities can be most effectively mobilized to increase tolerance among Muslims? Abou El Fadl's critics deserve attention in their effort to identify situations which are not cases for religious tolerance. One does not have to be a historical materialist to believe that tolerance, religious or otherwise, is not a panacea. To have a clear sense of what tolerance is and where it might serve as the best solution for a problem is a critical requirement for any complex religious agenda that promotes tolerance. For the philosopher Bouhdiba, the law plays a critical role in fostering tolerance. Abou El Fadl's "tolerance verses" too can fulfil such a purpose. The philosopher al-Fārābī had a method of moral improvement to offer which may still recommend itself today. Although not speaking of tolerance, he described an exercise of self-examination where we recognize how uncomfortable the practice of certain virtues is and then gradually habituate ourselves to them. A philosophically engaged approach to Islamic intellectual history which treats such voices of the past as interlocutors may borrow this method in encouraging us to expose ourselves to views and practices we find disagreeable.

Bibliography

Abou El Fadl, Khaled, *The Place of Tolerance in Islam*, ed. Joshua Cohen/Ian Lague for *Boston Review*, Boston: Beacon Press, 2002.

Acar, Ismail, "Theological Foundations of Religious Tolerance in Islam: A Qur'ānic Perspective," in: Jacob Neusner/Bruce Chilton (eds.), *Religious Tolerance in World Religions*, 297–313, West Conshohocken: Templeton Foundation Press, 2008.

Adamson, Peter, "Al-Kindi," published online: Edward N. Zalta/Uri Nodelman (eds.), *Stanford Encyclopedia of Philosophy*,
https://plato.stanford.edu/entries/al-kindi/ (accessed on 14.07.2024).

Addas, Claude, *Quest for the Red Sulphur. The Life of Ibn ʿArabī*, Cambridge: Islamic Texts Society, 1993.

Afsaruddin, Asma, "Tolerance and Pluralism in Islamic Thought and Practice," in: Vicki A. Spencer (ed.), *Toleration in Comparative Perspective*, 99–119, Lanham: Lexington Books, 2018.

Akasoy, Anna, "Gender and the Poetics of God's Alterity in Andalusi Mysticism," in: Megan Moore (ed.), *Gender in the Premodern Mediterranean*, 97–117, Tempe: Arizona Center for Medieval & Renaissance Studies, 2019.

Akasoy, Anna, "Imaginary Spaces of Devotion in Andalusi Mystical Poetry. Christian Monks and Monasteries in a *Qaṣīda* by al-Shushtarī," *The Maghreb Review* 45/4 (2020), 721–43.

Akasoy, Anna, "Paganism and Islam. Medieval Arabic Literature on Religions in West Africa," in: John Marenbon/Carlos Steel/Werner Verbeke (eds.), *Paganism in the Middle Ages. Threat and Fascination*, 207–38, Leuven: Leuven University Press, 2012.

Akasoy, Anna, "Was Ibn Rushd an Averroist? The Problem, the Debate, and its Philosophical Implications," in: Anna Akasoy/Guido Giglioni (eds.), *Renaissance Averroism and its Aftermath*, 321–47, Dordrecht: Springer, 2013.

Ali, Kecia, *The Lives of Muhammad*, Cambridge: Harvard University Press, 2014.
Ali, Tariq, "Theological Distractions," in: Khaled Abou El Fadl (ed.), *The Place of Tolerance in Islam*, 37–41, Boston: Beacon Press, 2002.
Alvarez, Lourdes, "The Mystical Language of Daily Life. Vernacular Sufi Poetry and the Songs of Abū al-Ḥasan al-Shushtarī," *Exemplaria* 17/1 (2005), 1–32.
Amirpur, Katajun, "Gegenwärtige islamische Konzeptionen von religiöser Toleranz: das Beispiel Iran," in: Myriam Bienenstock/Pierre Bühler (eds.), *Religiöse Toleranz heute und gestern*, 169–91, Freiburg: Karl Alber, 2011.
Angeles Gallego, María/Bleaney, Heather/García Suárez, Pablo, *Bibliography of Jews in the Islamic World*, Leiden: Brill, 2010.
Baer, Marc/Makdisi, Ussama/Shryock, Andrew, "Tolerance and Conversion in the Ottoman Empire. A Conversation," *Comparative Studies in Society and History* 51 (2009), 927–40.
Barkey, Karen, *Empire of Difference. The Ottomans in Comparative Perspective*, Cambridge: Cambridge University Press, 2008.
Bauer, Thomas, *Die Kultur der Ambiguität. Eine andere Geschichte des Islams*, Berlin: Verlag der Weltreligionen, 2011.
Bennison, Amira K., *The Almoravid and Almohad Empires*, Edinburgh: Edinburgh University Press, 2016.
Bouhdiba, Abdelwahab, "On Islamic Tolerance," *Diogenes* 176, vol. 44/4 (1996), 121–36.
Brown, Daniel W. (ed.), *The Wiley Blackwell Concise Companion to the Hadith*, Chichester: Wiley Blackwell, 2020.
Brown, Jonathan A. C., *Hadith. Muhammad's Legacy in the Medieval and Modern World*, London: Oneworld², 2018.
Coope, Jessica A., "Religious and Cultural Conversion to Islam in Ninth-Century Umayyad Córdoba," *Journal of World History* 4/1 (1993), 47–68.
Casewit, Yousef, *The Mystics of al-Andalus. Ibn Barrajān and Islamic Thought in the Twelfth Century*, Cambridge: Cambridge University Press, 2017.
Chittick, William C., *Imaginal Worlds. Ibn al-'Arabī and the Problem of Religious Diversity*, Albany: State University of New York Press, 1994.
Cohen, Mark R., *Under Crescent and Cross. The Jews in the Middle Ages*, Princeton: Princeton University Press, 1994.
Cook, Michael, *Ancient Religions, Modern Politics. The Islamic Case in Comparative Perspective*, Princeton: Princeton University Press, 2014.
Cook, Michael, *Commanding Right and Forbidding Wrong in Islamic Thought*, Cambridge: Cambridge University Press, 2000.
Cornell, Vincent J., "Mystical Doctrine and Political Action in Moroccan Sufism. The Role of the Exemplar in the Ṭarīqa al-Jazūliyya," *Al-Qanṭara* 13 (1992), 201–31.
Cornell, Vincent J., "Theologies of Difference and Ideologies of Intolerance in Islam," in: Jacob Neusner/Bruce Chilton (eds.), *Religious Tolerance in World Religions*, 274–96, West Conshohocken: Templeton Foundation Press, 2008.
Crone, Patricia, "'No Compulsion in Religion'. Q. 2:256 in Mediaeval and Modern Interpretation," in: Mohammad Ali Amir-Moezzi/Meir M. Bar-Asher/Simon Hopkins (eds.), *Le Shī'isme Imāmite quarante ans après. Hommage à Etan Kohlberg*, 131–78, Turnhout: Brepols, 2009.
Diouf, Mamadou, "The Public Role of the 'Good Islam': Sufi Islam and the Administration of Pluralism," in Mamadou Diouf (ed.), *Tolerance, Democracy, and Sufis in Senegal*, 1–35, New York Chichester, West Sussex: Columbia University Press, 2013.

Diouf, Mamadou, (ed.), *Tolerance, Democracy, and Sufis in Senegal*, New York Chichester, West Sussex: Columbia University Press, 2013.
Dutton, Yasin, "The Introduction to Ibn Rushd's Bidāyat al-Mujtahid," *Islamic Law and Society* 1 (1994), 188–205.
Ellethy, Yaser, *Islam, Context, Pluralism and Democracy. Classical and Modern Interpretations*, New York: Routledge, 2015.
Empey, Heather J., "The Mothers of the Caliph's Sons. Women as Spoils of War during the Early Almohad Period," in: Matthew S. Gordon/Kathryn A. Hain (eds.), *Concubines and Courtesans. Women and Slavery in Islamic History*, 143–62, Oxford: Oxford University Press, 2017.
Ess, Josef van, *Theology and Society in the Second and Third Centuries of the Hijra*, vol. 4, *A History of Religious Thought in Early Islam*, Leiden: Brill, 2017–2019.
Falaky, Fayçal, "Radical Islam, Tolerance, and the Enlightenment," *Studies in Eighteenth-Century Culture* 47 (2018), 265–68.
Fierro, Maribel, "The Legal Policies of the Almohad Caliphs and Ibn Rushd's Bidāyat al-Mujtahid," *Journal of Islamic Studies* 10/3 (1999), 226–48.
Fierro, Maribel, "Spiritual Alienation and Political Activism: The ġurabā' in al-andalus during the Sixth/Twelfth Century," *Arabica* 47 (2000), 230–60, JSTOR.
Fierro, Maribel, *'Abd al-Rahman III. The First Cordoban Caliph*, Oxford: Oneworld, 2005.
Fierro, Maribel, "A Muslim Land without Jews or Christians: Almohad Policies Regarding the 'Protected People'," in: Matthias M. Tischler/Alexander Fidora (eds.), *Christlicher Norden – Muslimischer Süden. Ansprüche und Wirklichkeiten von Christen, Juden und Muslimen auf der Iberischen Halbinsel im Hoch- und Spätmittelalter*, 231–47, Münster: Aschendorff, 2011.
Filios, Denise K., "Expulsion from Paradise: Exiled Intellectuals and Andalusian Tolerance," in: Simon R. Doubleday/David Coleman (eds.), *In the Light of Medieval Spain. Islam, the West, and the Relevance of the Past*, 91–113, New York: Palgrave Macmillan, 2008.
Finkel, Joshua, "A Risāla of al-Jāḥiẓ," *Journal of the American Oriental Society* 47 (1927), 311–34.
Friedmann, Yohanan, "Classification of Unbelievers in Sunni Muslim Law and Tradition," *Jerusalem Studies in Arabic and Islam* 22 (1998), 163–95.
Friedmann, Yohanan, *Tolerance and Coercion in Islam. Interfaith Religions in the Muslim Tradition*, Cambridge: Cambridge University Press, 2003.
Friedmann, Yohanan, "Tolerance and Coercion," in: Jane Dammen McAuliffe (ed.), *Encyclopaedia of the Qur'ān*, vol. 5, 290–94, Leiden: Brill, 2005.
Frishkopf, Michael, "Muslims, Music, and Religious Tolerance in Egypt and Ghana. A Comparative Perspective on Difference," in: Karin van Nieuwkerk/Mark Levine/Martin Stokes (eds.), *Islam and Popular Culture*, 323–46, Austin: University of Texas Press, 2016.
Gallego, María A./Bleaney, Heather/Suárez, Pablo Garcíam (eds.), *Bibliography of Jews in the Islamic World*, Leiden: Brill, 2010.
García-Arenal, Mercedes, "La práctica del precepto de *al-amr bi-l-ma'rūf wa-l-nahy 'an al-munkar* en la hagiografía magrebí," *Al-Qanṭara* 13 (1992), 143–65.
Al-Ghazālī, *Deliverance from Error. Five Key Texts Including His Spiritual Autobiography, al-Munqidh min al-Dalal*, trans. Richard J. McCarthy, Boston: Twayne Publishers, 1980.
Griffel, Frank, "Toleranzkonzepte im Islam und ihr Einfluß auf Jean Bodins Colloquium Heptaplomeres," in: Ralph Häfner (ed.), *Bodinus Polymeres. Neue Studien zu Jean Bodins Spätwerk*, 119–44, Wiesbaden: Harrassowitz, 1999.
Griffel, Frank, *Apostasie und Toleranz im Islam. Die Entwicklung zu al-Ġazālīs Urteil gegen die Philosophie und die Reaktionen der Philosophen*, Leiden: Brill, 2000.

Griffel, Frank, *Al-Ghazālī's Philosophical Theology*, Oxford: Oxford University Press, 2009.
Griffel, Frank, ""… and the Killing of Someone who Upholds these Convictions is Obligatory!" Religious Law and the Assumed Disappearance of Philosophy in Islam," in Andreas Speer/Guy Guldentops (eds.), *Das Gesetz – The Law – La Loi*, 214–26, Berlin: De Gruyter, 2014.
Griffel, Frank, "Al-Ghazālī's (d. 1111) *Incoherence of the Philosophers*," in: Khaled El-Rouayheb and Sabine Schmidtke (eds.), *The Oxford Handbook of Islamic Philosophy*, 191–209, Oxford: Oxford University Press, 2017.
Griffel, Frank, *Den Islam denken. Versuch, eine Religion zu verstehen*, Stuttgart: Reclam, 2019.
Griffith, Sidney H., "The Monk in the Emir's Majlis. Reflections on a Popular Genre of Christian Literary Apologetics in Arabic in the Early Islamic Period," in: Hava Lazarus-Yafeh et al (eds.), *The Majlis. Interreligious Encounters in Medieval Islam*, 13–65, Wiesbaden: Harrassowitz, 1999.
Griffith, Sidney H., *The Church in the Shadow of the Mosque. Christians and Muslims in the World of Islam*, Princeton: Princeton University Press, 2008.
Griffith, Sidney H., "Excursus I: Christian Theological Thought during the First 'Abbāsid Century," in: Sabine Schmidtke (ed.), *The Oxford Handbook of Islamic Theology*, 91–102, Oxford: Oxford University Press, 2016.
Hallaq, Wael B., *The Origins and Evolution of Islamic Law*, Cambridge: Cambridge University Press, 2005.
Halm, Heinz, *Shī'ism*, New York: Columbia University Press, ²2014.
Hartmann, Angelika, "Pluralismus und Toleranz aus der Sicht des Islam," in: Christian Augustin/Johannes Wienand/Christiane Winkler (eds.), *Religiöser Pluralismus und Toleranz in Europa*, 123–86, Wiesbaden: VS Verlag für Sozialwissenschaften, 2006.
Hashmi, Sohail, "A Conservative Legacy," in: Khaled Abou El Fadl (ed.), *The Place of Tolerance in Islam*, 31–36, Boston: Beacon Press, 2002.
Haykel, Bernard, "Reforming Islam by Dissolving the Madhāhib: Shawkānī and his Zaydī Detractors in Yemen," in: Bernard G. Weiss (ed.), *Studies in Islamic Legal Theory*, 337–64, Leiden: Brill, 2002.
Hoover, Jon, "Ibn Taymiyya Between Moderation and Radicalism," in: Elisabeth Kendall/Ahmad Khan (eds.), *Reclaiming Islamic Tradition: Modern Interpretations of the Classical Heritage*, 177–203, Edinburgh: Edinburgh University Press, 2018.
Ibn ʿArabī, *The Tarjumán al-Ashwáq. A Collection of Mystical Odes by Muḥyi'ddín Ibn al-ʿArabí*, ed. and trans. Reynold A. Nicholson, London: Royal Asiatic Society, 1911.
Israel, Jonathan I., *Enlightenment Contested. Philosophy, Modernity, and the Emancipation of Man 1670–1752*, Oxford: Oxford University Press, 2008, 618.
Jackson, Sherman A., *On the Boundaries of Theological Tolerance in Islam. Abū Ḥāmid al-Ghazālī's Fayṣal al-Tafriqa*, Oxford: Oxford University Press, 2002.
Janos, Damien (ed.), *Ideas in Motion in Baghdad and Beyond. Philosophical and Theological Exchanges between Christians and Muslims in the Third/Ninth and Fourth/Tenth Centuries*, Leiden: Brill, 2016.
Jong, Frederick de/Radtke, Bernd (eds.), *Islamic Mysticism Contested. Thirteen Centuries of Controversies and Polemics*, Leiden: Brill, 1999.
Kadri, Sadakat, *Heaven on Earth. A Journey through Shari'a Law from the Deserts of Ancient Arabia to the Streets of the Modern Muslim World*, New York: Farrar Straus & Giroux, 2012.
Kahera, Akel I./Benmira, Omar, "Damages in Islamic Law. Maghribī Muftīs and the Built Environment (9th–15th C.E.)," *Islamic Law and Society* 5 (1998), 131–64.

El Kaisy-Friemuth, Maha, "The Concept of Freedom in Islam," in: Georges Tamer/Ursula Männle (eds.), *The Concept of Freedom in Judaism, Christianity and Islam*, 101–46, Berlin: De Gruyter, 2019.

Kalin, Ibrahim, "Sources of Tolerance and Intolerance in Islam. The Case of the People of the Book," in: Jacob Neusner/Bruce Chilton (eds.), *Religious Tolerance in World Religions*, 239–73, West Conshohocken: Templeton Foundation Press, 2008.

Karamustafa, Ahmet T., *God's Unruly Friends. Dervish Groups in the Islamic Later Middle Period, 1200–1550*, Oxford: Oneworld, 1994.

Kokew, Stephan, *Annäherung an Toleranz. Ausgangspunkte, Kontexte und zeitgenössische Interpretationen des Toleranzbegriffs aus dem schiitischen Islam*, Würzburg: Ergon, 2014.

Kokew, Stephan, "Toleranz im Islam," in: Michael Klöcker/Udo Tworuschka (eds.), *Handbuch der Religionen*, 50. Ergänzungslieferung, Munich: Mediengruppe Oberfranken, 2016.

Kraemer, Joel L., *Humanism in the Renaissance of Islam. The Cultural Revival during the Buyid Age*, Leiden: Brill, 1993.

Krämer, Gudrun, "Toleranz im Islam. Ein Blick in Geschichte und Gegenwart," in: Angelika Neuwirth/Günter Stock (eds.), *Europa im Nahen Osten – Der Nahe Osten in Europa*, 39–52, Berlin: Akademie Verlag, 2010.

Lassner, Jacob, *Jews, Christians, and the Abode of Islam. Modern Scholarship, Medieval Realities*, Chicago: The University of Chicago Press, 2012, 177.

Lecker, Michael, *The "Constitution of Medina": Muhammad's First Legal Document*, Princeton: Darwin Press, 2004.

Levy-Rubin, Milka, *Non-Muslims in the Early Islamic Empire. From Surrender to Coexistence*, Cambridge: Cambridge University Press, 2011.

Levy-Rubin, Milka, "'Umar II's *ghiyār* Edict: Between Ideology and Practice," in: Antoine Borrut/Fred Donner (eds.), *Christians and Others in the Early Umayyad State*, 157–72, Chicago: Oriental Institute of the University of Chicago, 2016.

Marcotte, Roxanne D., "Suhrawardī al-Maqtūl, the Martyr of Aleppo," *Al-Qanṭara* 22/2 (2001), 395–419.

Marín, Manuela, "*Inqibād 'an al-sulṭān: 'ulamā'* and Political Power in al-Andalus," in: *Saber religioso y poder político en el Islam*, 127–40, Madrid: Agencia Española de Cooperación Internacional, 1994.

Massignon, Louis, *The Passion of al-Hallaj*, vol. 4, *Mystic and Martyr of Islam*, Princeton: Princeton University Press, 1982.

Mcginnis, Jon, *Classical Arabic Philosophy*, Indianapolis: Hackett, 2007.

Menocal, María Rosa, *The Ornament of the World. How Muslims, Jews, and Christians Created a Culture of Tolerance in Medieval Spain*, New York: Back Bay Books, 2012.

Moreen, Vera Basch (ed.), *In Queen Esther's Garden. An Anthology of Judeo-Persian Literature*, New Haven: Yale University Press, 2000.

Motzki, Harald (ed.), *The Biography of Muhammad. The Issue of the Sources*, Leiden: Brill, 2000.

al-Muqaddasī, *The Best Divisions for Knowledge of the Regions (Aḥsān al-Taqāsīm fī Ma'rifat al-Aqālīm)*, trans. Basil Collins, Reading: Garnet, 2001.

Musa, Aisha Y., *Ḥadīth as Scripture. Discussions on the Authority of the Prophetic Traditions in Islam*, Basingstoke: Palgrave Macmillan, 2015.

Neusner, Jacob/Chilton, Bruce (eds.), *Religious Tolerance in World Religions*, West Conshohocken: Templeton Foundation Press, 2008.

Noth, Albrecht, "Möglichkeiten und Grenzen islamischer Toleranz," *Saeculum* 29 (1978), 190–204.

Paret, Rudi, "Sure 2,256: lā ikrāha fī d-dīni. Toleranz oder Resignation?," *Der Islam* 45 (1969), 299–300.
Paret, Rudi, "Toleranz und Intoleranz im Islam," *Saeculum* 21 (1970), 344–65.
Peters, Francis E., *Muhammad and the Origins of Islam*, Albany: State University of New York Press, 1994.
Philpott, Daniel, *Religious Freedom in Islam. The Fate of a Universal Human Right in the Muslim World Today*, Oxford: Oxford University Press, 2019.
Powers, Paul R., *Intent in Islamic Law. Motive and Meaning in Medieval Sunnī Fiqh*, Leiden: Brill, 2006.
Poya, Abbas, *Anerkennung des Iğtihād – Legitimation der Toleranz. Möglichkeiten innerer und äußerer Toleranz im Islam am Beispiel der Iğtihād-Diskussion*, Berlin: Schwarz, 2003.
Rapoport, Yossef, *Marriage, Money and Divorce in Medieval Islamic Society*, Cambridge: Cambridge University Press, 2005.
Saeed, Abdullah/Saeed, Hassan, *Freedom of Religion, Apostasy and Islam*, Aldershot: Ashgate, 2005.
Safran, Janina M., "The Politics of Book Burning in al-Andalus," *Journal of Medieval Iberian Studies* 6/2 (2014), 148–68.
Sanders, Paula, *Ritual, Politics, and the City in Fatimid Cairo*, Albany: State University of New York Press, 1994.
Schirrmacher, Christine, *"Let There Be No Compulsion in Religion" (Sura 2:256). Apostasy from Islam as Judged by Contemporary Islamic Theologians. Discourses on Apostasy, Religious Freedom, and Human Rights*, Eugene: Wipf & Stock, 2016.
Schmidtke, Sabine (ed.), *The Oxford Handbook of Islamic Theology*, Oxford: Oxford University Press, 2016.
Schoeler, Gregor, *The Biography of Muḥammad. Nature and Authenticity*, Milton Park: Routledge, 2011.
Schulze, Reinhard, "Der Islam und die Toleranz," in: Romana Weiershausen/Insa Wilka/Nina Gülcher (eds.), *Aufgeklärte Zeiten? Religiöse Toleranz und Literatur*, 45–68, Berlin: Erich Schmidt, 2011.
Sen, Amartya, *Identity and Violence. The Illusion of Destiny*, New York: W.W. Norton & Co., 2006.
Shryock, Andrew J., "Attack of the Islamophobes. Religious War (and Peace) in Arab/Muslim Detroit," in: Carl Ernst (ed.), *Islamophobia in America: The Anatomy of Intolerance*, 145–74, 162, New York: Palgrave Macmillan, 2013.
Stevens, Cat, "Tolerance in Islam," published online: https://catstevens.com/think/spiritual-domain/tolerance-in-islam/ (accessed on 14.07.2024).
Stroumsa, Sarah, *Maimondes in his World. Portrait of a Mediterranean Thinker*, Princeton: Princeton University Press, 2009.
Stroumsa, Sarah, *Freethinkers of Medieval Islam. Ibn al-Rawāndī, Abū Bakr al-Rāzī and their Impact on Islamic Thought*, Leiden: Brill, 1999; reprint 2016.
Sweeney, Michael J., "Philosophy and Jihād: Al-Fārābī on Compulsion to Happiness," *The Review of Metaphysics* 60 (2007), 543–72.
Szpiech, Ryan, *Conversion and Narrative. Reading and Religious Authority in Medieval Polemic*, Philadelphia: University of Pennsylvania Press, 2013.
Thomas, David/Roggema, Barbara (eds.), *Christian-Muslim Relations. A Bibliographical History*, vol. 1 *(600–900)*, Leiden: Brill, 2009.
Treiger, Alexander, "Origins of Kalām," in: Sabine Schmidtke (ed.), *The Oxford Handbook of Islamic Theology*, 27–43, Oxford: Oxford University Press, 2016.
Walker, Paul E., *Caliph of Cairo. The Remarkable Story of the Ruler who Vanished. The Mysterious Case of Al-Hakim, Commander of the Believers*, London: I.B. Tauris, 2009.

Wasserstrom, Steven M., "Jewish-Muslim Relations in the Context of Andalusian Emigration," in: Mark D. Meyerson/Edward D. English (eds.), *Christians, Muslims and Jews in Medieval and Early Modern Spain*, 69–87, Notre Dame: University of Notre Dame Press, 2000.

Watt, John W., "The Strategy of the Baghdad Philosophers. The Aristotelian Tradition as a Common Motif in Christian and Islamic Thought," in: J.J. van Ginkel et al (eds.), *Redefining Christian Identity. Cultural Interaction in the Middle East since the Rise of Islam*, 151–65, Leuven: Peeters, 2005.

Woodward, Mark, et al, "Salafi Violence and Sufi Tolerance? Rethinking Conventional Wisdom," *Perspectives on Terrorism* 7/6 (2013), 58–78.

Suggestions for Further Reading

Barkan, Elazar/Barkey, Karen (eds.), *Choreographies of Shared Sacred Sites. Religion, Politics and Conflict Resolution*, New York: Columbia University Press, 2015.

Bender, Courtney/Klassen, Pamela E. (eds.), *After Pluralism. Reimagining Religious Engagement*, New York: Columbia University Press, 2010.

Bowering, Gerhard (ed.), *Islamic Political Thought. An Introduction*, Princeton: Princeton University Press, 2015.

Elverskog, Johan, *Buddhism and Islam on the Silk Road*, Philadelphia: University of Pennsylvania Press, 2010.

Emon, Anver M., *Religious Pluralism and Islamic Law. Dhimmīs and Others in the Empire of Law*, Oxford: Oxford University Press, 2012.

Gabbay, Alyssa, *Islamic Tolerance. Amīr Khusraw and Pluralism*, Abingdon: Routledge, 2010.

Heck, Paul L., *Common Ground. Islam, Christianity, and Religious Pluralism*, Washington, D.C.: Georgetown University Press, 2009.

Morgan, Llewelyn, *The Buddhas of Bamiyan*, Cambridge: Harvard University Press, 2012.

Thomas, David et al. (eds.), *Christian-Muslim Relations. A Bibliographical History*, Leiden: Brill, 2009.

Waardenburg, Jacques, *Muslims and Others. Relations in Context*, Berlin: De Gruyter, 2003.

Catharina Rachik and Georges Tamer
Epilogue

Tolerance is not a static or universally defined ideal, but rather a dynamic concept, shaped and reshaped across diverse historical, cultural, and theological contexts. Within the religious traditions of Judaism, Christianity, and Islam, sacred texts and authoritative traditions have generated a range of interpretations concerning the legitimacy, limits, and aspirations of tolerance. Contemporary discussions must therefore ask whether a narrow conception of tolerance — such as permitting minority faiths to exist only in private spheres or endorsing coexistence merely to avoid conflict — remains sufficient in increasingly pluralistic societies.

Echoing the spirit of Goethe's provocation, that "tolerance should be a temporary attitude only: it must lead to recognition. To tolerate means to insult,"[1] this volume seeks to explore whether and how Judaism, Christianity and Islam offer resources for moving beyond mere coexistence toward mutual respect and acceptance. What theological, legal, or philosophical mechanisms within each tradition can support this shift? And how can these mechanisms be activated without requiring communities to relinquish their core truth claims?

This challenge is especially pressing in light of the enduring paradox of toleration: how can religions that assert exclusive claims to truth engage in genuine tolerance, without falling into relativism or compromising their doctrinal integrity?

The following epilogue begins by providing brief summaries of the individual contributions to this volume. It then offers a comparative reflection on commonalities and differences in how Judaism, Christianity, and Islam conceptualize tolerance, and how these conceptions might respond to the complexities of interreligious life today.

---

[1] Forst, Rainer, "Toleration," published online: Edward N. Zalta (ed.), *The Stanford Encyclopedia of Philosophy*, Fall 2017 Edition, https://plato.stanford.edu/archives/fall2017/entries/toleration/ (accessed on 27.03.2025).

1 The Concept of Tolerance from a Jewish Perspective

In his essay, Menachem Kellner explores the concept of religious tolerance within Judaism, aiming to define a framework that avoids the extremes of relativism and absolutism. He advocates for a "strong tolerance," which respects the intrinsic dignity and worth of other religions without abandoning truth claims. Drawing primarily on Maimonides' theological principles, Kellner seeks to develop a model of Jewish tolerance that traditionalists from other faiths could also embrace.

Kellner critiques simplistic definitions of tolerance as mere "putting up with" others or pitying those with differing views. Instead, he calls for a robust model of mutual respect that acknowledges the inherent value of other religious traditions. This is especially challenging in monotheistic traditions, such as Judaism, Christianity, and Islam, which traditionally assert exclusive claims to divine truth. Kellner identifies several tensions that are central to this endeavor. The first one is the "paradox of toleration," which raises the question of how one can respect beliefs they find false or harmful without compromising their own commitment to truth. The second tension pertains to the relationship between monotheism and exclusivism. While monotheism is theoretically universalist, it has historically fostered exclusivist attitudes by deeming alternative religious expressions illegitimate. Finally, the text addresses the particularism within Judaism, noting that the religion's dual identity, manifesting as both a religious tradition and an ethnic identity, complicates its position on religious pluralism.

Kellner's analysis of the historical evolution of Jewish tolerance suggests that, prior to the modern era, Jewish communities placed a greater emphasis on securing tolerance for themselves than on extending it to others. This focus stemmed from the weak and persecuted position of these communities during that historical period. The establishment of the State of Israel and the modern engagement of Judaism with global religious communities have led to a pressing need for theological tolerance. A case in point is the subject of idolatry ('avodah zarah), which in classical Judaism is regarded as one of the three cardinal sins. Given the growing ties with Hindu India, for instance, a reinterpretation of this concept is imperative. Moreover, Jewish communities outside Israel must define their collaboration with non-Jews in a secular environment. In this context, Kellner's analysis illuminates the seminal contribution of Moses Mendelssohn, who pioneered a conceptual framework for tolerance anchored in Jewish thought. Mendelssohn, influenced by the Enlightenment, advanced a doctrine of religious tolerance and pluralism grounded in the theorization of natural religion, which he conceived as accessible to all human beings through rational thought. However, Kellner ultimately rejects pluralism, as it is predicated upon a notion of epistemological relativism. His objective is to formulate a conception of tolerance that does not repudiate the claim that truth matters.

Additionally, he critiques traditionalist approaches, such as the Noahides and Messianic Universalism. Within the Noahide framework, adherents posit that non-Jews can attain righteousness through observance of the seven Noahide laws, which Kellner finds paternalistic. This viewpoint is particularly contentious when considering the perspective of Maimonides, who asserted that adherence to the Torah is an indispensable criterion for identifying a true Noahide. Consequently, this stipulation effectively excludes individuals who are either unaware of the Torah or do not acknowledge its authority. Messianic Universalism emerges as another strategy to circumvent intolerance within Jewish thought. According to Maimonides, in the era of the Messiah, Judaism will transition from its status as an ethnic religion to a universal religion that encompasses all of humanity. Maimonides affirms that Christianity and Islam play preparatory roles in the eventual universal acceptance of Judaism, which still excludes other religions from ultimate legitimacy. Additionally, Kellner expounds on the absence of tolerance within Judaism. The Bible instructs believers to "love the stranger (ger)" (Dt 10:19) and to "love thy neighbor (re'a)" (Lev 19:18); statements which have historically been interpreted in a particularistic fashion. According to the Jewish tradition, the term "stranger" is understood to refer to a proselyte, while the term "neighbor" is interpreted as referring to a fellow Jew, not to any non-Jew. This particularism, characterized by its exclusive nature, manifested prominently during the medieval period.

Kellner proposes a constructive resolution to the theological tension between exclusive truth claims and the aspiration for genuine interreligious tolerance. The crux of his argument is that one can acknowledge the truth of the Torah while recognizing human limitations in fully grasping divine truth — a stance he calls "epistemological humility." Kellner underscores that asserting the truth of the Torah does not necessitate the claim of complete understanding of that truth. To substantiate this claim, Kellner employs Maimonides' teachings, particularly his portrayal of Moses as the most exalted prophet who still could not fully comprehend God. This, according to Kellner, demonstrates that even the most exalted human intellect is limited. He underscores that this acknowledgment of human limitation — already embedded in the Jewish tradition — should encourage humility in theological claims and openness toward others.

Kellner's analysis demonstrates that even Maimonides, despite his towering authority, made theological claims (e. g., denying the possibility of sincere theological error) that were challenged by figures such as Rabbi Abraham ben David. The contemporary reception of Maimonides' theological stance, particularly with regard to his rigid exclusivism concerning corporeal conceptions of God, suggests that modern Jewish theology is already operating within a more tolerant framework, albeit one that is often unacknowledged. Kellner's argument underscores the significance of acknowledging this theological fallibility in fostering a culture of respectful tolerance.

Despite his personal inclination toward religious pluralism, Kellner rejects it as a final solution, primarily because it dilutes the Jewish commitment to truth and ignores Judaism's ethnic and national dimensions. Judaism is not just a religion but also a peoplehood, and the covenantal identity of the Jews resists being reduced to a relativistic religious claim. Moreover, Kellner sees religious pluralism as insufficiently rigorous in its treatment of truth — which, despite being contested, still matters deeply to theological discourse.

Ultimately, Kellner offers epistemological modesty as a middle path between absolutism and relativism. This approach, he believes, allows Jews — as well as adherents of other faiths — to take their own truths seriously while treating the religious other not merely with forbearance but with genuine respect.

2 The Concept of Tolerance from a Christian Perspective

Christian Polke's posthumously completed essay offers a comprehensive exploration of tolerance within Christianity, examining its historical, theological, and ethical dimensions. It delves into the evolution of Christian attitudes toward tolerance, particularly in light of its foundational texts, doctrinal developments, and practical implications in interfaith and sociopolitical contexts. Polke highlights how Christian tolerance evolved from periods of exclusivism and violence to modern frameworks emphasizing religious freedom and human dignity.

Polke notes that the concept of tolerance, as understood today, is largely a product of modernity. The word *tolerantia* is found in old Latin translations of the Bible as well as in the writings of a few church fathers where it is used in the sense of endurance in relation to others. Here, enduring evil, misfortune and persecution becomes a sign of faith and trust in God. Thus, tolerance was initially a virtue of the weak. The concept of tolerance is alien to the biblical worldview. But biblical texts have influenced the development of Christian tolerance. For example, Paul in several of his letters thematizes the "handling of the strong with the weak" (Rom 14–15; 1Cor 8) and aims at a basically tolerant attitude within the context of religious commandments and social circumstances, emphasizing the importance of personal conscience. However, his rejection of divergent beliefs shows limited tolerance by modern standards. Jesus, on the other hand, taught love for enemies (Matthew 5:44), a principle that Polke argues goes beyond passive endurance to active concern for others' well-being.

Polke chronicles Christianity's transformation from a persecuted minority to a dominant global religion, which significantly influenced its stance on tolerance. Early Christians, under Roman rule, developed strategies for coexistence. However, after Christianity became the state religion, dissenters, pagans, and heretics were widely suppressed, reversing the earlier Christian plea for tolerance. Theologians like Augustine contributed to this shift by justifying coercion to protect doctrinal purity and social order, linking heresy with political destabilization. Polke highlights how this newfound dominance created internal pressures for conformity, as the Church sought to unify the empire through a single, orthodox faith. Councils, such as those at Nicaea, were convened to resolve doctrinal disputes, often with the backing of imperial authority. This transformation marked a pivotal moment in the history of Christian tolerance, as the faith moved from advocating for freedom to imposing its own orthodoxy. This shift also became visible in the interpretation of key Bible passages, like the *Parable of the Wheat and Tares* (Mt 13:24–30.). In the Middle Ages this passage was taken up by Thomas Aquinas to justify killing heretics for the common good, because it was argued that theologians were able to identify the tares. In the High Middle Ages, this perspective culminated in the Inquisition, where heresy was equated with treason.

The Protestant Reformation introduced new tensions around tolerance and produced the perception of confessional differences. But reformers like Martin Luther and John Calvin still supported the suppression of heretics and their writings don't include the acceptance of followers of other religions (Jews, Muslims) or atheists. Ideas of tolerance in the modern sense came from the dissenters e.g. the left wing of the reformation. Radical reformers, such as the Anabaptists, became pioneers of religious tolerance by rejecting coercion. Polke highlights the contributions of two thinkers in particular, Roger Williams and Pierre Bayle, who both stood out for their ideas of tolerance in their time. Williams, a Puritan dissenter, advocated for the separation of church and state and defended the "liberty of conscience" for all, including Jews, Muslims, and non-believers. His writings emphasized the coexistence of truth and peace, rejecting forced religious conformity. Bayle, influenced by his experience as a persecuted Huguenot, argued for the "rights of erroneous conscience," asserting that finite human reason prevents absolute certainty in religious matters. He condemned coercion, emphasizing moral reciprocity and the importance of engaging in dialogue to correct misconceptions.

Polke examines how the Roman Catholic Church's stance on religious tolerance evolved, particularly in response to modernity. During the nineteenth century, the Church strongly opposed secularization, modernism, and the separation of church and state, reaffirming its claim to absolute religious truth. However, in the twentieth century, especially after World War II, the Catholic Church gradually embraced a more tolerant attitude. The Second Vatican Council (1962–65), particularly through the declaration *Dignitatis Humanae*, marked a turning point by affirming religious freedom as a fundamental human right. The Church acknowledged that faith must be a free act, and that coercion is incompatible with human dignity. This shift was influenced by broader social changes, interfaith engagement, and the experiences of totalitarianism, which underscored the dangers of religious oppression. Polke acknowledges ongoing tensions within the church, particularly between conservative and progressive factions. He stresses that modern Christian tolerance is shaped not only by theological reflection but also by historical experiences of violence and the need for peaceful coexistence in pluralistic societies.

Polke then lines out a systematic hermeneutics of the idea of tolerance in the spirit of Christianity, which he bases on four points: truth and faith on the one hand and, on the other hand, moral universalism and the dialogical character of tolerance. He proposes that Christian tolerance must navigate the tension between a commitment to truth and a deep respect for human dignity and freedom. This model is grounded in the recognition of human fallibility, which fosters humility in theological claims and prevents dogmatic certainty from stifling dialogue. It emphasizes the importance of separating spiritual and temporal authority, allowing for pluralism and the coexistence of diverse beliefs in public life. Polke argues that Christian tolerance, at its core, is defined not by passive acceptance, but rather by active engagement with the principles of love, humility, and a commitment to justice.

For Polke, tolerance requires active engagement in dialogue, especially between different faiths and worldviews, as a way of fostering mutual understanding while upholding the integrity of one's own beliefs. This dialogue does not seek to erase differences but instead respects and learns from them. Ultimately, Christian tolerance reflects the teachings of Jesus, particularly the call to love one's neighbor and even one's enemies. By embodying these principles, Christians can contribute to a model of coexistence that transcends religious, cultural, and ideological divides, offering a way forward for peaceful engagement in a pluralistic world.

3 The Concept of Tolerance from an Islamic Perspective

The concept of tolerance in Islam, as explored in Anna Ayse Akasoy's article, is deeply intertwined with historical, theological, and political considerations. She starts with a critical examination of how the concept of tolerance, traditionally framed within a Western European historical and philosophical context, can be applied universally, particularly in Islamic contexts. She critiques the Eurocentric assumption that Islamic history lacks a comparable tradition of tolerance, arguing that Western tolerance emerged in response to specific crises, such as religious wars and the power of the Catholic Church — conditions that did not exist in the Islamic world in the same form. She proposes a reinterpretation of tolerance as a means to address the challenge of religious coexistence, emphasizing its role as a political and theological strategy rather than an ideological commitment to pluralism. In Islamic thought, tolerance is often conceptualized as a pragmatic necessity rather than an inherent moral value, with debates centering on accommodating beliefs deemed incorrect while maintaining religious truth claims. Akasoy also addresses the difficulty of defining intolerance, questioning whether polemics or literary condemnations should be considered intolerant alongside more obvious acts of persecution. Ultimately, she argues that universalizing tolerance requires moving beyond a Western-centric framework and recognizing the diverse ways societies, including Islamic ones, have historically navigated religious and ideological differences.

Akasoy highlights the central role of the Qur'ān in shaping Islamic thought while emphasizing the significant variability in interpretations of its verses among Muslims. She underscores the absence of any term in the Qur'ān that can be translated as "tolerance." Consequently, scholars are compelled to meticulously identify and interpret verses that can be interpreted as referring to tolerance. Scholars who argue for a positive stance on tolerance cite verses such as 2:256 ("There is no compulsion in religion") and 109:6 ("You have your religion, and I have mine"). However, it is contended by others that subsequent verses advocating for defensive measures against non-believers may supersede earlier, more inclusive messages. While medieval scholars frequently viewed tolerance as a pragmatic necessity under Islamic rule, contemporary reformists argue that the Qur'ān provides a foundation for universal religious freedom. This ongoing discourse underscores the intricate and enduring nature of the Islamic theological tradition, wherein the question of whether the Qur'ān inherently endorses tolerance or if it is subject to abrogation by subsequent, more restrictive verses remains a central tenet.

While the Qurʾān remains the primary reference for discussions on religious diversity, prophetic traditions provide additional ethical and legal guidance. Several prophetic traditions (ḥadīth/aḥādīth) promote values such as tasāmuḥ (tolerance), ṣabr (patience), and modārā (magnanimity), which reinforce a broader ethical framework for coexistence. However, other traditions, such as the one stating that only one of seventy-three sects will be saved, suggest a more exclusivist outlook. The authenticity and interpretation of aḥādīth have been debated since the classical period, with scholars differing on methods of verification and application. Some traditions emphasize diversity of opinion (ikhtilāf) as a blessing, particularly within the Muslim community, while others have been used to justify punitive measures against apostasy. The varied nature of prophetic traditions, therefore, permits both tolerant and intolerant interpretations, depending on the historical and theological perspective employed.

Akasoy highlights Islamic law as a source for examining interreligious tolerance as well as intrareligious tolerance. Regarding interreligious tolerance legal frameworks were established that regulated the relationship between Muslims and non-Muslims. The Qurʾān and ḥadīth serve as primary sources for these legal regulations, which formalized the status of non-Muslims, particularly the "People of the Book" (traditionally Jews and Christians), who were granted protected status (dhimmī) in exchange for paying the jizya tax. Historic documents, like the *Pact of ʿUmar*, demonstrate, that non-Muslims apart from Arab polytheists were allowed to continue practicing their religion under Muslim rule. In academic discourse, this fact is interpreted as indicative of Islamic tolerance or met with criticism, as non-Muslims did not enjoy the same degree of religious freedom as Muslims. This dichotomy of views reflects the varying definitions of tolerance among scholars, leading to divergent conclusions regarding Islamic tolerance. Intrareligious tolerance is reflected by the principle of difference (ikhtilāf), which, in Islamic law, serves as a technical term for variations in legal opinion, although the degree of acceptance of these variations varied in different historical eras. Similarly, the concept of ijtihād, which signifies the individual endeavor of a scholar to reach an accurate conclusion, exemplifies tolerance, as these efforts were endorsed even if the outcome proved to be erroneous. The significance of these concepts is demonstrated by their practical implementation across various historical periods. These principles were not confined to Islamic legal doctrine but were also evident in the broader context of Islamic intellectual history.

Islamic history offers varied examples of tolerance and intolerance. Muslim rule in al-Andalus and the Ottoman Empire is frequently cited as historical precedents of tolerance. However, these periods also contained instances of persecution, demonstrating that tolerance was often contingent on political and social conditions rather than a fixed doctrinal stance. The treatment of non-Muslims under Islamic rule was largely dictated by Islamic law, which granted *dhimmīs* (People of the Book) the right to practice their religion while imposing certain restrictions, such as the payment of the *jizya* tax. Akasoy also highlights misconceptions about Sufi-movements within Islamic history which are usually perceived or labeled as more tolerant than other branches of Islam. She points out that Sufism by popular reputation may be irenic, pacifist and pluralist, but the historical reality is considerably more complicated and there is evidence of Sufi militancy as well. The example of the mystic Ibn ʿArabī reveals both tolerant and intolerant attitudes. By exploring his writings, it is suggested that Ibn ʿArabī's reputation as a paragon of tolerance should be critically examined.

Modern discussions on tolerance in Islam are shaped by global political dynamics. Figures such as Khaled Abou El Fadl have argued for an Islamic tradition of tolerance based on historical and scriptural evidence, while critics challenge whether such interpretations accurately reflect traditional Islamic thought. The discourse surrounding tolerance often intersects with broader human rights debates, particularly concerning freedom of speech, women's rights, and the treatment of LGBTQ communities in Muslim societies.

Ultimately, the study suggests that tolerance in Islam is not a monolithic concept but a fluid and historically contingent practice. The diversity of Islamic traditions, legal interpretations, and historical experiences underscores the complexity of defining and implementing tolerance within Muslim societies. The ongoing challenge lies in reconciling historical precedents with contemporary ethical and political frameworks, ensuring that discussions of tolerance in Islam are both intellectually rigorous and socially relevant.

4 Commonalities and Differences

As the articles of this volume illustrate, faith and tolerance exist in a complex and often paradoxical relationship. Religious commitment typically entails adherence to a particular truth revealed by the divine, which may appear to be in tension with the openness and pluralism that tolerance demands. Tolerance, by contrast, implies acceptance of different beliefs — even those considered false — raising the fundamental question: If one holds his or her faith to be true, how can one respect or even esteem those who believe otherwise? Does tolerance dilute faith, or can it be reimagined as a virtue grounded in faith itself?

This tension is particularly acute in Judaism, Christianity, and Islam, where religious identity is not only personal but communal and covenantal, tied to divine guidance and sacred law. Yet despite their exclusive truth claims, each tradition has developed theological, legal, and philosophical mechanisms to accommodate or engage with religious difference. The following section examines two prominent pathways through which the monotheistic traditions have addressed the challenge of tolerance: first, through legal and ethical frameworks that recognize moral values across religious boundaries; and second, through mystical and philosophical traditions that emphasize the limitations of human knowledge in approaching the divine. These pathways illuminate how historical models of tolerance continue to inform and challenge modern developments of tolerance conceptions as well as interreligious engagement.

In Jewish tradition, the Noahide Laws offer a foundational model for recognizing the righteousness of non-Jews without requiring conversion. These seven ethical commandments — believed to have been given to Noah and his descendants — constitute a moral code intended for *all* humanity. Rabbinic literature teaches that righteous gentiles who observe these laws merit a place in the World to Come.[2] While Judaism affirms its own covenant as uniquely binding for Jews, it acknowledges that non-Jews may also attain divine favor by living ethically. This framework navigates the tension between particularist theology and universal moral order by affirming that ethical monotheism, rather than covenantal status, is the criterion for righteousness.[3]

Jewish interpretations of the Noahide Laws have evolved over time, reflecting varying theological and philosophical orientations toward non-Jews. In the medieval period, Menahem Ha-Meiri (1249–ca. 1315) redefined the boundaries of religious legitimacy by arguing that monotheists such as Christians and Muslims — being "nations bound by religion" — are not idolaters and thus fall within God's covenantal concern. This inclusive stance has influenced modern rulings in Israel regarding the civil rights of non-Jews and has informed broader approaches to interfaith engagement. In contrast, Maimonides (1138–1204) presents a more exclusivist position in his legal writings. In the *Mishneh Torah*, he states that only those non-Jews who observe the Noahide Laws because they are divinely revealed through Moses qualify as righteous gentiles. This view is criticized by figures such as Rabbi Abraham ben David (1125–1198) for lacking clear precedent in rabbinic tradition. Yet Maimonides' *Guide of the Perplexed* offers a different emphasis: there, he envisions human perfection as the pursuit of rational knowledge and metaphysical truth — an ideal accessible to all people, regardless of religious affiliation. Many scholars interpret this duality as deliberate: Maimonides' legal

---

[2] *Sanhedrin* 56a–59b, published online: sefaria.org, https://www.sefaria.org/Sanhedrin.56a.13?lang=bi (accessed on 17.03.2025).
[3] Barnes, Bruce R., "The Noahide Laws and the Universal Fellowship with God," *Rocznik Teologii Katolickiej* XX (2021), 6–32.

corpus establishes communal boundaries, while his philosophical writings gesture toward a universalist theology grounded in reason.[4]

This tension finds a powerful echo in the thought of Moses Mendelssohn (1729–1786), a key figure of the Jewish Enlightenment. While upholding the binding nature of Jewish law for Jews, Mendelssohn argued that reason and conscience are universally accessible sources of moral obligation. For him, the Noahide Laws represented not merely a legal structure, but the reflection of a universal moral order inscribed into creation. He maintained that divine justice would not deny salvation to righteous individuals simply because they did not recognize Mosaic revelation. Mendelssohn's integration of natural law into Jewish ethics laid the groundwork for Jewish engagement with modern liberalism and inspired Reform Jewish emphasis on ethical monotheism as a shared human heritage.[5]

Building on this trajectory, modern Jewish thinkers have sought to expand the Noahide tradition into a comprehensive ethical philosophy that promotes justice, human dignity, and moral responsibility beyond the bounds of *halakhic* particularism.[6] Among them, David Novak offers one of the most rigorous theological reconstructions. While affirming the value of the Seven Laws of Noah as Judaism's expression of natural law, Novak critiques their traditional formulations for falling short of a fully pluralistic ethic. He argues that the Noahide Laws tolerate other religions only to the extent that they approximate monotheism and moral order, thereby offering instrumental rather than principled tolerance. Novak proposes reinterpreting the Noahide framework not as a static legal code but as a dynamic, speculative moral theology grounded in creation, reason, and human personhood.[7] This reinterpretation allows for a deeper engagement with non-monotheistic traditions while maintaining Jewish theological commitments. By rooting moral obligation in the *imago dei* — the human being as created in God's image — Novak opens the door to a broader, theologically grounded ethic of interreligious respect. However, he acknowledges the ongoing challenge: affirm-

---

[4] Zuesse, Evan M., "Tolerance in Judaism: The Medieval and Modern Sources," in: Jacob Neusner/Alan J. Avery-Peck/William S. Green, *The Encyclopaedia of Judaism*, vol. 4, 2694–99, Leiden: Brill, 2005; Novak, David, *Image of the Non-Jew in Judaism: A Historical and Constructive Study of the Noahide Laws*, Liverpool, 2011, published online: Liverpool Scholarship Online, https://doi.org/10.3828/liverpool/9781906764074.003.0016 (accessed on 13.03.2025); Twersky, Isadore, *Introduction to the Code of Maimonides*, New Haven: Yale University Press, 1980, 356 ff.; Kellner, Menachem, *Maimonides on Judaism and the Jewish People*, Albany: SUNY Press, 1991, 33 ff.

[5] Zuesse, "Tolerance in Judaism," 26 f.

[6] Ibid. 31.

[7] Novak, *Image of the Non-Jew*, https://doi.org/10.3828/liverpool/9781906764074.003.0016 (accessed on 13.03.2025), 226 ff.

ing particular revelation while participating in a shared moral conversation that can support pluralism in a globalized world.[8]

Within the Christian theological framework, the concept of tolerance is intricately intertwined with the interpretation of Scripture, particularly the writings of Saint Paul. Specifically, *Romans* 2:14–15 occupies a central role in debates concerning the moral status of non-Christians. The passage describes Gentiles who, "though not having the Law, do by nature what the Law requires," thereby showing that "the Law is written on their hearts." This has traditionally been interpreted to suggest that Gentiles — without access to Mosaic revelation — can nevertheless act morally and will be judged accordingly. This passage has thus shaped Christian reflection on natural law, moral conscience, and the salvific potential of those outside the Christian covenant.[9] While some theological interpretations of Paul emphasize particularism — maintaining that salvation comes solely through Christ — others draw from *Romans* 2 to develop a more universalist ethic, where moral conscience functions as a divine imprint on all human beings. This latter strand laid the groundwork for the Christian natural law tradition, which affirms that basic moral truths are accessible to all through reason and conscience, regardless of religious affiliation.[10]

Matthew Levering offers a contemporary defense of this tradition, arguing that natural law provides a theologically grounded basis for interreligious tolerance. Drawing on *Romans* 2 and the writings of early Church Fathers such as Origen (185–253/54) and John Chrysostom (d. 407), Levering shows how early Christian thinkers affirmed the idea that non-Christians could access moral truth and live virtuously through the use of reason. Chrysostom, for example, emphasized that all human beings are created with rationality and conscience, which enable them to discern good from evil. He cited figures like Job, Melchizedek, and Cornelius as examples of righteous non-Jews who were morally upright despite lacking the fullness of revelation. For Chrysostom, these Gentiles could receive "glory and honor and peace" not by covenantal status, but through virtuous action

---

[8] Novak, David, *Natural Law in Judaism*, Cambridge: Cambridge University Press, 2009, chap. 6, "Noahide Law and Human Personhood."
[9] Atkins, Jed W., *The Christian Origins of Tolerance*, Oxford: Oxford University Press, 2024, 75.
[10] Nikki, Nina, "Was Paul Tolerant?: An Assessment of William S. Campbell's and J. Brian Tucker's "Particularistic" Paul," in: Outi Lethipuu/Michael Labahn (eds.), *Tolerance, Intolerance, and Recognition in Early Christianity and Early Judaism*, 114–37, Amsterdam: Amsterdam University Press, 2021, 115 ff.

grounded in natural law.¹¹ Levering interprets Chrysostom's position as affirming a universal moral order accessible to all humanity while maintaining the Christocentric structure of salvation. This approach reflects a nuanced theological universalism: while all people participate in moral truth and are judged justly, the fullness of communion with God is ultimately mediated through Christ. Levering thus envisions natural law as a resource for interreligious ethics and civic tolerance, allowing Christians to affirm the moral dignity of others without abandoning the doctrinal centrality of Christ. It is a model of inclusivity without relativism, where shared ethical commitments coexist with particular theological claims.¹²

This balance between inclusivity and exclusivity also appears in modern Catholic theology. The twentieth-century theologian Karl Rahner (1904–1984) famously introduced the concept of the "anonymous Christian", arguing that individuals outside the explicit bounds of Christianity could still receive salvation through their authentic moral commitment and existential openness to the divine. According to Rahner, divine grace is operative wherever human beings respond to truth and goodness, even if they do not consciously recognize Christ. This perspective, rooted in a theological reading of natural law, emphasizes that the human orientation toward transcendence is universal, and thus salvation must be universally accessible.¹³ While Rahner's theory shaped Catholic thinking after the Second Vatican Council, it has also drawn criticism — particularly from religious pluralists who argue that it subordinates other religious traditions to Christianity by interpreting them through a Christian lens. Critics contend that Rahner's model, though inclusive in intent, fails to fully affirm the autonomy and internal coherence of other faiths. Despite this, his thought has significantly expanded the church's theological openness to religious diversity by suggesting that tolerance need not be a compromise of faith, but rather an affirmation of the universal reach of divine grace.¹⁴

Thus, within Christian thought, natural law has served as a crucial bridge between particular revelation and universal moral insight. Whether through Chrysostom's early formulations or Rahner's modern inclusivism, Christian theology has sought to affirm the moral dignity of non-Christians, often locating the source of this dignity in reason, conscience, and the human capacity to seek

---

11 Levering, Matthew, "Christians and Natural Law," in: Anver M. Emon/Matthew Levering/David Novak (eds.), *Natural Law: A Jewish, Christian, and Islamic Trialogue*, Oxford: Oxford University Press, 2014, 66–110.
12 Ibid., 78 ff.
13 Karen Kilby, *Karl Rahner: Theology and Philosophy*, London: Routledge, 2004, 116 ff.
14 Bresnahan, James F., "Rahner's Ethics: Critical Natural Law in Relation to Contemporary Ethical Methodology," *The Journal of Religion* 56,1 (1976), 36–60; Kilby, *Karl Rahner*, 117 f.

truth. Yet as in Judaism, this path is marked by tensions: between universal ethics and theological particularism, between inclusivist generosity and the boundaries of doctrinal orthodoxy.

In Islamic thought, the tension between religious truth and tolerance is mediated through a combination of revelatory guidance, juridical categories, and moral reasoning. While Islam affirms the finality of the Qur'ān and the prophethood of Muhammad, it also recognizes the existence of previous divine revelations. The Qur'ān refers to Jews and Christians as *ahl al-kitāb* (People of the Book), acknowledging them as recipients of earlier scriptures. This recognition establishes a framework for qualified inclusion: believers in earlier revelations, if righteous and faithful to their own traditions, may be rewarded by God, as expressed in Qur'ān 5:69.[15] Historically, this principle was institutionalized through the legal category of *dhimma*, a status granted to non-Muslims — especially Jews and Christians — living under Islamic rule. The *dhimma* system provided legal protections, including freedom of worship and communal autonomy, in exchange for the payment of a special tax (*jizya*) and acceptance of certain social restrictions. Though often cited as an early model of Islamic tolerance, the *dhimma* system reflects a hierarchical arrangement: it offers coexistence and protection, but not full equality, as non-Muslims were subject to legal and civic limitations within the broader Islamic polity. Some classical scholars adopted a broader interpretation of *dhimma*. The eighth-century jurist ʿAbd ar-Raḥmān al-Awzāʿī (707–774/88–157), for example, argued that even religious communities outside the traditional scope of *ahl al-kitāb*—such as Hindus or religions of sub-Saharan west Africa —could be treated analogously to Zoroastrians (*majūs*) and granted protected status. His approach reflected a pragmatic jurisprudence responsive to the realities of religious diversity, especially in regions like al-Andalus, where interreligious contact was constant. Al-Awzāʿī's inclusive reasoning, grounded in the necessity of governance rather than abstract theological pluralism, exemplifies how premodern Islamic law negotiated difference through flexible legal reasoning within a theological framework.[16]

However, contemporary scholars urge caution when interpreting the *dhimma* system as a direct precursor to modern religious tolerance.[17] Mark Cohen reminds

---

[15] Q 5:69: "For the believers, the Jews, the Sabians, and the Christians — those who believe in God and the Last Day and do good deeds — there is no fear: they will not grieve." Cf. Translation of the Qur'ān by M.A.S. Abdel Haleem, published online: Quran.com, https://quran.com/5?startingVerse=69 (accessed on 01.04.2025).
[16] Cf. Akasoy in this volume.
[17] Fernández-Morera, Darío, *The Myth of the Andalusian Paradise: Muslims, Christians, and Jews under Islamic Rule in Medieval Spain*, Simon and Schuster, 2023, chapters 6 and 7.

us that in premodern contexts, tolerance was often perceived not as a virtue, but as a political concession.[18] Anver Emon likewise critiques simplistic binaries of tolerance versus intolerance. In his analysis, the *dhimma* system is best understood as a form of managed diversity — a legal solution to the challenge of ruling over a religiously plural population, rather than a moral endorsement of theological pluralism.[19] In this context, Emon explores the limits of Islamic natural law theories in supporting modern conceptions of tolerance. He argues that while Islamic legal traditions incorporate rational tools such as *maṣlaḥa* (public interest) and *maqāṣid ash-sharīʿa* (objectives of the law), these tools are theologically tethered to divine revelation and are often insufficient to ground a fully universal ethic. The *dhimma* system, he notes, was based not on rational moral insight into shared human dignity, but rather on a revelatory legal accommodation extended to particular religious communities. As such, it reflects a model of pragmatic coexistence rather than one of natural rights. For Emon, this example underscores a broader challenge: while Islamic jurisprudence incorporates reason to derive legal norms in certain contexts, its theological foundations constrain the development of a natural law tradition capable of supporting robust interreligious pluralism.[20]

This tension is further illustrated in the contrasting positions of contemporary and modern Islamic thinkers. Abdullahi An-Naʿim advocates for a reformist reading of Islamic law through *ijtihād* (independent reasoning), arguing that minority rights and religious pluralism can be justified internally by appealing to the ethical objectives of the *sharīʿa*. He calls for a harmonization of Islamic tradition with international human rights norms, without abandoning Islamic identity. By contrast, Abū al-Aʿlā Mawdūdī (1903–1979/1320–1399) defends the traditional *dhimma* framework as a divinely sanctioned system of hierarchical tolerance, in which non-Muslims are protected but remain legally subordinate. For Mawdūdī, this asymmetry is not a flaw, but an expression of divine justice as articulated in Islamic law. Legal scholar Timothy William Waters analyzes both positions and critiques the inherent limitations in each. An-Naʿim's approach, while normatively appealing, risks being theologically marginal in communities where traditional in-

---

[18] Cohen, Mark R., "The Myth of the Andalusian Paradise: Muslims, Christians, and Jews under Islamic Rule in Medieval Spain by Darío Fernández-Morera (Review)," *The Catholic Historical Review* 104,3 (2018), 541–43.
[19] Emon, Anver M., *Religious Pluralism and Islamic Law: Dhimmis and Others in the Empire of Law*, Oxford University Press, 2012, 315 ff.
[20] Emon, Anver M., "Islamic Natural Law Theories," in: Anver M. Emon/Matthew Levering/David Novak (eds.), *Natural Law: A Jewish, Christian, and Islamic Trialogue*, Oxford: Oxford University Press, 2014, esp. 179–83.

terpretations dominate. Mawdūdī's account, though internally coherent, is incompatible with modern conceptions of equal citizenship and human rights. Waters argues that Islamic legal discourse must grapple with the tension between cultural legitimacy and liberal universalism, particularly when reimagining minority rights in pluralistic societies.[21]

As in Judaism and Christianity, Islamic legal and theological traditions offer a form of bounded tolerance — one that allows for coexistence, but often within a framework of theological or political hierarchy. While modern thinkers have sought to rearticulate these traditions in light of contemporary norms, the challenge remains: how to affirm the moral and theological dignity of the religious "other" without abandoning the core tenets of Islamic faith and law. In comparison, these traditions illustrate that while religious law can support forms of pragmatic or moral tolerance, genuine pluralism often demands theological creativity and philosophical reorientation.

In addition to legal and ethical frameworks, the mystical and philosophical traditions within Judaism, Christianity, and Islam have advanced profound resources for religious tolerance by emphasizing the inaccessibility of *absolute* divine knowledge. These traditions often suggest that all religious expressions, while partial and conditioned by human limitations, reflect a yearning for and orientation toward the ungraspable divine. Rather than denying the truth of one's own faith, this mystical-philosophical approach cultivates a humility grounded in the recognition of human fallibility, which opens space for interreligious respect and dialogue.

In Islam, the thought of Ibn ʿArabī (1165–1240) has become a central point of reference in contemporary discussions of tolerance. While he did not explicitly theorize tolerance in the modern sense, his metaphysical framework — particularly as expressed in his poetry — has been widely interpreted as offering a pluralistic theology of religions. Ibn ʿArabī suggests that all religious paths reflect the limited human attempts to apprehend the divine, whose essence infinitely transcends human comprehension. Since God manifests himself in multiple forms, religious diversity is not only inevitable but divinely willed. He famously wrote, "My

---

21 For a comparative analysis of these thinkers, see Waters, Timothy William, "Reconsidering Dhimmah as a Model for a Modern Minority Rights Regime," in: Modjandeh, Habibi (ed.), *Theoretical Foundations of Human Rights. Collected Papers of the Second International Conference on Human Rights, May 2003*, Qom: Mofid University Publications, 9–11. See also Abdullahi An-Na'im, *Human Rights in Cross-Cultural Perspectives*, Philadelphia: University of Pennsylvania Press, 1992; and Abul A'la Maududi, *Rights of Non-Muslims in Islamic State*, Lahore: Islamic Publications, 1961.

heart has become capable of every form [...] it is the religion of Love." This verse has often been cited as a poetic expression of a universal mystical openness.²²

At the same time, Ibn 'Arabī does not affirm the equality of all paths. He speaks of Islam as the sunlight compared to the starlight of other traditions — indicating Islam's perceived finality and comprehensiveness. He further argues that the property of the other revealed religions has been transferred to the last revealed religion — Islam. Modern scholars have debated the implications of this position. While some see it as an affirmation of salvific diversity, others — like Mohammad Hassan Khalil — argue that Ibn 'Arabī recognizes the reality of other religions but reserves perfection and completeness for Islam. His mystical universalism, then, remains hierarchical, rather than fully egalitarian.²³ Importantly — as noted by Akasoy in this volume — Ibn 'Arabī's ideas must be understood within their historical context. Living through periods of religious persecution under the Almohads, and later in the pluralistic milieu of Anatolia, his writings evolved in tone. While early works exhibit openness, later texts contain critiques of Christianity, reflecting the shifting socio-political environment. Despite these fluctuations, Ibn 'Arabī's central metaphysical insight — that all religions are human responses to a transcendent divine reality — has provided scholars with a basis for advocating interreligious tolerance.²⁴

The influence of Ibn 'Arabī extended beyond Islamic thought. Abraham Abulafia (1240–1291) was among the Jewish mystics engaged with Neoplatonic and Islamic mystical ideas.²⁵ In Judaism, the most prominent philosophical articulation of epistemological humility comes from Maimonides. While not a mystic in the conventional sense, Maimonides emphasized that God's essence is unknowable, and that true knowledge of the divine lies in understanding human limitation. In the *Guide of the Perplexed*, he argues that even Moses, the greatest of prophets, did not fully comprehend God — implying that no theological system can claim finality or totality. He rejects the claim that Jews are different than non-Jews, but affirms that Judaism is unique as such, suggesting it ultimately will be accept-

---

22 Cf. Akasoy in this volume.
23 Khalil, Mohammad Hassan, *Islam and the Fate of Others*, Oxford: Oxford University Press, 2012, 57 f.; Shah-Kazemi, *The Spirit of Tolerance*.
24 Cf. Akasoy in this volume.
25 Wasserstrom, Steven M., "Jewish-Muslim Relations in the Context of Andalusian Emigration," in: Mark D. Meyerson/Edward D. English (eds.), *Christians, Muslims and Jews in Medieval and Early Modern Spain*, 69–87, Notre Dame: University of Notre Dame Press, 2000.

ed by all humans. This leads to a form of rationalist modesty, where truth is pursued with conviction but held with humility.[26]

This epistemological stance forms the basis for modern Jewish reconstructions of tolerance, particularly in the work of Kellner as shown in this volume. Drawing on Maimonides, Kellner proposes a model of Jewish tolerance rooted in "epistemological modesty": the idea that while Judaism claims truth, it must also recognize the limits of human understanding and the possibility that others, too, are in relationship with the divine. Kellner maintains that this posture allows for a firm commitment to Jewish theology without descending into exclusivism, and enables genuine dialogue with other faiths.[27] Parallel insights appear in contemporary Islamic philosophy, notably in the work of Abdolkarim Soroush, an Iranian intellectual influenced by both Sufi mysticism and modern religious pluralism. Building on the medieval poet Ḥāfeẓ (ca. 1325–1390/725–792) and mystic Rūmī (1207–1273/606–671), Soroush emphasizes the fallibility of human religious understanding, arguing that multiple interpretations — and even multiple paths — can coexist within the broader search for truth. His concept of *sarāṭhā-ye mustaqīm* ("the many straight paths"), derived from the Qurʾān's reference to "the straight path," reimagines guidance as plural rather than singular. Like Ibn ʿArabī and Maimonides, Soroush affirms that God transcends all conceptual frames, and that religious diversity may be theologically meaningful, not merely tolerated.[28]

In Christianity, similar currents are visible in the mystical philosophy of Nicholas of Cusa (1401–1464). Drawing on Neoplatonic metaphysics, Nicholas argued that God is beyond all categories, and that all religious knowledge is partial and symbolic. He shares with Ibn ʿArabī the fundamental premise, that God is indefinable and both distinct from and inseparable from the world. Both thinkers view humanity as central — for Nicholas of Cusa, the human mind mirrors the divine intellect and can rationally grasp the structure of reality, while for Ibn ʿArabī, the human being is the complete manifestation of divine attributes, ensuring the continuity of divine presence in time. However, their epistemologies diverge: Nicholas affirms that reason can attain divine knowledge, whereas Ibn ʿArabī insists that true knowledge is a gift of divine revelation.[29] In *De pace fidei* (1453), written in response to the fall of Constantinople, Nicholas envisioned

---

[26] Kellner, Menachem, *We Are Not Alone: A Maimonidean Theology of the Other*, Boston, USA: Academic Studies Press, 2021, 91 ff.
[27] Cf. Kellner in this volume.
[28] Cf. Akasoy in this volume.
[29] Smirnov, Andrey V., "Nicholas of Cusa and Ibn ʿArabī: Two Philosophies of Mysticism," *Philosophy East and West* 43,1 (1993), 65–85.

a unity of religions under the concept of *una religio in rituum varietate* — "one religion in a variety of rites." This idea reflects a deep-seated mystical conviction that all religious traditions ultimately seek the same divine truth, though expressed differently. However, Nicholas's later work (*Cribratio Alkorani*) reveals the limits of his pluralism, as he attempts to interpret Islam through a Christian lens. Despite this shift, he maintained a dialogical theology, believing that interfaith understanding — rather than military confrontation — was the best path to peace. His intellectual journey thus reflects the tension between philosophical inclusivity and doctrinal exclusivity, a challenge that remains central to interreligious dialogue today.[30]

This line of thought finds a contemporary echo in the work of Christian Polke portrayed in this volume, who argues that tolerance is not a compromise of truth, but a consequence of it. According to Polke, the recognition that only God possesses ultimate truth demands that believers approach others with humility, dialogue, and respect. Tolerance becomes a virtue grounded in theological anthropology: since human beings are finite, no single community can claim to fully grasp divine truth. Faith, in this model, is not diminished by openness to others — it is strengthened by the awareness that all knowledge of God is mediated and partial.[31]

Together, these mystical and philosophical traditions across Judaism, Christianity, and Islam and their modern interpretations offer a shared insight: divine truth is ultimately beyond human mastery. This insight yields not relativism, but a profound humility that invites openness to the other. Tolerance, then, is not merely a social necessity or political strategy — it is a spiritual imperative, born from the awareness that all faiths stand before a mystery that exceeds their grasp. Furthermore, this faith is connected to confidence in the belief that God exists. This common principle serves as the foundation for the theological frameworks of tolerance within each tradition and provides a compelling basis for interfaith engagement. Faith in God whose existence cannot be proven by humans scientifically or otherwise is what unites the religions and makes them equal partners, because on this metaphysical level, they all belong to the community of faith. Moreover, in each religious tradition humans carry a heavy responsibility: Created in God's image according to the Bible, and, according to the Qur'ān, as the representative of God on earth, it is the duty of the believer to care for each other and the world, as well as to promote justice. This responsibility includes striving for

---

30 Watanabe, Morimichi, "Cusanus, Islam, and Religious Tolerance," in: Ian Christopher Levy/ Rita George-Tvrtković/Donald Duclow (eds.), *Nicholas of Cusa and Islam*, 9–19, Leiden: Brill, 2014.
31 Cf. Polke in this volume.

knowledge — especially religious knowledge. The interconnectedness of the three religions necessitates engagement and knowledge of the other in order to facilitate a more profound comprehension of one's own faith.[32]

Therefore, interfaith engagement, manifesting in interfaith dialogue and interfaith education, serves as the foundational framework for the embodiment and promotion of religious tolerance. The cultivation of knowledge about other religious traditions serves as a pivotal form of moving from mere tolerance to respect and acceptance.

An example of interfaith dialogue serving as a crucial mechanism for reducing religious conflict, fostering tolerance, and ultimately promoting acceptance, is Perry Schmidt-Leukel's approach. He argues that religious conflicts are often fueled by in-group vs. out-group dynamics and exclusive universalist claims, which frame the religious "other" as a threat. Dialogue helps deconstruct these biases, allowing religious traditions to recognize their shared values while acknowledging differences. While tolerance enables peaceful coexistence by enduring differences, true acceptance emerges when religious communities view diversity as enriching rather than divisive. Through open and reciprocal exchange, interfaith dialogue transforms rigid identities, shifting from a "we vs. them" mindset to an inclusive "we all" perspective. This shift is essential for lasting peace, as it redefines religious pluralism not as a challenge to overcome, but as a shared reality to embrace.[33] Schmidt-Leukel's broader work explores how interfaith encounters not only foster tolerance but actively transform religious identities. In *Transformation by Integration*, he argues that genuine interreligious engagement leads to a shift from passive coexistence to active appreciation of religious diversity. Moving beyond tolerance means no longer merely enduring religious differences but recognizing their potential for enriching one's own faith. This is particularly evident in the rise of multi-religious identity formations and double belonging, where individuals draw spiritual insights from multiple traditions. Such developments challenge rigid exclusivism and call for a reassessment of syncretism, not as a dilution of faith but as a natural outcome of deep interreligious engagement. In this view, dialogue is not just about peaceful relations — it is

---

[32] Tamer, Georges, "From Tolerance to Acceptance. Towards a New Paradigm of Interreligious Coexistence," in: Anne Sarah Matviyets,/Giuseppe Veltri/Jörg Rüpke (eds.), *Tolerance and Intolerance in Religion and Beyond Challenges from the Past and in the Present*, 141–45, London/New York: Routledge, 2024.

[33] Schmidt-Leukel, Perry, "In What Sense Can Inter-Faith Dialogue Contribute to Inter-Faith Peace?" *Ching Feng* 22.1/2 (2024), 1—19.

about mutual transformation, where religions evolve by learning from one another.[34]

The recognition that truth transcends religious boundaries offers a profound foundation for interfaith discourses. Within the religions, not only scripture matters, but also tradition and ideas. These remain important for contemporary theologians to build conceptions of tolerance which have the potential to lead to acceptance. Not only interreligious engagement is already visible in these sources, also engagement with the secular sphere: For Clement of Alexandria (c. 150–215) whatever has been well said within philosophy, should be accepted. For him, Jewish, Greek and Alaxandrian heritage of speculation is united and used for the exposition of Christian wisdom which shows his recognition of the universal nature of truth.[35] Similarly, in Islam, the Prophet Muhammad declared, "Wisdom is the lost property of the believer — wherever he finds it, he has the right to it."[36] Such statements echo the sentiment famously expressed by Maimonides: "Accept the truth whatever its source is."[37] These shared affirmations across traditions remind us that interreligious engagement is not merely about managing differences, but about recognizing the divine spark in the other, and being open to truth wherever it appears. In this light, discourse becomes not only a path to peace, but a shared journey toward wisdom, one that honors both our distinctiveness and our common human search for the transcendent. This is the spirit which leads the work of our Bavarian Research Center for Interreligious Discourses.

---

34 Schmidt-Leukel, Perry, *Transformation by Integration: How Inter-Faith Encounter Changes Christianity*, London: Hymns Ancient and Modern Ltd, 2009, 30 ff.
35 Okafor, Boniface, *The Theory of Knowledge in Clement of Alexandria*, Univ. diss. Pamplona, 1993, 93.
36 Narrated by Abū Huraira, *Sunan at-Tirmidhī*, Hadīth 2687, published online: Sunna.com, https://sunnah.com/tirmidhi:2687 (accessed on 21.03.2025).
37 Cf. Kellner in this volume.

List of Contributors

Menachem Kellner is Wolfson Professor emeritus of Jewish Thought at the University of Haifa and founding chair of the Department of Philosophy and Jewish Thought, Shalem College, Jerusalem (retired). He received his Ph.D. from Washington University. His research focuses on medieval Jewish philosophy with a particular focus on the philosophy of Maimonides. His most recent book is *We Are Not Alone: A Maimonidean Theology of the Other* (2021).

Christian Polke (†) was Professor of Ethics within the field of Systematic Theology at the Faculty of Theology, Georg-August-University Göttingen. He earned his doctorate in 2008 with a dissertation on the ideological neutrality of the state. After holding academic assistant positions in Heidelberg and Hamburg, he completed his habilitation in 2015. Polke was a founding member of the *Initiative Niedersächsischer Ethikrat* (INE), established in response to the COVID-19 pandemic. His publications include *Expressiver Theismus: vom Sinn personaler Rede von Gott* (2020). Christian Polke passed away in April 2023.

Anna Ayşe Akasoy is Professor of Islamic intellectual history at the Graduate Center of the City University of New York. She received her Ph.D. in 2005 from the Johann Wolfgang Goethe-University, Frankfurt. Her research focuses on three subjects: the cultural history of falconry in the Middle East until the Ottoman period, Muslim-Buddhist contacts, and theories and narratives of decision-making in the Islamic world. Her publications include *Islam and Tibet: Interactions Along the Musk Route* (2010), *Rashīd al-Dīn, Agent and Mediator of Cultural Exchanges in Ilkhanid Iran* (2013) and *Al-Kindī, Die Erste Philosophie: Arabisch-Deutsch* (2011).

Catharina Rachik is currently research associate at the Friedrich-Alexander-Universität Erlangen-Nürnberg (FAU) where she coordinates the book-series "Key Concepts in Interreligious Discourse". Before she joined the Bavarian Research Center for Interreligious Discourses, she has been research associate and coordinator in the Center for Islamic Theology at the University of Münster. She received her M.A. in Islamic Studies from the University of Münster and is writing her dissertation on Moses in the Qurʾān. Her research focuses on Qurʾānic Studies and Tafsīr (classical and modern), the Qurʾān in Late Antiquity, as well as on the field of Islamic art. Her publications include "Der Exodus im Qurʾān," in: Carolin Neuber (ed.), *Der immer neue Exodus*, Stuttgart, 2018.

Georges Tamer holds the Chair of Oriental Philology and Islamic Studies and is founding director of the Bavarian Research Center for Interreligious Discourses at the Friedrich-Alexander-Universität Erlangen-Nürnberg. He received his Ph.D. in Philosophy from the Free University Berlin in 2000 and completed his habilitation in Islamic Studies in Erlangen in 2007. His research focuses on Qurʾānic hermeneutics, philosophy in the Islamic world, Arabic literature and interreligious discourses. His publications include: *Zeit und Gott: Hellenistische Zeitvorstellungen in der altarabischen Dichtung und im Koran*, 2008; *Hermeneutical Crossroads: Understanding Scripture in Judaism, Christianity and Islam in the Pre-Modern Orient* (2017), *Islamic Philosophy and the Crisis of Modernity* (2024), *Handbook of Qurʾānic Hermeneutics*, 7 volumes (2023–).

Index of Persons

'Abd al-Ghanī an-Nābulūsī   123
Abdel Haleem, Muhammad   91, 97, 162
Abou El Fadl, Khaled   96–98, 100, 106, 129 f., 136 f., 140 f., 157
Abraham   15, 18, 28 f., 35, 101, 165
Abraham ben David (Rabad)   30, 151, 158
Abraham ben Maimonides   15
Acar, Ismail   87, 98
Adam   19, 53, 97
al-'Adawīya, Rābi'a   121
Addas, Claude   125
Afsaruddin, Asma   87, 102
Akasoy, Anna Ayse   83, 108, 117, 123, 155–157, 162, 165 f.
'Alī   134
Ali, Kecia   105
Ali, Tariq   130 f.
Altmann, Alexander   7, 9, 20 f., 35
Alvarez, Lourdes   123
Amartya, Sen   133
Amirpur, Katajun   138 f.
Angeles Gallego, María   98
Angenendt, Arnold   46, 48 f., 51, 53
Aquinas, Thomas   11, 49, 153
Arendt, Hannah   75
Aristotle   114, 116 f.
al-Ash'arī   112
Assmann, Jan   45, 64, 66
Augustine of Hippo   48 f., 64, 79, 153
al-Awzā'ī, Abd ar-Raḥmān   108, 162

Baer, Marc   133
Balk, Hanan   17
Barkey, Karen   133
Barton, Stephan C.   46 f.
Batnitzky, Leora   8
Bauer, Thomas   111, 123
Bayle, Pierre   44, 54, 58–61, 76, 153
Benamozegh, Elijah   12
Benmira, Omar   109
Bennison, Amira K.   117
Benson, Ophelia   4
Bleaney, Heather   98

Blidstein, Gerald   13
Blumenthal, David   27
Bodin, Jean   120
Bouhdiba, Abdelwahab   130, 141
Boyarin, Daniel   28
Brague, Remi   24
Brill, Alan   1, 3, 10, 12 f., 19, 28, 91, 98, 105, 109 f., 112, 114 f., 121, 128, 134, 159, 167
Brown, Daniel W.   104
Brown, Jonathan A. C.   104
al-Bukhārī   103

Calvin, John   52 f., 56, 153
Casewit, Yousef   127
Chilton, Bruce   83, 87
Chittick, William   123
Cicero   45
Cohen, Herman   9
Cohen, Mark R.   98, 163
Cook, Michael   118, 128, 140
Cornell, Vincent   83, 87, 128, 140
Crellius, Johannes   53
Crescas, Hasdai ben Abraham   30
Crone, Patricia   91–94, 96, 99–101, 118
Cyprian   45

Daifallah, Nouréddine   122
Daniel   9, 13, 30, 35
David   4, 7, 10, 19 f., 22, 31, 73, 113, 115, 133
Davidson, Herbert A.   4, 29
Diamond, James   18, 25, 35
Dutton, Yasin   117

El Kaisy-Friemuth, Maha   92, 112
Ellenson, David   9, 19
Ellethy, Yaser   99
Empey, Heather J.   119
Ernst, Simon   19, 71, 120
Ess, Josef van   112

Fackenheim, Emil   25
Falaky, Fayçal   139
al-Fārābī   111, 114, 118, 141

Index of Persons

Farber, Zev 8
Feldmann-Kaye, Miriam 25
Ferziger, Adam 9f.
Fierro, Maribel 110, 117, 126, 128
Filios, Denise K. 133
Finkel, Joshua 108
Forst, Reiner 43, 45f., 49f., 58, 75, 149
Foucault, Michel 53, 129
Freudenthal, Gad 25
Friedmann, Yohanan 84, 91, 108
Frimer, Dov 11
Frishkopf, Michael 138

García-Arenal, Mercedes 128
García Suárez, Pablo 98
Gellman, Jerome (Yehuda) 1, 8, 17, 25f., 35
al-Ghazālī 114f., 129
Gillis, David 4, 13, 15f.
Goldin, Joshua L. 28
Goodman, Lenn Evan 27
Greenberg, Irving 10f.
Griffel, Frank 111, 114, 120
Griffith, Sidney H. 115

Ḥāfeẓ 121, 138, 166
al-Ḥākim bi-Amri-llāh 134
Halbertal, Moshe 3
Halevi, Hayyim David 19, 22
Halevi, Judah 11, 17f., 24, 32
al-Ḥallāj 127
Hallaq, Wael B. 112
Halm, Heinz 134
Harris, Michael J. 2, 19, 25
Harris, Sam 137
Hartmann, Angelika 86, 103
Harvey, Zev 30
Hashmi, Sohail 140
Hayes, Christine 28
Haykel, Bernard 110
Heilman, Samuel C. 1
Herberg, Will 3
Herzog, Isaac 6
Heschel, Abraham Joshua 2, 21
Hirshman, Menachem (Marc) 13
Hyamson, Moses 30

Ibn ʿArabī 121–126, 128, 137, 139, 157, 164–166

Ibn Bājja 118
Ibn Barrajān 127
Ibn Ḥazm 99
Ibn Luṭf, Bābāī 119
Ibn Rushd 109f., 113f., 117, 124, 127
Ibn Sīnā 114
Ibn Taymīya 117
Isaac 18, 28, 33, 35
Isaiah 14, 18, 67
Israel, Jonathan I. 5–9, 11–17, 21, 26, 31f., 139, 150, 158
Ivry, Alfred 27

Jackson, Sherman 114
Jacob 13, 18, 35
al-Jāḥiẓ, ʿAmr ibn Baḥr 108
Jan, Abid Ullah 91, 130
Jesus 13, 47f., 57–59, 62, 65, 67, 78, 97, 153f.
Jonah 21, 94
Jospe, Raphael 8f., 11, 35

Kadri, Sadakat 92, 133
Kahera, Akel I. 109
Kalin, Ibrahim 87, 95
Kaminsky, Joel S. 13, 19
Kant, Immanuel 23, 33, 71
Karamustafa, Ahmet T. 126f.
Kasher, Hannah 17, 21, 27, 30
Katz, Jacob 9, 22
Kaykāʾūs 125
Kellner, Menachem 1, 4, 6, 8f., 12–19, 21f., 24–28, 30–33, 35, 150–152, 159, 166, 169
Kimelman, Reuven 1f., 7, 10f., 15
al-Kindī 116
Klein-Braslavy, Sara 28
Kokew, Stephan 86, 102f.
Kook, R. Abraham Isaac 26, 29
Korn, Eugene 2, 9f., 12, 21, 28f., 35
Kraemer, Joel L. 4, 134
Krämer, Gudrun 86
Kreisel, Howard 11
Kurtz, Stanley 130
Kymlicka, Will 4

Lachter, Hartley 17
Lasker, Daniel J. 3, 17, 29, 32, 35
Lassner, Jacob 88, 98

Index of Persons

Lecker, Michael 105
Lessing, Gotthold Ephraim 60, 68, 86
Levenson, Jon D. 13, 19
Levy-Rubin, Milka 107
Lieberman, Phillip 27
Locke, John 68, 86
Lubitch, Ronen 22
Luther, Martin 44, 52 f., 56, 67 f., 78, 153

Maimonides, Moses 3 f., 6–9, 11–16, 18 f., 21, 24–33, 109, 124, 134, 150 f., 158 f., 165 f., 169
Makdisi, Ussama 133
Mālik 110
al-Ma'mūn 117
Marcotte, Roxanne D. 127
Marín, Manuela 126
Massignon, Louis 127
Melamed, Abraham 8
Mendelssohn, Moses 8 f., 150, 159
Mendus, Susan 4
Menocal, María Rosa 133
Montaigne, Michel de 58
Montesquieu, Charles de Secondat, Baron de 120
Moses 12, 18, 26–29, 97, 151, 158, 165
Muḥammad 90, 92–95, 97–103, 105 f., 113, 119, 131, 139
Musa, Aisha Y. 101
al-Muqaddasī 110

Nathan the Wise 68, 86
Nawaz, Maajid 137
Nehorai, Michael Zvi 22
Nelson, Cary 5
Neusner, Jacob 83, 87, 159
Nicholas of Cusa 124, 166 f.
Noth, Albrecht 89, 98, 101, 106, 132, 135
Novak, David 11, 159–161, 163

Oestreich, Gerhard 53
Orpah (Moabite) 20

Paret, Rudi 83, 101, 131 f., 135
Paul the Apostle 46 f., 79, 152, 160,
Peters, Francis E. 105
Philpott, Daniel 104

Plato 116
Plotinus 116
Pope Gelasius 50
Pope Gregory IX 48
Powers, Paul R. 109
Poya, Abbas 109

Rabinovitch, Nachum 6
Rapoport, Yossef 110
Rappoport, Chaim 14
Rashi 29
Ravitzky, Aviezer 7, 27
Rawls, John 55, 71
ar-Rāzī, Abū Bakr 127
Ricoeur, Paul 69–71, 74
Roosevelt, Eleanor 128
Ross, Tamar 26
Roth, Leon 19
Rūmī, Jalāl ad-Dīn 121, 139, 166
Ruth (Moabite) 20
Rynhold, Daniel 2, 19, 25

Sa'adia Gaon 20
Saeed, Abdullah 104
Saeed, Hassan 104
Safran, Janina M. 127
Sand, Shlomo 20
Sanders, Paula 134
Schechter, Solomon 20
Schirrmacher, Christine 104
Schlossberg, Eliezer 3
Schoeler, Gregor 105
Schulze, Reinhard 86, 103
Schwarz, Dov 11, 109
Schwarzfuchs, Simon-Raymond 16
Schwarzschild, Steven 9, 11, 21, 33
Shabestari, Mohammad Mojtahed 139
Shapiro, David 6
Shapiro, Marc 6
Shryock, Andrew J. 120, 133
Sklare, David 13
Solomon 20
Soloveitchik, Joseph B. 2 f., 25, 33
Soroush, Abdolkarim 138 f., 166
Spinoza 9, 30, 33, 68
Stangroom, Jeremy 4
Stevens, Yusuf Cat 96, 113

Stone, Suzanne 8
Strauss, Leo 24
Stroumsa, Sarah 46f., 109, 128
Suárez, Francesco 70
as-Suhrawardī, Shihāb ad-Dīn 127
ash-Shushtarī, Abū al-Hasan 123
Sweeney, Michael J. 118
Szpiech, Ryan 98

Tertullian 45
Tillich, Paul 73
Treiger, Alexander 115
Troeltsch, Ernst 50f., 73, 77
Turkel, Eli 2

ʿUmar 106f., 125
Urbach, Ephraim E. 24

Walker, Paul E. 134
Wasserman, Elhanan 25
Wasserstrom, Steven M. 124f., 165
Watt, John W. 115
Weiss, Raymond L. 24, 29, 110
Williams, Bernard 4
Williams, Roger 44, 54–57, 61, 153
Wolfson, Elliot 17
Woodward, Mark 121, 126

Zephaniah 14

Index of Subjects

abrogation (*naskh*) 99, 155
apostasy 9, 48, 51, 85, 92, 104, 156
Ash'arites 112
'avodah zarah (Idolatry) 6f., 12, 31, 150

Chosen People 1, 15, 32
coercion 49, 59, 62, 65f., 74, 84, 91, 153f.
Confessional Age 44, 52
conscience 46, 54, 56–60, 62, 66, 152f., 159–161
Constitution of Medina 105
conversion 5–7, 15, 47, 49, 74, 77, 91, 98, 133, 135f., 158

dhimmī 156
dialogue 1f., 55, 59f., 64, 71–75, 77f., 115, 153f., 164, 166–168
Divine Image 22f.
Divine Justice 112f., 159, 163
dogma 9, 26, 30f., 50f., 61, 132

ethical monotheism 33, 158f.
ethos 43f., 60, 68, 70f., 73

freedom of conscience 2, 65f., 68, 130
free will 94, 112f.
fundamentalism 51, 78

halakhah 6
heresy 8, 31, 44, 48–50, 53, 127, 153
hermeneutics 60, 63, 104, 131, 154
human dignity 152, 154, 159, 163
Human Rights 8, 62, 70f., 104, 137, 157, 163f.

ijtihād 109, 156, 163
ikhtilāf (disagreement) 103, 109, 111, 156
inculturation 63, 72
interreligious dialogue 64, 71f., 167
intolerance 11, 13, 20, 22, 34, 45–47, 49, 63–65, 68, 70, 74, 78, 83–85, 87, 94f., 100f., 103, 105, 107f., 114, 116, 120, 126, 131–135, 137, 139, 141, 151, 155f., 160, 163, 168

Islamic Law 91f., 102f., 106, 108–112, 114, 117, 123, 128, 156f., 162f.
Islamic Philosophy 114, 124, 166
Islamic Theology 111, 115

jizya 92, 106, 156f., 162
justification 43, 55, 59, 67, 141

martyrdom 6f.
Māturīdites 112
messianism 13, 15f.
monotheism 3, 7, 16, 22, 24, 33, 45f., 63, 66–68, 139, 150, 159
Mosaic distinction 45, 66
Mu'tazilites 94, 112f., 117, 120

Natural Law 9, 11, 61, 70, 159–161, 163
Noahide Laws 11, 151, 158f.

Pact of 'Umar 106f., 125, 156
particularism 13, 17, 19, 24, 150f., 159f., 162
peace 14, 23, 27, 50, 52f., 55–57, 76, 101, 103, 120, 125f., 134, 153, 160, 167, 169
People of the Book 87, 106–108, 156f., 162
persecution 4, 44f., 49f., 54–57, 59, 61, 96, 99, 126, 136, 152, 155f., 165
pluralism 1, 4, 7–12, 17f., 31, 33, 51, 55f., 61, 63, 66, 69, 72f., 75, 77, 99, 138, 140, 150f., 154f., 157, 160, 162–164, 167
Postmodernism 4, 25
Prophecy 27, 127
Prophetic Traditions 99, 101–105, 156
proselyte 17–20, 151

Qur'ān 32, 90–92, 94–96, 100–102, 104–107, 111, 117, 122, 125, 128, 130, 138, 140, 155f., 162, 166f.

rationalism 116–121, 124,
relativism 1, 11, 25, 63, 68f., 72f., 75, 149–152, 161, 167
religious diversity 10, 52, 58, 69, 83f., 89–92, 95f., 98–100, 102, 105f., 108, 112, 120,

122 f., 131, 133 f., 138, 156, 161 f., 164, 166, 168
religious freedom   49, 51–53, 57 f., 61 f., 66–68, 76, 91 f., 94, 104, 107, 122, 132, 152, 154–156
religious other   10, 35, 86, 100, 112, 152
religious pluralism   25, 32, 61, 71, 122, 150, 152, 163, 166, 168
revelation   5, 9, 11, 27, 29, 31, 61, 92, 97, 99–101, 104, 106, 111, 127, 131, 159–163, 166

scriptural interpretation   90, 98
sectarianism   10, 119, 132
secularism   2, 7
Soteriology   63, 67,
Sword Verse   92, 99

theological certainty   28
tolerance   1, 3 f., 6–11, 17–22, 25, 33–35, 43–49, 51–58, 60–78, 83–92, 94–100, 102–124, 126–141, 149–169
truth   1, 3 f., 6 f., 9, 11, 17, 22, 24–26, 28 f., 32, 34 f., 47 f., 51 f., 55–59, 61–69, 72–75, 77, 85, 92–94, 109, 113, 116, 118, 124, 128 f., 131, 136, 138, 140 f., 149–155, 157 f., 160–162, 164, 166 f., 169
Two Kingdoms Doctrine   50

universalism   13, 17–19, 24, 46, 63, 68, 70 f., 73, 151, 154, 161, 164 f.

virtue   4, 20, 43–45, 48, 56, 60, 63, 67, 70, 72, 74–77, 96, 103, 120, 141, 152, 157, 163, 167